ArcGIS *and the* Digital City

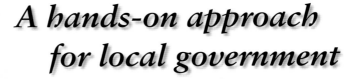

A hands-on approach for local government

William E. Huxhold, Eric M. Fowler, and Brian Parr

ESRI PRESS
REDLANDS, CALIFORNIA

First printing July 2004.

Printed in the United States of America.

Library of Congress Cataloging-in-Publication Data
Huxhold, William E.
ArcGIS and the digital city : a hands-on approach for local government / William E. Huxhold and Eric M. Fowler.
   p. cm.
    Includes bibliographical references.
    ISBN 1-58948-074-0 (pbk. : alk. paper)
    1. Local government-Data processing. 2. City planning-Data processing. 3. Geographic information systems.
    4. ArcGIS. 5. Graphical user interfaces (Computer systems)
   I. Fowler, Eric M., 1966- II. Title.
JS100.H89 2004
352.3'8214'028553--dc22   2004013025

Published by ESRI, 380 New York Street, Redlands, California 92373-8100.

Books from ESRI Press are available to resellers worldwide through Independent Publishers Group (IPG). For information on volume discounts, or to place an order, call IPG at 1-800-888-4741 in the United States, or at 312-337-0747 outside the United States.

Contents

Acknowledgments

At ESRI, thanks to Laura Feaster and Sheila Ferguson for their initial review of the material and editorial comments, to Brandon Whitehead for testing all of the exercises, and to Claudia Naber for moving the project along.

Others who have assisted in the development of the text include our students in the Department of Urban Planning advanced GIS course at the University of Wisconsin-Milwaukee in the spring semesters of 2002, 2003, and 2004. These students were required to wade through photocopy after photocopy of the exercises, riddled with typos and, sometimes, bad grammar. Without their eyes and their GIS knowledge, this book would be much more difficult for those who are not familiar with ArcGIS software. Our teaching assistants during those years were Owen Manske and Brian Clarke. We appreciate the time they spent cleaning up most of the errors in the data and helping us understand the learning process that the students were experiencing.

Introduction

Geographic information in local government

When the municipality of Burnaby, British Columbia, Canada, studied their needs for an urban geographic information system in 1986, they discovered that between 80 and 90 percent of all the information collected and used by the municipality was related to geography (Municipality of Burnaby 1986). This is pretty much the case all over the world—most of the data collected, maintained, and used by local governments (cities, counties, and other forms of municipalities) contain some geographic reference.

Think of the data that local governments collect by address: tax assessment records, building permits, liquor licenses, birth and death records, crime incidents, building inspection records, dog licenses, water meter readings, and much more. Think of data they collect on other geographic references: street pavement records; street intersection traffic control devices; harbor and river traffic and events; public transit route volume, revenue, and schedules; block and census tract summaries of housing and population. Almost every function of local government—garbage collection, nursing districts, urban forestry districts, school districts, fire response zones, etc.—uses some geographic area to manage its resources.

The use of geographic information systems (GIS) technology by cities and counties over the past twenty-five years has shown that the geographic nature of the data they process provides almost unlimited opportunities for improving the service-delivery, management, and policy-making activities in those governments. GIS allows digital map information to be combined with attribute information about features on the maps, thereby providing local governments with new ways to use the enormous amounts of data that, in most cases, is already in computerized form to solve complex urban problems and manage resources more efficiently and effectively.

In a GIS, maps contain links to attribute data that are used to display and analyze that data. These links also allow the data to be integrated horizontally throughout the organization. Horizontal data integration makes it easy to share data among different functions. For example, addresses from the historical register in the Planning Department can be compared to addresses from building demolition permit records in the Building Inspection Department to prevent a historical building from being demolished; or census tract statistics from population data can be related to census tract statistics from crime records to identify census tracts that are unusually high in per capita crime. These links also allow data to be aggregated vertically to larger geographic areas so that crime data, tax assessment data, water-main break data, and other data collected by address can be summarized by census tract, aldermanic district, or other geographic area. Governments are more effective when they apply GIS technology to urban problems because GIS makes it easier to integrate data horizontally and aggregate data vertically throughout the organization (Huxhold 1991).

GIS in local government

The role of GIS in an organization is to provide expanded computer applications within the organization's overall information technology (IT) infrastructure. Geographic information systems are, after all, information technology, and the information technology in an organization exists to support the information needs of the organizational structure.

A city government organizes itself into functional units (offices, bureaus, and departments) in order to fulfill its responsibilities. These functional units address many of the issues and problems and day-to-day services related to the state or activities of the people, businesses, properties, and facilities within the city's jurisdiction. Collecting data about those entities and their activities helps these organizational units perform their duties. That data is what GIS implementers need to know about when designing a GIS for an organization. That allows them to build a model of what data the organization needs.

This data model is a logical description of the information needed by an organization to perform its functions (Huxhold and Levinsohn 1995, 7–18). More specifically, a data model is a list of all the data needed by an organization or an organizational unit to meet its mission. On an organization-wide basis, a data model defines all the data needed by the organization for all of the functional units within its structure.

The GIS data model is a record of the data and data structure for the entire city government. Each functional area (Tax Assessor, Building Inspection, Water Service, etc.) is identified with a list of the data items needed for it to operate. The data can be integrated horizontally across the entire organization because of common links that allow integration to occur (addresses, water-main numbers, parcel numbers, etc). This relational structure of the logical design of the data model for the city is what makes data useable throughout the organization, and that is why relational database management systems are so valuable in geographic information systems.

About this book

This book consists of a series of exercises using ESRI® ArcGIS® software. ArcGIS uses a relational database management system to analyze, store, retrieve, and update data. ArcGIS is one of the most popular geographic information system software products currently used by local governments and other governmental and private-sector organizations. In the exercises in this book you will create and use a database consisting of land parcel maps and property attributes as well as census data and street centerlines. The exercises begin with the construction of the spatial (map) database by converting maps from a CAD (.dxf) format, extend through the processes of building topology and editing, then querying and analyzing the data, and end with updating the data with a new subdivision.

We developed the exercises to serve two purposes. First, the exercises provide an exposure to the technical operation and capabilities of ArcGIS for building and using a geographic information system for a local government; and, second, they give the reader exposure to real data from a real local government. Thus, they provide a controlled "hands-on" environment where you can use digital maps and feature attribute databases to address issues in the operations, management, and policy-planning activities of a local government in a hypothetical city we call Arc City.

Once you have completed the exercises, you will have experience creating and working with geographic data common to local government. The exercises do not cover all the requirements in a local government or all of the functions of which ArcGIS is capable. These exercises, though, do serve as an introduction to many of the tasks that really happen with local governments.

For additional information on ArcGIS, we strongly recommend using the reference manuals and books, especially *Getting to Know ArcGIS,* available from ESRI at www.esri.com.

To gain full benefit from the exercises in this book, it's best if you have previously been exposed to the basic concepts of geographic information systems and introduced to various applications of this technology in local government. This user guide is designed to be cumulative: the skills acquired in one exercise will help you complete subsequent exercises. Exercises in the early chapters contain detailed step-by-step tasks necessary to create and organize the data needed to complete the analysis and report exercises in the later chapters. In later chapters less direction is given because the needed data and commands will have been discussed in detail in the earlier chapters.

Welcome to Arc City

Arc City has many of the characteristics of a real city, although it is somewhat smaller. It has 646 land parcels, 2,035 housing units, and 3,372 residents. Within Arc City, 26 streets and a river define 30 blocks and 3 bridges. Three city supervisors govern Arc City, each having been elected from one of three supervisory districts. And, like most local governments, changes are taking place in Arc City as new development occurs, people move in and out, and problems arise.

The supervisors have decided that the city needs a geographic information system to help manage and analyze the land-related information about the city. A GIS needs assessment was completed which revealed that the city's maps and data about property and people are scattered among different municipal departments. City staff created some of the data the city uses and some is obtained from other levels of government such as the U.S. Census Bureau and the Federal Emergency Management Agency (FEMA). All of this map and attribute data will need to be integrated into the Arc City GIS so that city officials and staff can more efficiently manage services and analyze and solve problems.

You are one of the GIS specialists on the GIS project team established by the supervisors to gather the maps and data and prepare them for conversion to the GIS. As you create the GIS, the supervisors recognize its value and charge you with solving additional issues within Arc City.

The exercises are organized into chapters, each emphasizing a major capability of GIS technology using the commands available in ArcGIS. The main topics covered are the following:

- importing CAD data and building topology to create a geodatabase
- establishing, querying, editing, and geocoding attribute data
- producing maps and reports from the results of spatial analysis
- updating map and attribute data

Arc City data

Arc City is not a real city, but it does use real city maps and attribute data. The maps are parcel maps typically found in the offices of the tax assessor, surveyor, or property lister of municipalities and counties in the United States. They are from two quarter-sections in the City of Milwaukee and, like most local governments, are in CAD (Computer Aided Drafting) format. Street centerlines and blocks and districts are additional map features that were obtained from the U.S. Census Bureau's TIGER® files and then refined by the city. The attribute data used in Arc City consists of parcel records from the City of Milwaukee's Tax Assessor's Office and census data from the U.S. Census Bureau.

Note: Both the parcel maps and attribute data for the entire city of Milwaukee can be seen at the city's Web site: *www.milwaukee.gov.* Just click the "Neighborhoods" icon, then click the link Map Milwaukee: Property Data and Interactive Mapping, and follow the instructions. To download parcel attribute data for another area of the city, click the "GIS Home" link, then "Download Tabular Data," then "Download Map Data."

Chapter 1

Creating a geodatabase

After the needs analysis and planning are complete, one of the first tasks in implementing a local government GIS is to create the spatial database. This is usually the most expensive and time-consuming task in the development of a GIS (Huxhold and Levinsohn, 191). It is often referred to as data compilation or data conversion because the digital data for a GIS must be pulled together from different sources. Typical sources include surveyor's records, hard-copy maps, CAD (computer aided drafting) files, and digital files in a variety of GIS or other formats.

Converting data

All local governments implementing GIS use one or more of the following methods for converting map data to digital form for a GIS spatial database:

☐ **Compiling**—The process of taking x,y coordinates from GPS (Global Positioning Satellite) receivers or COGO (coordinate geometry) bearings and distances from surveyor's measurements to create a map.

☐ **Digitizing**—The process of placing a hard-copy map on a digitizing tablet connected to the GIS then using an electronic mouse to trace the lines on the map to a vector format in the GIS software.

☐ **Scanning**—The process of placing a hard-copy map on a scanning device that converts the map features to a raster image. The image must then be "scrubbed" to clean errors introduced during scanning and prepare the features for a vector database.

☐ **Screen digitizing**—The process of taking a digital orthophotographic image or scanned map image, displaying it on a screen, and tracing the lines and other features on the image with a mouse to create a digitized file. Sometimes called "heads up" digitizing.

⌐ **Importing**—The conversion of digital map data created in the format of a different software system (CAD or other GIS software) to the format of the GIS used by the organization. Importing digital map data from CAD software (such as AutoCAD® software) is very common in local governments because many of them convert their paper maps to the CAD format long before they decide to implement GIS.

In Arc City, converting the existing data to a GIS database will not be a trivial process, even though the city is small and most of the data is already in some digital form (CAD files, dBASE® files, and ArcGIS shapefiles). To begin with, careful planning and preparation have already taken place. The needs assessment revealed the geographic features and attributes that must be included in the GIS database. From this information a data model was developed, as well as a database design that shows exactly how the data is to be organized in a geodatabase. Now, much work remains to create the GIS database.

Registering maps on a continuous coordinate system

As in many cities, the Arc City Engineer's Office converted its paper maps to digital form years ago using CAD software. These digital maps were stored in the digital exchange format (.dxf extension after each file name) in individual files—one for each quarter section. A quarter section is an area of land that is approximately one-half mile square. It is a common division of land in the United States as part of the Public Land Survey System—except for the original thirteen states (Huxhold 1991, 197–200).

The fact that each map is stored individually creates difficulties when it comes time to use the files in a GIS. As individual maps, they are not tied to their location on the earth's surface, and all you have is a series of digital maps—an atlas, if you will. To take full advantage of the analysis capabilities of the GIS, the Arc City digital quarter-section maps will be combined into a seamless map and placed on a continuous coordinate system—the State Plane Coordinate System, in this case.

Building polygon topology

Using topology in the spatial data within a geographic information system ensures that spatial analysis will produce reliable results. Topology defines the spatial relationships among the points, lines, and polygons that are implicit to the human, but the computer must have them explicitly defined to preserve and protect spatial relationships.

Consider the following features commonly represented in a municipal GIS and the spatial relationships between them:

Features	Spatial relationship
Fire hydrants and waterlines	Fire hydrants must be connected to waterlines.
Roads and census blocks	Census block boundaries must be covered by (align with) major road lines.
Voting districts	Voting districts must not overlap.

In each example above, a type of spatial relationship is inherent to the way the features relate to each other within their real-world context. Topology provides a way to model and protect the spatial relationships in digital data.

In a geodatabase, spatial relationships are protected by topology rules. Topology rules are used to define the spatial relationships that are important to the integrity of data and allow you to correctly model the geometry of real-world features in your spatial data. Topology rules define connectivity relationships, for example, enforcing connectivity between sewer lines and manhole points; define containment policies, for example, requiring parcels to contain address points; and govern relationships among shared boundaries, for example, requiring a perfect match between subdivision boundaries and the outer boundaries of the bordering parcels.

The Arc City CAD files are topologically incorrect. Parcels and buildings exist as line features instead of area features (polygons), and block polygons still need to be created from the street segments. As a result, no polygon processing (area computation, shading or color filling, polygon overlay, etc.) can be performed on parcels and blocks.

It will be up to you to import the CAD data into the Arc City geodatabase then clean it up so that the features it represents are topologically correct and ready to be used for analysis.

Adding location identifiers

The digital records of all geographic features (points, lines, and polygons) in a GIS database are automatically given a unique identification number that links them to records in an attribute table. However, an organization often has its own numbering systems (e.g., parcel identification numbers) and attribute data (e.g., property ownership data) stored in databases (called legacy systems) that exist before the GIS is implemented. In order to use a legacy system's attributes in a GIS, both the legacy database table and the digital map table must contain the same unique feature identifiers so the map features and their attributes can be linked.

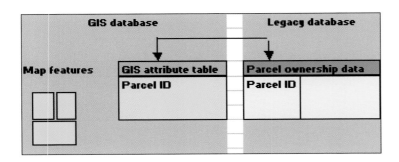

For years, Arc City's tax assessor has used dBase database management software to manage attribute data about parcels in the tax assessment files. This legacy system will now be linked to the digital parcel maps through a parcel identifier: the tax key number. Digital block maps and the Census Bureau's population data must be linked in a similar fashion using block numbers.

Creating the Arc City spatial database with ArcGIS

In this chapter, you will create an Arc City geodatabase and populate it with parcels, buildings, streets, blocks, and address points. All of the data you will use to populate the geodatabase comes from the source data that has been provided to you. To prepare the Arc City geodatabase, you will perform several tasks that incorporate the following work flow:

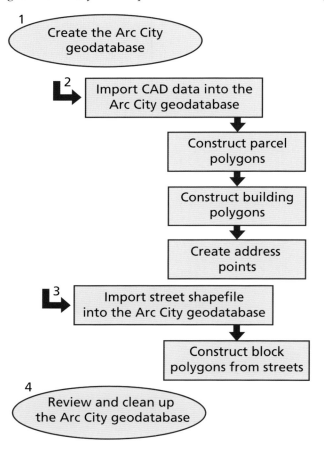

Within the major tasks shown on the flowchart are several smaller tasks that include defining the coordinate system for the data in the geodatabase; using geodatabase topology rules to identify errors in your data; repairing the errors found in the source data; converting parcel lines, building lines, and street centerlines to polygons; backing up your data sources; and removing the unnecessary data from the geodatabase created during the database construction process.

This process has been organized into nine exercises that must be completed correctly in order to have an accurate spatial database for later exercises that produce maps and reports for Arc City.

Exercise 1a

Examine the existing Arc City data

You have already obtained the existing digital data sources from the different city departments and have placed all of the files into a single folder named SourceData on your computer. Now you need to take a closer look at the data to see just what you have.

In this exercise, you will examine the city's existing data files with ArcCatalog™ to understand characteristics such as file names and formats, geographic features, attributes, and metadata. You will also create a folder connection and create data thumbnails to make it easier to access and browse the data as you work.

In this section you will perform the following tasks:
- Start ArcCatalog and create a folder connection.
- Preview CAD data.
- Create thumbnails for the quarter-section maps.
- Preview streets data and create thumbnails.
- Browse source data thumbnails.
- Preview tax assessment database tables.

The exercise instructions assume you have installed the data to the default directory (**C:\DigitalCity**). If you have installed the data elsewhere, you'll need to substitute the correct paths.

Start ArcCatalog and create a folder connection

1. Start ArcCatalog.

2. On the Standard toolbar, click the Connect to Folder button.

3. In the Connect to Folder dialog, navigate to your **C:\DigitalCity** folder then click it.

4. Click OK.
   A connection to **C:\DigitalCity** appears in the Catalog Tree.

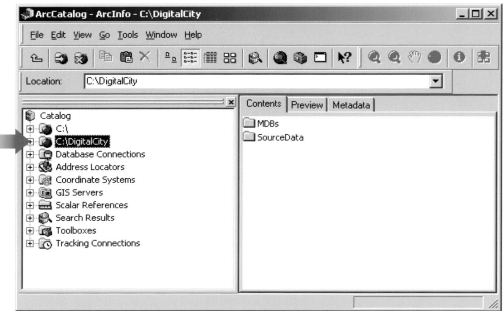

5. Expand the DigitalCity folder then the SourceData folder. Examine the contents of the SourceData folder. (Note: When exploring data, it can be helpful to display file extensions. If extensions do not appear in your Catalog Tree to display them, click the Tools menu, then click Options. In the General tab, uncheck Hide File Extensions and click OK.)

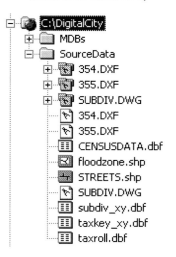

As you can see, the SourceData folder contains a number of data sources of different types. Different icons next to each data source indicate the format (e.g., CAD, shapefile, table) or feature type (e.g., polygon, line, point) of the data.

You will use some of these data sources for the exercises in this chapter to build the initial GIS database. You will use others in later chapters.

To begin building the GIS database, you will create four of the most important feature classes you need for the Arc City basemap: parcels, buildings, streets, and blocks. The table below shows the data sources you will use to build these basemap features and their attributes.

GIS feature class	Feature data sources	File names	Attribute data sources	File names
Parcels	Quarter section # 354 Quarter section # 355	354.DXF 355.DXF	Tax assessment database	taxroll.dbf taxkey_xy.dbf
Buildings	Quarter section # 354 Quarter section # 355	354.DXF 355.DXF	None	
Streets	TIGER street file	STREETS.shp	TIGER street file	STREETS.shp
Blocks	To be created from streets		Census block data	CENSUSDATA.dbf

Preview CAD data

Notice that there are two entries in the Catalog Tree for each quarter section (354.DXF and 355.DXF). One (with the blue icon) is a CAD feature data set. A feature data set contains multiple feature classes such as points, lines, polygons, and annotations. The other (with the white icon) is a CAD drawing file with all features grouped into a single layer.

6. In the Catalog Tree (the lower left side panel that lists the folders and files), expand the **354.DXF** CAD feature data set by clicking the plus sign to the left of its name and icon. Note that the plus sign turns to a minus sign and five feature classes are listed.

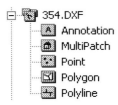

7. In the Catalog Display (the large panel on the right side that displays folders and files), click the Preview tab, then, in the Catalog Tree, click each feature class in the **354.DXF** CAD feature data set to preview its features.

8. In the Catalog Tree, click the **354.DXF** CAD drawing file (the one with the white icon) to preview it.

Unlike the CAD feature data set, the CAD drawing contains all of the features in a single layer.

9. Click the Preview drop-down list at the bottom of the Catalog Display. Notice that Geography is the only preview option.

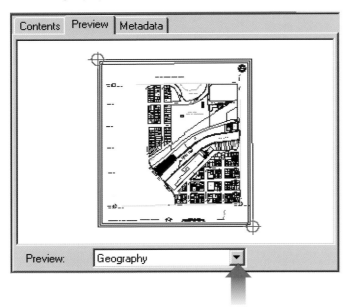

Typically, you expect to see a Table option along with the Geography option when previewing your geographic data, but no attribute table is associated with the CAD drawing. However, the CAD feature classes in the CAD feature data set do have attribute tables.

10. In the Catalog Tree, click the Polyline feature class within the **354.DXF** CAD feature data set.

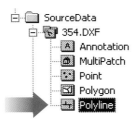

11. Click the Preview drop-down list and choose Table. Scroll across the table and examine the data.

Although the table contains a number of fields, not much useful attribute information exists in the CAD polyline table. For example, no identifier can be linked to other attribute data.

One potentially useful field is the Layer field. The values in this field designate which layer the CAD features belong to, for example, building outlines (layer code 28), lot and parcel lines (layer code 09), and so on.

Create thumbnails for the quarter-section maps

Next, you will create thumbnail images of the CAD data so that you can browse it in ArcCatalog.

12. Change the preview back to Geography. If you have zoomed or panned the display, click the Full Extent button that's located on the Geography toolbar.

13. Click the Create Thumbnail button to take a snapshot of the data as it is currently displayed.

14. In the Catalog Display, click the Contents tab to confirm that the thumbnail was created and looks the way you want it to look.

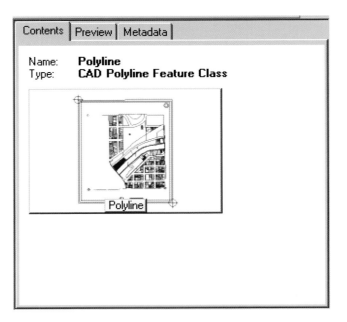

15. Preview the Polyline feature class for the other quarter-section map (**355.DXF**) and then create a thumbnail for it. (If you can't remember how to create a thumbnail, select the Polyline feature class for **355.DXF**, then repeat steps 12 and 13.)

◻ Preview streets data and create thumbnails

The streets data that you have exists in the shapefile format. You should also preview it.

16. Click **STREETS.shp** in the Catalog Tree and preview its geography. Then preview its attribute table.

The streets shapefile contains all the attributes associated with the name of the streets and the address ranges along each street segment.

Just like you did for CAD data, you will create a thumbnail for the streets data.

17. In the Catalog Display, choose Geography from the Preview drop-down list. If necessary, zoom to the full extent of the streets. Click the Create Thumbnail button.

18. To check your work, in the Catalog Display, click the Contents tab.

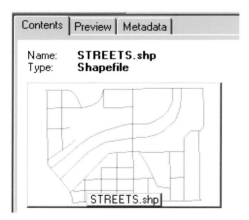

◻ Browse source data thumbnails

Thumbnail views of data provide you a quick look at your data's geography when browsing folders that contain many data sources. As the amount of data in your GIS database grows, thumbnails will help you quickly find the data you need.

19. In the Catalog Tree, click the SourceData folder, then, if necessary, click the Contents tab in the Catalog Display. On the Standard toolbar, click the Thumbnails button.

The display changes to show the thumbnail images of each file. For some of the files, no thumbnail was created; these files still appear as icons.

Preview tax assessment database tables

There are two more data sources to preview—the tables from the city assessor's tax assessment database. Unlike the other data, these sources contain tabular information with no geographic component.

20. In the Catalog Display, click the icon for the **taxroll.dbf**, then click the Preview tab. Examine the contents of the table.

| Contents | Preview | Metadata |

OID	PARITY	MPROP_TAXK	YRASSMT	PLATPAGE
0	O	3540001000	1998	35409
1	O	3540002000	1998	35409
2	E	3540003100	1998	35409
3	E	3540005000	1998	35409
4	E	3540006000	1998	35409
5	E	3540007100	1998	35409
6	E	3540007200	1998	35409
7	E	3540008000	1998	35409

Record: ◄◄ ◄ [1] ► ►◄   Show: All Selected Records (of 644)

Preview: Table ▼

The taxroll table contains many fields that are useful to the assessor, such as the address of the property, name and address of the owner, assessed value, date of assessment, number of housing units, and zoning code.

21. In the Catalog Tree, click **taxkey_xy.dbf** and preview the table.

Taxkey_xy.dbf contains the information that you will need to associate the records in the taxroll table with the GIS parcel features you create from the CAD data. The fields X_ORIGIN and Y_ORIGIN identify the location of a point inside each parcel. TKXY_TAXKE contains unique identifiers for each parcel.

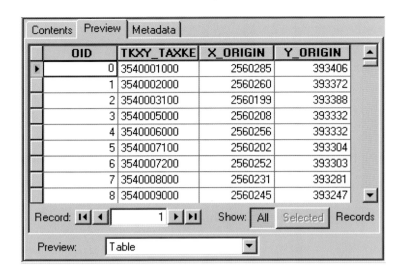

22. Look closely at the values in the TKXY_TAXKE field, then preview the taxroll table again. Look for a field containing the Tax Key identifiers that you can use to link the taxroll records with the parcel locations.

You should have noticed that the field MPROP_TAXK has the Tax Key numbers in the taxroll table. You now have a way to link the attributes with the map features.

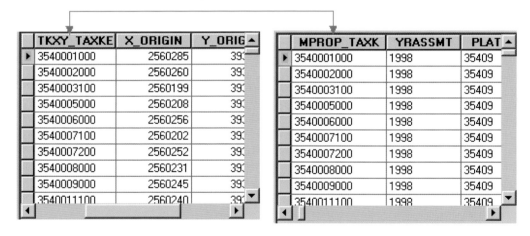

Now that you are more familiar with your source data, you are ready to begin converting the CAD data to GIS feature classes.

23. If you are continuing to Exercise 1b, keep ArcCatalog open. Otherwise, exit ArcCatalog.

Exercise 1b

Create the Arc City geodatabase and import CAD data

Now that you have seen how the quarter-section maps are represented in the CAD data format, you are ready to create a geodatabase and import the parcel and building features into it.

The initial creation of a geodatabase involves only a few mouse clicks to create an empty container for storing your spatial data. Once the geodatabase is created, you must add spatial data to it. This can involve importing data from other sources, creating the data from scratch, or generating feature classes from tabular and text-based sources. (Map layers stored in a geodatabase are referred to as feature classes.)

In this exercise, you will create the Arc City geodatabase and import the two quarter-section CAD maps into it. Once the two quarter sections are inside the geodatabase, you will merge them into a single feature class.

In this exercise you will perform the following tasks:
- Create a workspace folder and a personal geodatabase.
- Make a copy of the source data.
- Create the Arc City geodatabase.
- Import the CAD files to your geodatabase as feature classes.
- Remove unneeded CAD layers.
- Merge layers from the two quarter sections.

Create a workspace folder and a personal geodatabase

You will begin your work by creating a working folder in which you will place the Arc City geodatabase and a copy of your source data.

1. If necessary, start ArcCatalog.

2. In the Catalog Tree, right-click your **C:\DigitalCity** folder, point to New and click Folder. Name the new folder **MyArcCity**. (If you are working in a classroom environment where multiple students are accessing the same DigitalCity folder, you may need to use a unique folder name. For example, you could name the folder **MyArcCity_abc** where abc are your initials).

Next you will copy your original data into the **MyArcCity** folder.

Make a copy of the source data

In order to protect your original data from accidental edits or deletion, you'll make a copy of the data. By working with copies of the source data, you will know that you can always go back to the original data should something go wrong.

3. In the Catalog Tree, click the **SourceData** folder. In the Catalog Display, click the Contents tab, then on the Standard toolbar click the Details button.

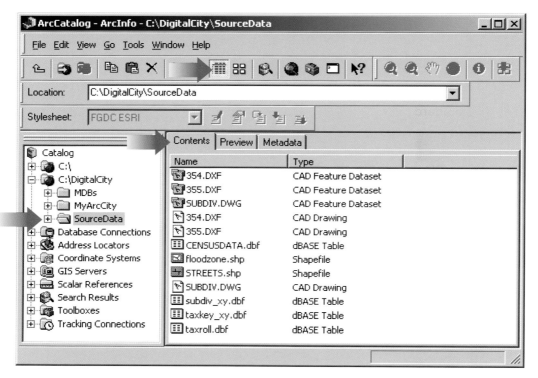

4. Inside the Catalog Display, hold down the Control key and click all the files except for the three CAD Feature Datasets (ArcCatalog will recreate the data sets when it copies the drawing files).

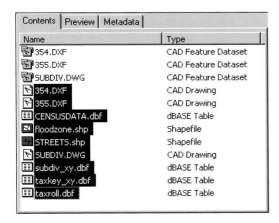

5. On the Standard toolbar, click the Copy button.

6. In the Catalog Tree, click the **MyArcCity** folder, then click the Paste button on the Standard toolbar (The Paste button is just to the right of the Copy button.)

Now that you have a backup of the source data, you can begin creating the geodatabase without worrying about corrupting the original files.

Create the Arc City geodatabase

7. Right-click your **MyArcCity** folder. Point to New, then click Personal Geodatabase. Name the geodatabase **ArcCity.mdb**. (To remove the geodatabase right-click the geodatabase, choose Rename, then type in the new name).

You now have an empty geodatabase. Your next step is to import two CAD feature classes into it.

⌐ Import the CAD files to the geodatabase

8. In the Catalog Tree, right-click **ArcCity.mdb**, point to Import, then click Feature Class (single).

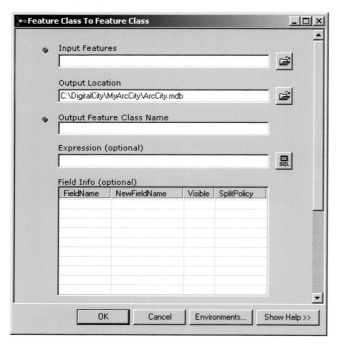

In the Feature Class to Feature Class dialog, you need to pick which CAD feature class you want to import and a name for it.

9. If necessary, position your windows so you can see the Catalog Tree and the Feature Class to Feature Class dialog at the same time.

10. In the Catalog Tree, expand **354.DXF**, then click and drag the Polyline feature class from the Catalog Tree and drop it in the Input Features box. For the Output Feature Class Name, enter **arcs354**.

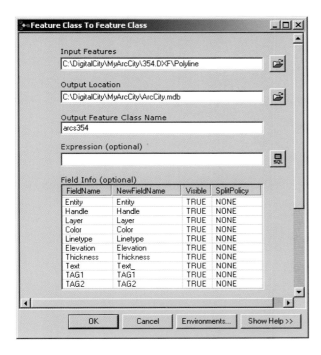

11. Click OK. When the process completes, click Close.

12. Using the same process that you used in steps 8–11, import the Polyline feature class from **355.DXF** into your ArcCity geodatabase. Name the output **arcs355**.

13. In the Catalog Tree, expand the ArcCity geodatabase, then preview the two new feature classes (**arcs354**, and **arcs355**) in the Catalog Display. (Click the Preview tab in the Catalog Display, then click on each new feature class in the Catalog Tree).

14. Use the Pan and Zoom tools on the Geography toolbar to explore the features in **arcs354** and **arcs355**.

Among the many features present, some are buildings and parcels, while others are symbols used in the CAD file, like hatching or x's.

Your next task is to refine these feature classes by removing features from them that do not represent parcel lines or building lines.

☐ Remove unneeded CAD layers

As you have seen, there are quite a few features in **arcs354** and **arcs355** that are not parcels or buildings and that you don't need in the geodatabase. To remove them, you will use ArcMap™ to edit the feature classes.

15. On the Standard toolbar, click the Launch ArcMap button.

16. In the ArcMap dialog, click the option to start using ArcMap with a new, empty map, then click OK.

17. Close ArcCatalog.

18. On ArcMap's Standard toolbar, click the Add Data button.

19. In the Add Data dialog, navigate to **C:\DigitalCity\MyArcCity\ArcCity.mdb**. Hold down the Shift key and click the **arcs354** and **arcs355** feature classes, then click Add, and then click OK on the warning message about missing spatial reference information.

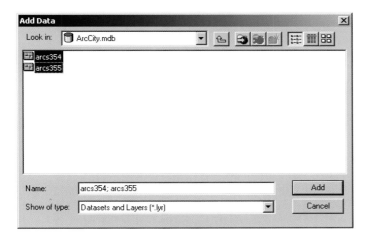

The message about missing spatial reference appeared because there is no information about the projection and coordinate system stored with **arcs354** or **arcs355**. In other words, ArcMap does not know where on the face of the earth these features are located. ArcMap can still display the data, but the software lets you know that it's not finding any information about the spatial reference of the feature classes in question. Right now this is not a problem, and later on you will define the spatial reference for your data.

The two feature classes are displayed as map layers inside of ArcMap. (In ArcMap, feature classes are referred to as layers or map layers.)

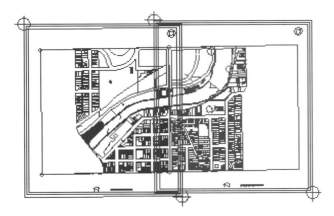

Remnants from the CAD drawings, like boundary lines and scale bars, still exist and are overlapping in the center of the display. You will remove these features by selecting the lines that belong to certain CAD layers, using the codes in the Layer attribute field, and then deleting your selection.

20. Click the Selection menu, then click Select By Attributes. In the Select By Attributes dialog, click the Layer drop-down arrow and click **arcs354**. In the Method drop-down menu, choose Create a new selection.

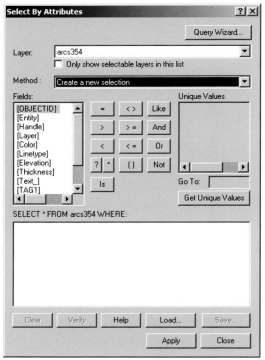

Next, you will create a query statement to select the lines you want to delete. The following table summarizes the information for a few of the extraneous layers. (In a real project, additional or different layers may need to be deleted.)

Layer	Definition
0	Map frame
26	Quarter-section frame and title block
32	Section lines
48	Quarter-section shapes

21. To create the selection query, you can either type it in the expression box or construct it using the Fields list, operator buttons, and the Unique Values list. (Hint: To see all values select [Layer] in the Fields list, then click Get Unique Values.) Enter the following query:

    [Layer] = '0' OR [Layer] = '26' OR [Layer] = '32' OR [Layer] = '48'

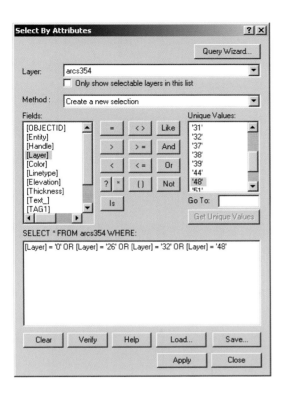

22. Click Verify to confirm your query was entered correctly.

If there is an error in the expression, delete the expression and re-enter it. If the verification was successful, go on to the next step.

23. Click Apply, then click Close to dismiss the dialog box. Several features should be highlighted on the map.

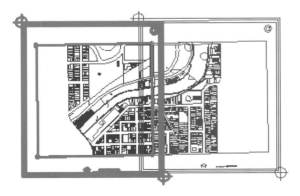

To delete the selected features, you'll need to load the Editor toolbar and start an edit session.

24. On the Standard toolbar, click the Editor button to load the Editor toolbar.

25. From the Editor drop-down menu, click Start Editing.

26. In the Target drop-down list, select **arcs354**.

27. Click the Sketch tool button.

28. Press the Delete key.

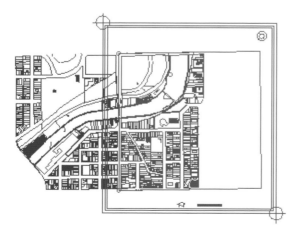

29. Repeat steps 21 through 29 to delete the extraneous features in the **arcs355** feature class. (Remember to use **arcs355** for the layer in the Select By Attribute dialog as well as for the editing target. Also, you won't need to start an editing session or load the Editor toolbar.)

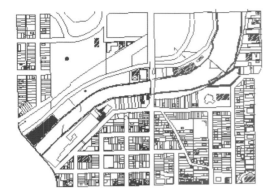

30. From the Editor menu, choose Stop Editing and click Yes to save your edits.

31. Close ArcMap. You do not need to save the changes to your map.

Merge layers from the two quarter sections

Now that the two CAD layers have been imported into the geodatabase and stripped down to essential features, you will merge them into a single feature class. Before you can do this, you will create a new feature class that will hold the results of the merge.

32. Start ArcCatalog.

33 In the Catalog Tree, right-click the ArcCity geodatabase, point to New, and click Feature Class.

34. In the First Panel of the New Feature Class dialog, name the new feature class **Combo354355**.

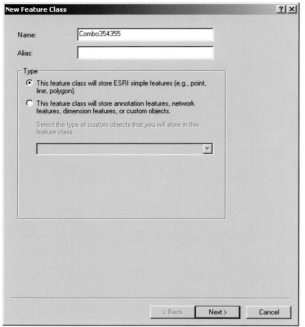

35. Click Next. Accept the default setting on the second panel and click Next.

The third panel is where you define the attribute fields for the new feature class. Because you are going to append **arcs354** and **arcs355** together and place the results in this feature class, this feature class must have the exact same attribute fields as **arcs354** and **arcs355**. To avoid the process of creating these fields from scratch, you can import the field definitions from an existing feature class. In this case you will import them from **arcs354**.

36. In the lower-right portion of the New Feature Class dialog, click the Import button.

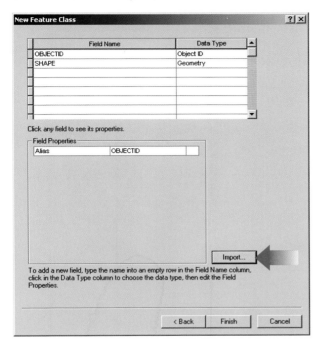

37. In the Browse for table/feature class dialog, navigate to your Arc City geodatabase and select the **arcs354** feature class.

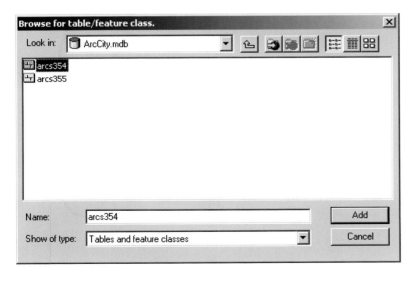

38. Click Add.

The attribute fields in the **arcs354** feature class were ported over to the feature class you're creating. Only the schema of the attribute fields (e.g., field names, field types, and field widths) was imported into the new feature class; no attribute values were imported.

39. In the list of fields, click the SHAPE field.

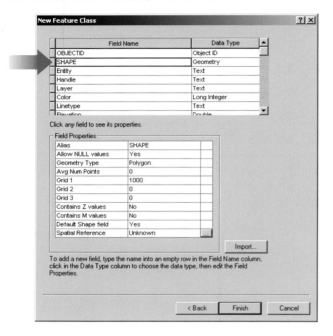

The SHAPE field stores the geometry of each feature in a feature class. Clicking this field in the New Feature Class dialog gives you access to its properties. Using its properties you can, among other things, define what type of geometry the feature class can store (e.g., point, line, or polygon) and the spatial reference of the features. You will learn more about working with the spatial reference in this chapter. For now, you can think of it as a way to define where on the planet the features in the feature class are located and how much area the feature class covers.

40. In the right-hand side of the Field Properties frame, click on Polygon in the Geometry Type column, then choose Line from the drop-down list.

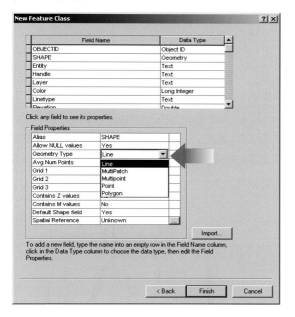

This setting defines the new feature class as a line feature class.

41. In the lower-right corner of the Field Properties frame, click the Ellipses button.

This opens the Spatial Reference Properties dialog. At this point, you want to create a spatial reference for the new feature class that matches the one used by the two feature classes your are going to append. Instead of defining the spatial reference, you will import the one that's being used by **arcs355**.

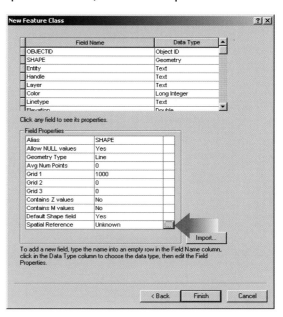

42. In the Spatial Reference Properties dialog, click the Import button, then browse to your Arc City geodatabase, select the **arcs355** feature class, and click Add.

After importing the spatial reference of **arcs355**, the Name of the Coordinate System will still read Unknown, and the Details box will still be empty. This is because there still is no coordinate system defined for two feature classes in your geodatabase. At this point, what you have done is matched the X/Y Domain (the spatial extent) of your new feature class to that of **arcs355**.

43. Click OK in the Spatial Reference Properties dialog, then click Finish in the New Feature Class dialog.

Combo354355 now exists within your geodatabase; it has the same spatial extent and the same attribute fields as **arcs355** and **arcs354**. You are now ready to append **arcs354** and **arcs355** and put the results in your new feature class.

44. On the Standard toolbar, click the Show/Hide ArcToolbox Window button.

45. In ArcToolbox, expand the Data Management Tools toolbox, then expand the General toolset.

46. In the General toolset, double-click the Append tool.

47. In the Append dialog, click the Browse button located to the right of the Input Features box. In the Input Features dialog, navigate to your **Arc City** geodatabase and select the **arcs354** and the **arcs355** feature classes, then click Add. (You can select multiple items by holding down the Ctrl key while you click them.) Click the Browse button at the right of the Output Features box. Navigate to your **Arc City** geodatabase and select **Combo354355**. (If you don't see the **Combo354355** feature class in the **Arc City** geodatabase, choose the **MyArcCity** folder from the Look in drop-down list, then double-click the **ArcCity.mdb** in the contents list). Leave the Schema Type option set to TEST.

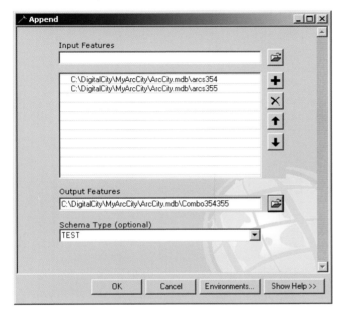

Based on these settings, the features in **arcs354** and **arcs355** will be appended together inside of the **Combo354355** feature class. When the Schema Type is set to Test, the append function requires that the attribute fields in the feature classes perfectly match and are in the same order within their respective tables.

48. Click OK. When the process finishes, close the Status window.

49. On the Standard toolbar, click the Show/Hide ArcToolbox Window button to close ArcToolbox.

50. Use ArcCatalog to preview the geography of **Combo354355**.

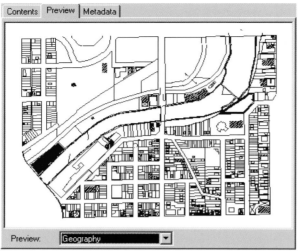

You should also take a look at the attributes of this feature class.

51. Preview the attribute table of Combo354355.

Entity	Handle	Layer	Color	Linetype	Eleva
▶ Polyline	126	27	27	BYBLOCK	
Polyline	12E	27	27	BYBLOCK	
Polyline	132	27	27	BYBLOCK	
Polyline	136	27	27	BYBLOCK	
Polyline	13A	27	27	BYBLOCK	
Polyline	13E	27	27	BYBLOCK	
Polyline	142	27	27	BYBLOCK	
Polyline	146	27	27	BYBLOCK	
Polyline	14A	27	27	BYBLOCK	
Polyline	14E	27	27	BYBLOCK	
Polyline	152	27	27	BYBLOCK	
Polyline	156	27	27	BYBLOCK	
Polyline	15A	27	27	BYBLOCK	

Contents | Preview | Metadata

Preview: Table

Record: 1   Show: All Selected Records (of *20

You now have a single feature class that contains all the features from arcs354 and arcs355.

52. Close ArcCatalog.

Symbolize Combo354355 to distinguish the CAD layers

53. Start ArcMap™ with a new, empty map.

54. Click the Add Data button. Add **Combo354355** from the **Arc City** geodatabase. When it appears, click OK on the warning message about the missing spatial reference information.

(Since you imported a spatial reference for this feature class, you may be wondering why you still got the warning message. Even though you imported the spatial reference, all the software did was match the spatial reference information that was available from **arcs355** and carry this over into **Combo354355**. Since there was no coordinate system defined for **arcs355**, there is still a missing component in the spatial reference for **Combo354355** and ArcMap is reporting this to you when it encounters the feature class. At this point, this is still not a problem and you will fully define the spatial reference information in exercise 1c).

Right now all the features in **Combo354355** are drawn in the same color. If you symbolize these features based on their CAD layer code, you will be able to distinguish different types of features such as parcels and buildings.

55. In the Table of Contents panel (to the left of the map and where the displayed layers are listed), right-click **Combo354355** and then click Properties. On the Layer Properties dialog, click the Symbology tab.

56. In the show box, click Categories. From the Value Field drop-down list choose Layer, then click Add All Values. Click the Color Scheme drop-down list, and choose the first color scheme in the list.

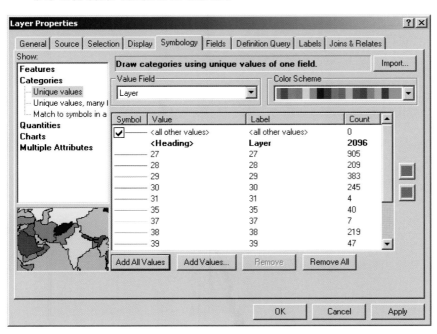

57. Click OK.

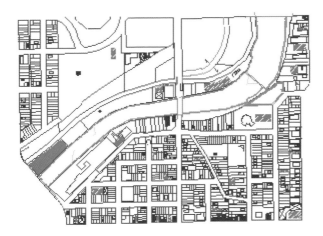

58. Use the Zoom and Pan tools on the Tools toolbar to examine the map display.

Notice that buildings and parcels are not the only features. Do not delete the other features because they may be useful in the future for Arc City reference maps.

You have finished importing the CAD data into the **Arc City** geodatabase. In the next exercise, you will extract the building and parcel features from **Combo354355** and place them in separate feature classes.

59. From the File menu, click Save As. Navigate to your **C:DigitalCity\MyArcCity** folder, and save the map document as **my_ex01b.mxd**.

60. Exit ArcMap.

Exercise 1c

Create separate parcel and building feature classes

Now that the CAD data is contained in one seamless geodatabase feature class, your next task is to separate the parcel and building features into their own feature classes. You also need to create point features from the tax key table so that you will be able to associate the tax key identification numbers with the parcels.

The feature classes you will create in this exercise will be placed in a feature data set within the **Arc City** geodatabase. Feature data sets act as individual containers within a geodatabase and are typically used to organize and hold data that is spatially related. In this case, the spatial relationship is one of containment—the parcels contain the buildings and the tax key points.

The spatial reference of a feature class must match the spatial reference of the feature data set within which they exist. (The spatial reference is comprised of the coordinate system, map projection, and spatial extent of a feature class or feature data set.) By defining the spatial reference of a feature data set, you set up an automatic control over the spatial reference of any feature class it contains.

You have no metadata for the CAD data, but you know that the engineering draftsperson, using notes provided by the city's surveyor, drew the quarter-section maps so that the features in the maps are correctly positioned within the south zone of the Wisconsin State Plane Coordinate System. You also know that the map units are feet. This is the coordinate system you will define for the feature data set and the data you add to it.

In this exercise, you will create a feature data set, define its spatial reference, and move the **Combo354355** feature class into it. Once the feature data set is created, you will add the parcels, buildings, and tax key points to it.

In this exercise you will perform the following tasks:
- Review the current coordinate settings.
- Define the coordinate system of **Combo354355**.
- Create a feature data set.
- Create parcel and building features.
- Import parcel identifiers.

Review the current coordinate settings

1. Start ArcCatalog.

2. In the Catalog Tree, navigate to **C:\DigitalCity\MyArc-City**. Click the plus sign next to the **Arc City** geodatabase to expand it, then click **Combo354355**.

3. In the Catalog Display, click the Metadata tab. In the Metadata panel, click the Spatial tab. Review the spatial metadata for the **Combo354355** feature class. (If you don't see the three tabs, shown in the graphic below, on the Metadata toolbar, choose FGDC ESRI from the Stylesheet drop-down list.)

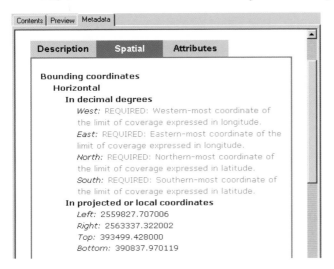

Notice that there is no information about the horizontal bounding coordinates in decimal degrees. This is because the spatial reference has not been defined for this data.

Projected or local coordinates are present, however, because these are read directly from the data's geometry. These are real-world coordinates used by the draftsperson to create the CAD files, but until the coordinate system is formally defined, ArcGIS will have no way of knowing to which area on the earth these coordinates correspond. Using data with an undefined coordinate system has several downsides, two of which include uncertainty with measurements made from the data and the inability to align the data with feature classes stored in different coordinate systems.

☐ Define the coordinate system of Combo354355

4. In the Catalog Tree, right-click **Combo354355** and choose Properties. In the Feature Class Properties dialog, click the Fields tab.

5. In the Field Name list, click the Shape field. In the list of field properties, click the Ellipses button in the right-hand column of the Spatial Reference property.

6. On the Spatial Reference Properties dialog, click Select.

As mentioned in the exercise introduction, you know that the CAD maps were created using the Wisconsin State Plane Coordinate System—South, and that the units are measured in feet. You will use this information to assign a map projection and coordinate system to your data.

7. In the Browse for Coordinate Systems dialog, double-click the **Projected Coordinate Systems** folder to open it. Next, open the **State Plane** folder and then open the **Nad 1927** folder. Scroll across the list of coordinate systems and click the **NAD 1927 StatePlane Wisconsin South FIPS 4803.prj** file.

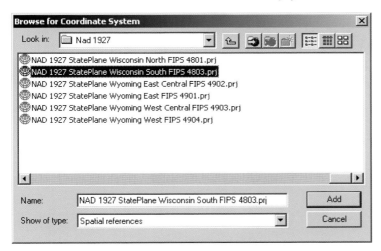

8. Click Add.

The coordinate system parameters are displayed in the Details box of the Spatial Reference Properties dialog.

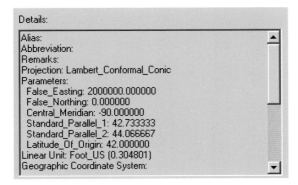

9. Click OK to close the two open dialogs.

10. Preview the spatial metadata of **Combo354355** using the same method you followed in step 3. (If the metadata did not change from the last time you looked at it, click the Create/Update metadata button on the Metadata toolbar).

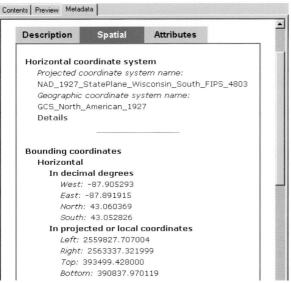

A definition of the horizontal coordinate system that you defined for the feature class now exists in the metadata. ArcGIS was able to determine the bounding coordinates in decimal degrees even though you defined your data in State Plane Coordinates. You can review the details by clicking the Details link.

☐ Create a feature data set

In this task, you will create a new feature data set inside the **Arc City** geodatabase and define its spatial reference. Once the new feature data set is created, you will add the **Combo354355** feature class to it.

11. In the Catalog Tree, right-click the **Arc City** geodatabase, point to New, and click Feature Dataset.

12. Name the new feature data set **ParcelBldg**.

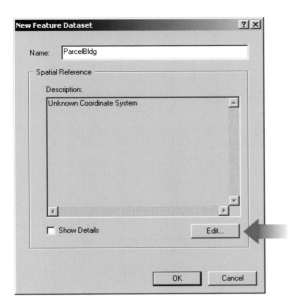

13. In the lower-right corner of the New Feature Dataset dialog, click the Edit button.

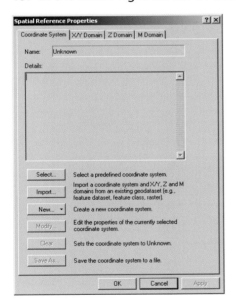

The Spatial Reference Properties dialog appears. You will use this dialog to import the spatial reference from **Combo354355** and assign it to the feature data set.

14. On the Spatial Reference Properties dialog, click Import. In the Browse for Dataset dialog, select **Combo354355**, then click Add.

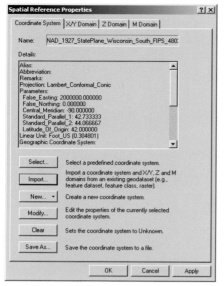

15. In the Spatial Reference Properties dialog, click OK.

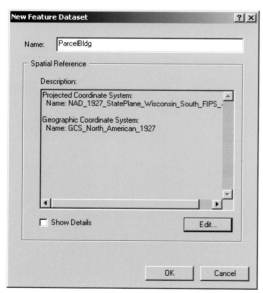

The spatial reference that you defined for **Combo354355** has been applied to the **ParcelBldg** feature data set.

16. In the New Feature Dataset dialog, click OK.

Within the **Arc City** geodatabase, the **ParcelBldg** feature data set now exists with the State Plane coordinate system, NAD 27, Wisconsin South Zone assigned to it, but it is still empty.

17. In the Catalog Tree, drag and drop **Combo354355** into the **ParcelBldg** feature data set. (To do this, click **Combo354355**, then, while holding down the mouse button, move your cursor over the top of the **ParcelBldg** feature data set and release the mouse button.)

18. In the Catalog Tree, expand the **ParcelBldg** feature data set.

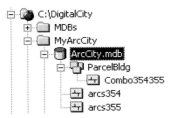

The spatial properties of the feature class match the spatial properties of the feature data set in which it exists. This is true for all feature data sets and the feature classes they contain because a feature data set can only contain feature classes that have the same spatial reference systems as it does.

Now when you use this data in ArcMap, it will recognize this coordinate system allowing you to accurately work with scale, measurements, and feature classes stored in different coordinate systems.

19. Close ArcCatalog.

Create parcel and building features

Next, you will use ArcMap to extract the parcel and building features from **Combo354355** and place them in respective feature classes inside the **ParcelBldg** feature data set. Use the following table as a guide for selecting the features in the next steps.

Layer	Definition
27	Real estate basemap (parcels)
28	Building outlines

20. Start ArcMap and open a new, empty map.

21. Click the Add Data button, then navigate to your **C:\DigitalCity\MyArcCity** folder. Double-click the **ArcCity.mdb**, then double-click the **ParcelBldg** feature data set. Click the **Combo354355** feature class and click Add.

First you will select the lines belonging to the parcel layer.

22. Click the Selection menu and click Select by Attributes. Enter the query: [Layer] = '27'.

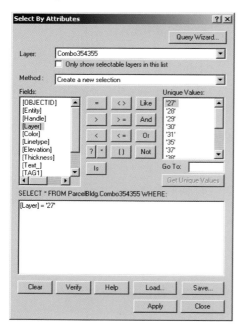

23. Click Apply, then click Close.

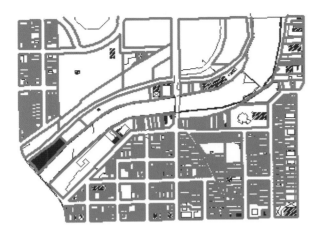

The selected line features are highlighted on the map. Now you will export them to a new Parcel feature class within the **ParcelBldg** feature data set.

24. In the table of contents, right-click **Combo354355**, point to Data, then click Export Data. In the Export Data dialog, make sure the Export drop-down list is set to Selected features and that Use the same Coordinate System as this layer's source data option is chosen.

25. Click the Output Browse button. In the Saving Data dialog, make sure the Look In Dropdown list is set to the **ParcelBldg** feature data set and name the new feature class **Parcel_L**. Click Save.

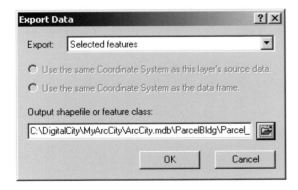

26. Click OK in the Export Data dialog. After ArcMap processes the export procedure, click Yes to add the new data to your map.

27. Right-click **Combo354355** in the table of contents, point to Selection, and click Clear Selected Features.

28. Repeat the procedure used in steps 22 through 27 to select then export the building features to a new feature class. (Your query should be [Layer] = '28'). Name the new feature class **Building_L**, and add it to ArcMap. (When you open the Selection by Attribute dialog, make sure that **Combo354355** is chosen in the Layer drop-down list).

29. In the table of contents, uncheck **Combo354355** to turn it off.

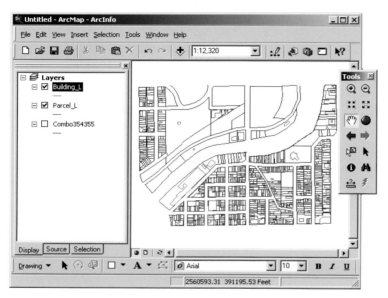

You now have buildings and parcels for the entire city in separate line feature classes.

Import parcel identifiers

The next step is to create a point feature class from the tax key table so that you can associate a tax key number with each parcel. To do this, you will add the **taxkey_xy.dbf** table to the map document, display the *x,y* coordinates as point locations on the map, and then export them to a point feature class in the **ParcelBldg** feature data set.

30. Click the Add Data button and navigate to your **MyArcCity** folder. Select **taxkey_xy.dbf** and click Add.

The table of contents switches to the Source tab when the table is added to ArcMap. The table is not listed on the Display tab because it is not associated with a feature class.

31. In the table of contents, right-click taxkey_xy and choose Open.

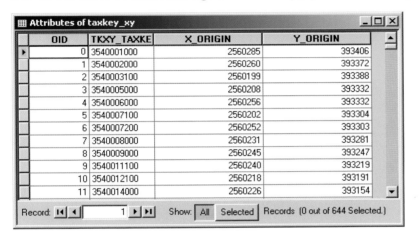

Remember that the X_ORIGIN and Y_ORIGIN fields contain the *x,y* coordinates of the locations for each tax key number. You will use these fields to create a point on the map display for each tax key.

32. Close the Attributes of taxkey_xy table.

33. Right-click taxkey_xy, and choose Display XY Data.

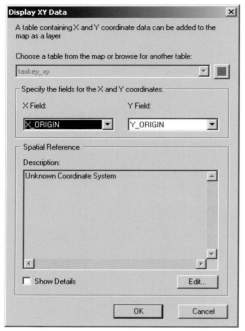

In the Display XY Data dialog, the fields X_ORIGIN, and Y_ORIGIN are selected by default as the appropriate *x,y* coordinates. Notice that the Spatial Reference Description is "Unknown Coordinate System".

34. In the Display XY Data dialog, click OK.

The points are displayed on the map display and are stored in a temporary layer named taxkey_xy Events.

ArcGIS has dynamically mapped the *x,y* coordinates from the values in the table, but they are stored in a temporary file. To make the points permanent features in your geodatabase, you must convert them to a feature class.

35. In the table of contents, turn off the Building_L layer so you can see the points more clearly in relation to the parcels.

36. Right-click taxkey_xy Events and click Data, then Export Data.

37. In the Export Data dialog, choose to export all features using the same coordinate system as the source data, then click the Browse button. In the Saving Data dialog, navigate to your **ParcelBldg** feature data set in your **Arc City** geodatabase and name the feature class **TaxKeyXY,** then click Save. (You may have to click the Save as type drop-down menu and choose Personal Geodatabase feature classes.)

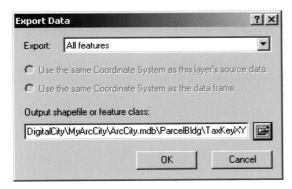

38. Click OK in the Export Data dialog and then No when prompted to add the data to ArcMap. For now, you do not need to display the new feature class in ArcMap.

You now have three new feature classes in your **Arc City** geodatabase: parcel lines, building lines, and tax key points. In the next exercise, you'll add the parcel tax key numbers to the parcel features.

39. From the file menu click Save. Name the map document **my_ex01c.mxd** and save it in your **MyArcCity** folder.

40. Close ArcMap.

Exercise 1d

Correct digitizing errors and create a topology

You now have parcels and buildings in your GIS database, but they are represented as line features. You need them to be represented as polygons because parcels are area features and you want to create a one-to-one relationship between the records in the assessor's parcel attribute data files and the parcel features. In this exercise, you will use the parcel boundaries to create parcel polygon features.

When you previewed the CAD maps in exercise 1a, you were interested in getting an overall, general idea of the data. Because you did not zoom in to examine the data in detail, you could not see any errors that may have been introduced when the maps were digitized. Two common errors are overshoots and undershoots—places where lines that should meet extend too far or fall short.

Overshoot   Undershoot

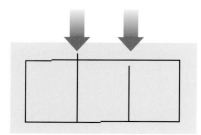

Overshoots could cause extra polygon features to be created and undershoots could prevent the creation of polygons. Because of this, you'll need to find and fix these errors before you convert the line features to polygons.

Visually searching for errors like overshoots and undershoots (also called dangles) would be a tedious job: you would have to zoom in·to a large scale and then pan around extensively. Fortunately, ArcGIS offers a way to automate the process of identifying and fixing data errors. To do this, you build a topology.

Topology defines the spatial relationships among points, lines, and polygons in a GIS. The human eye can see these topological relationships (adjacency of polygons, containment of polygons, and connectivity of lines) implicitly just by looking at a map, but the computer cannot "see" the map. It has only data. It doesn't store the map—it stores the data needed to produce the map. Thus, topology must be defined explicitly in the GIS database.

In this exercise you will perform the following tasks:
- Preview the parcel boundaries feature class.
- Determine what topology rules to use.
- Create and validate the topology.
- Add the topology and feature class to a map document.
- List the errors using the Error Inspector.

- Find and fix an error.
- Fix the remaining undershoots.
- Find and fix overshoot errors.
- Fix an error using the editing tools.

Note: In this and the following exercises, you will learn how to edit the data to eliminate topology errors. In real life, however, you would first need to check with official records from the county surveyor's office or similar office that is responsible for the legal placement of parcel boundaries.

Geodatabase topology

In a geodatabase, a topology is a set of rules that defines the spatial relationships you want to model and preserve in your spatial data. Each topology rule applies to a particular type of spatial relationship. For example, Must Not Have Gaps is a topology rule that defines a spatial relationship among polygon boundaries.

You can use topology rules to monitor the spatial relationship between the features within a single feature class, as well as between features of two feature classes. Topology rules don't prevent errors from occurring, but they do make it easy for you to find and fix them.

ArcCatalog contains tools for managing geodatabase topology. In ArcCatalog, you can create a topology, define and manage its properties, and preview and summarize topology errors. In ArcCatalog you can also copy, rename, and delete a topology.

ArcMap contains tools for exploring and fixing topology errors. With ArcMap topology tools, you can uniquely symbolize different types of topology errors, generate an interactive list of topology errors, examine topology errors on a case-by-case basis, and access predefined fixes for specific types of topology errors.

Preview the parcel boundaries feature class

1. Start ArcCatalog. If necessary, expand the **Arc City** geodatabase and the **ParcelBldg** feature data set.

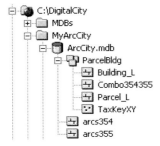

2. Preview the Parcel_L feature class. It contains the parcel boundary line features you will be working with in this exercise.

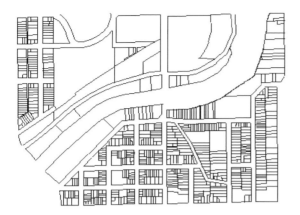

In the following steps, you will create a geodatabase topology and add rules to identify spatial errors that may exist in the parcel boundaries data. More than twenty topology rules are available in ArcGIS that define various possible relationships among point, line, and polygon features. To keep this exercise simple, you will use only those topology rules needed to find any undershoots or overshoots in the parcel boundary lines. In a real project, you would use additional rules to ensure all of the necessary spatial relationships between features.

Determine what topology rules to use

3. From the Help menu, click ArcGIS Desktop Help. In the help system's table of contents, click the Contents tab. Expand the Editing in ArcMap category, expand the Editing topology subcategory, then click the Topology rules topic.

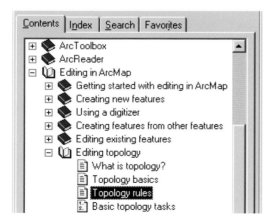

4. After reading the introduction, click the blue bullet next to Line Rules. In the Line rules table, read the description for the Must Not Have Dangles rule.

You'll use the Must Not Have Dangles rule to find both overshoots and undershoots in your parcel lines.

5. After reading the information about the Must Not Have Dangles rule, close ArcGIS Desktop Help.

Create and validate the topology

6. In the Catalog Tree, right-click the **ParcelBldg** feature data set, point to New, and click Topology.

The first panel of the New Topology wizard gives a brief explanation of topology.

7. Click Next. On the second panel, accept the default settings for the topology name, read the description about cluster tolerance, then change the cluster tolerance to 0.2 US survey feet.

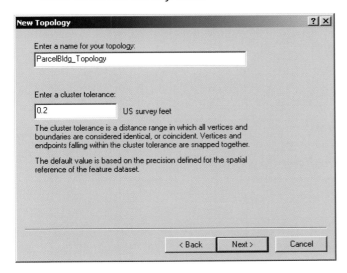

8. Click Next. On the third panel, check Parcel_L to add the parcel lines to the topology.

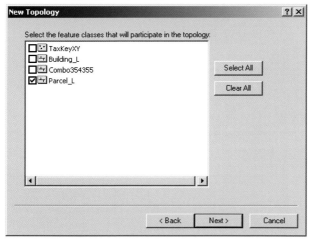

9. Click Next.

The fourth panel gives you the option to specify ranks. Ranks are used to prioritize which features snap to which during the topology validation process. For example, if you had section lines and section corners participating in the same topology, and you knew that the section corners had a higher positional accuracy than the section lines, you could give the section corners a higher rank than the section lines. Then, when you validate the topology, the section corners will stay put and the section lines will snap to the section corners.

Since you only have one feature class in this topology, ranks do not apply to your current situation.

10. Click Next, then click Add Rule. From the Rule drop-down list, choose Must Not Have Dangles. After choosing the rule, read the Rule Description. (Toggling the Show Errors option helps you visualize what types of errors the rule will identify).

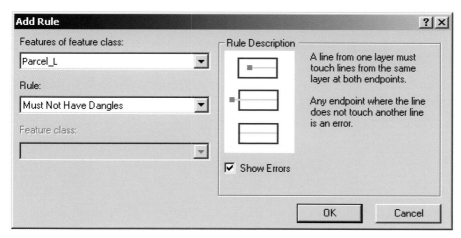

11. Click OK, then click Next. In the final panel of the wizard, review the choices you made.

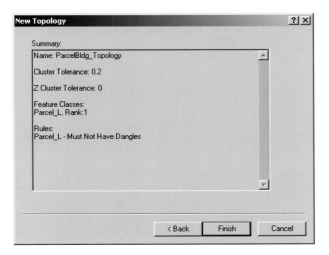

If you've made any mistakes, use the Back button to go back and fix them.

12. Click Finish. After a moment, a message asks if you want to validate the topology.

During the validation process, vertices and line segments that fall within the specified cluster tolerance are made coincident and topology errors are identified.

13. Click Yes. After the validation process ends, an icon representing the topology you just created appears in the **ParcelBldg** feature data set.

14. In the Catalog Tree, click the **ParcelBldg_Topology**, then, if necessary, click the Preview tab.

Each red square represents a violation of the Must Not Have Dangles topology error. Your next task is to use ArcMap to fix these errors.

15. Close ArcCatalog.

☐ Add the topology and feature class to a map document

16. Start ArcMap and open a new, empty map.

17. Click the Add Data button. Navigate to your **Arc City** geodatabase, double-click the **ParcelBldg** feature data set, click the **ParcelBldg_Topology**, and click Add. When prompted, click Yes to add the participating feature classes.

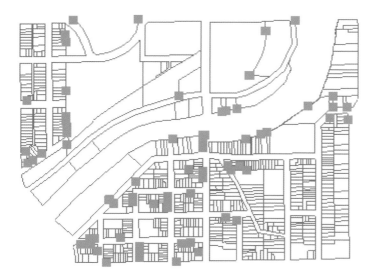

As you can see, a topology can be added to ArcMap as a layer, and after being added to ArcMap, the topology displays all the errors in the feature class(es) for which it stores rules.

List the errors using the Error Inspector

You'll use the Error Inspector to find and repair the errors. To access this functionality, you'll need to display the Topology toolbar and the Editor toolbar.

18. From the View menu, point to Toolbars and choose Topology to open the Topology toolbar. After you open the Topology toolbar, open the Editor toolbar.

19. From the Editor menu, choose Start Editing.

20. On the Topology toolbar, click the Error Inspector button.

21. Position the Error Inspector so you can also see the map display (e.g., move it out of the way by docking it horizontally underneath the map and table of contents).

22. In the Error Inspector, make sure Errors is checked and uncheck Visible Extent only, then click Search Now.

With the complete list of all the topology errors, you can take a systematic approach to fixing the troublesome geometries.

Find and fix an error

23. In the Error Inspector, click the Feature 1 field to sort the fields in ascending order.

24. Right-click on the top row and choose Zoom To.

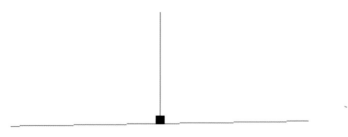

The error is an undershoot; you will have to zoom in closer to see it.

25. Click the Zoom In tool and zoom in closely to the error.

Later on, you will convert the parcel lines to polygons. Polygons require complete closure, that is, there can be no opening along its edges. An undershoot, like the one here, can be a burgeoning polygon's worst enemy. The topology environment contains predefined methods for fixing all sorts of topology errors. There is a predefined fix for undershoots, but before you can use it, you need to determine the length of the undershoot.

26. **Click the Measure tool.**

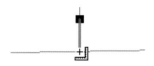

27. **Measure the distance between the error feature and the line perpendicular to it.**

The distance measure is displayed in the Status Bar below the table of contents and is approximately 1.2 feet.

28. **In the Error Inspector, right-click on the top row again and choose Extend from the context menu. In the Maximum Distance dialog, type 1.5.**

Measurements made with the Measure tool can vary depending on the accuracy of your clicks, which means your initial measurement could be off by a few inches. By choosing to extend the line by a maximum distance of 1.5 feet, you are ensuring that the line is extended enough to correct the undershoot. You don't need to worry about creating an overshoot, because the line extension will stop when it crosses another feature.

29. Press Enter.

The error is corrected and its entry is removed from the Error Inspector. You could continue to fix each undershoot error individually, but it will be much faster to apply the fix to all of the errors at the same time.

Fix the remaining undershoots

30. On the Tools toolbar, click the Full Extent button.

Zooming to the full extent will allow you to see which errors are fixed.

31. In the Error Inspector, select all of the rows by holding down the Shift key, clicking on the top row, scrolling to the bottom of the list, and clicking the bottom row.

32. With all of the rows selected, right-click on one of the rows and choose Extend. This time, enter **2** as the Maximum Distance and press Enter. (If you were to continue examining the errors, you would find that some of the undershoots were close to two feet.)

ArcMap searches all of the errors and, where appropriate, extends the undershoots up to two feet. Any errors that are fixed are removed from the topology layer and the Error Inspector.

Not all errors have been fixed, however. There are still forty-six errors remaining.

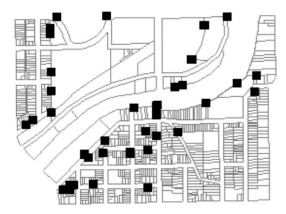

Find and fix overshoot errors

33. In the Error Inspector, scroll to the top and click the record at the top of the list. Right-click the top record and click Zoom To. Then use the Zoom In tool to zoom in close enough to see the error.

This error is an overshoot. You'll need to use the Trim fix to correct this error and the others like it.

34. Zoom out to the full extent of the map display.

35. In the Error Inspector, select all of the rows. Then right-click on a row and choose Trim. In the Maximum Distance dialog, type **2** and press Enter.

This time, you are left with eighteen errors. These errors have various causes: the line needs to be extended or trimmed more than two feet; a different predefined fix is required or you would need to use the editing tools to correct the error. You'll fix one of these errors to get some practice using the editing tools.

36. Close the Error Inspector.

Fix an error using the editing tools

The next error you'll fix is located in the northeast portion of the city, as the arrow in the graphic below indicates.

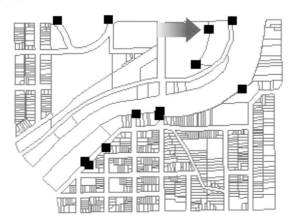

37. Zoom in to the error until you can clearly see its cause.

Two lines are offset from one another where there should be a single line defining the parcel boundary. If this data belonged to your city instead of Arc City, you would need to check with other departments to determine the correct location of the lines. For the purposes of this exercise, however, you will assume that the endpoint of the southern line is in the wrong location. To fix the problem, you will set the snapping environment and then snap it to the northern endpoint to form a single line feature.

38. Turn off the topology layer. (Uncheck **ParcelBldg_Topology** in the table of contents.)

39. Click the Editor menu and click Options. In the Editing Options dialog, click the General tab. In the Snapping Tolerance box, type **2**. In the Snapping tolerance drop-down list, choose map units.

40. Click OK.

41. Click the Editor menu and click Snapping. In the upper box of the Snapping dialog, check End for Parcel_L.

Layer	Vertex	Edge	End
Parcel_L	☐	☐	☑

Based on the settings you just made, the endpoints of the parcel lines will automatically snap together if they are moved within two feet of one another while you are editing.

42. Close the Snapping Environment dialog.

43. Click the Edit Tool on the Editor toolbar.

44. In the map display, double-click the southern line feature to display its vertexes.

45. Hover your mouse over the endpoint of the southern line. When the icon changes to the small box with the four arrows, click and hold down the left mouse button, then drag the endpoint directly over the endpoint of the northern line and release the mouse button.

46. Click on the Map display, but not on a feature to unselect the line.

The error is fixed. Ordinarily, you would need to fix each of the remaining errors and validate the topology again to make sure that you have not introduced any new errors.

However, for the purposes of this exercise, it is enough for you to see how to find and repair topology errors. You'll get more practice fixing errors in later exercises.

47. Click the Editor menu and click Stop Editing. Click Yes to save your edits.

48. From the File menu, click Save As. Navigate to your **C:\DigitalCity\MyArcCity** folder and save the map document as **my_ex01d.mxd**.

49. Exit ArcMap. You do not need to save the map document.

Exercise 1e

Create parcel polygon features

The errors in the parcel lines are all fixed and you are ready to create polygons. (All of the errors that remained at the end of exercise 1d have been fixed in the exercise 1e data.) In this exercise, a new polygon feature will be created wherever the lines intersect to create a closed shape. At the same time, attributes from the TaxKeyXY point feature class, which you created in exercise 1c, will be associated with the new polygons. Any polygon containing a point will be assigned the attributes of that point.

The new feature class may contain errors. Sliver polygons or missing polygons are two likely examples. In this exercise, you'll use topology rules to check for errors in the parcel polygon features and to make sure that the attributes were assigned correctly.

In this exercise you will perform the following tasks:
- Update the Arc City geodatabase.
- Create polygons and add attributes.
- Delete unnecessary attribute fields.
- Add feature classes and rules to the topology.
- Validate the topology and preview errors.

Update the Arc City geodatabase

Before you start this exercise, you must replace your current **Arc City** geodatabase with the version designed for use within this exercise. To do this, you will copy the replacement geodatabase into your **MyArcCity** folder and delete the version you have been working with up to this point.

1. Start ArcCatalog.

2. In the Catalog Tree, navigate to and then expand the **C:\DigitalCity\MDBs** folder.

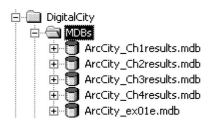

3. Right-click the **ArcCity_ex01e.mdb** and choose Copy.

4. Right-click the **MyArcCity** folder and choose Paste. Expand the **MyArcCity** folder in the Catalog Tree.

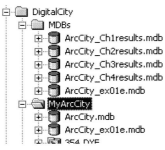

5. Inside the **MyArcCity** folder, right-click the **ArcCity.mdb** and choose Delete. Click Yes on the warning message.

6. Right-click the **ArcCity_ex01e.mdb** and choose rename. Type **ArcCity** then press Enter.

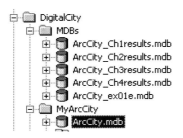

This version of the Arc City geodatabases has the same contents as the Arc City geodatabase you used in the last chapter. The only difference is that most of the errors in the Parcel_L feature class that existed at the end of the last exercise have been repaired.

☐ Create polygons and add attributes

7. In the Catalog Tree, expand the **Arc City** geodatabase. Right-click the **ParcelBldg** feature data set, point to New, then click Polygon Feature Class from Lines.

8. In the Polygon Feature Class From Lines dialog, name the new feature class **Parcel_P.** Accept the default cluster tolerance. Check Parcel_L for the feature class that will contribute lines. From the drop-down list at the bottom of the dialog, choose TaxKeyXY as the point feature class to establish attributes for the polygon features.

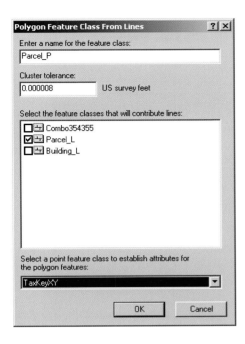

9. Click OK. After a moment, the new Parcel_P feature class is added to the feature data set.

10. Preview the Parcel_P polygon features.

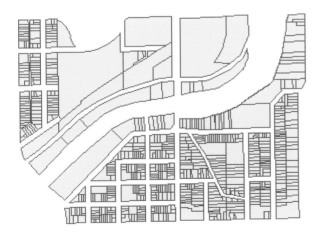

11. Preview the Parcel_P attribute table.

TKXY_TAXKE	X_ORIGIN	Y_ORIGIN
▶ 3540794000	2561287	390881
3540767000	2560712	390859
3540768000	2560748	390862
3540769000	2560765	390875
3540777000	2560963	390882
3540795000	2561303	390904

The TKXY_TAXKE, X_ORIGIN, and Y_ORIGIN fields were added to the Parcel_P feature class and came from the TaxKeyXY feature class. As you saw in exercise 1c, there is one TaxKeyXY point feature in each parcel. During the conversion process the attributes from each TaxKeyXY point were added to the corresponding record of the parcel the point fell within.

The TKXY_TAXKE field contains the tax key of each parcel. TKXY_TAXKE contains crucial information because it uniquely identifies each parcel and will allow you to join the parcel feature class with the assessor's data. The other two fields from the TaxKeyXY feature class are not needed within the Parcel_P feature class. In the next step you will delete them.

⊔ Delete unnecessary attribute fields

12. In the Preview panel, click the X_ORIGIN column heading to select the column.

TKXY_TAXKE	X_ORIGIN	Y_ORIGIN
3540794000	2561287	390881
3540767000	2560712	390859
3540768000	2560748	390862
3540769000	2560765	390875
3540777000	2560963	390882
3540795000	2561303	390904
3550847000	2562167	390912
3550846000	2562211	390910
3540766000	2560738	390915
3540796000	2561305	390930

13. Right-click the column heading and choose Delete Field. When prompted, click Yes to confirm the deletion. Repeat the procedure to delete the Y_ORIGIN column.

⊔ Add feature classes and rules to the topology

To check for errors in the new Parcel_P feature class, you'll add the Parcel_P and TaxKeyXY feature classes to the **ParcelBldg_Topology** and define two new rules for the topology. The first rule will find any lines in the Parcel_L feature class that are not covered by the boundaries in the Parcel_P feature class. The second rule will check each polygon in the Parcel_P feature class to make sure it contains a point in the TaxKeyXY feature class.

14. In the Catalog Tree, right-click **ParcelBldg_Topology** and choose Properties. In the Topology Properties dialog, click the Feature Classes tab.

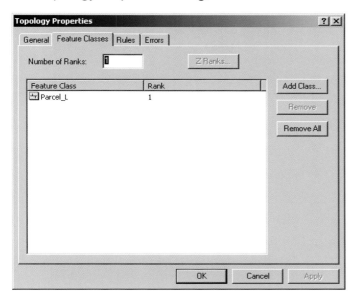

15. Click Add Class. In the Add Class dialog, hold down the Ctrl key and select both TaxKeyXY and Parcel_P.

16. Click OK, then click Apply to add the two feature classes to the topology.

17. In the Topology Properties dialog, click the Rules tab.

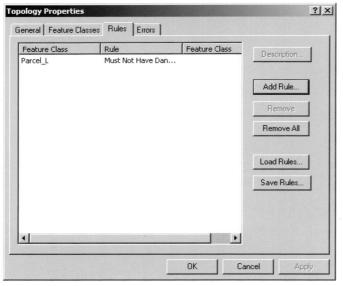

You see the Must Not Have Dangles rule that you added earlier for the Parcel_L feature class. You'll remove this rule before adding your two new ones.

18. On the Rules tab click Remove All then click Add Rule.

19. In the Add Rule dialog, make sure that Parcel_L is the selected feature class. For Rule, choose Must Be Covered By Boundary Of. Parcel_P is automatically selected as the second feature class. Take a moment to read the rule's description.

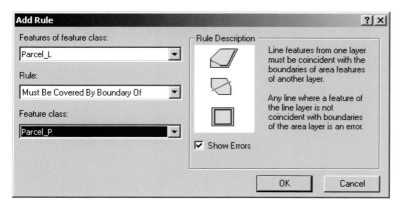

20. Click OK, then click Add Rule again.

This time you will add a rule that makes sure there is a tax key point within each parcel.

21. In the Add Rule dialog, chose Parcel_P in the Features of feature class drop-down list. Choose Contains Point from the Rule drop-down list. Choose TaxKeyXY from the Feature class drop-down list.

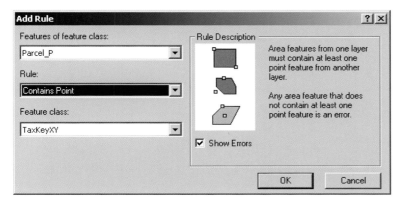

22. Click OK in the Add Rule dialog, then click OK in the Topology Properties dialog.

Validate the topology and preview errors

23. Preview the updated **ParcelBldg_Topology**.

Currently, the catalog display shows only a blue, hatched rectangle, which represents a dirty area. The software uses dirty areas to indicate areas in a topology that have not been validated. (Validation is the process used to check for topology errors.) When you add or remove feature classes or rules from a topology, the entire extent of the data in the feature data set is considered dirty.

24. In the Catalog Tree, right-click **ParcelBldg_Topology** and click Validate. When the validation is complete, click OK to close the validation message.

25. From the View drop-down menu, click Refresh.

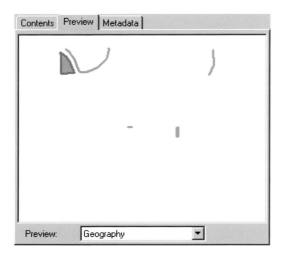

The new topology errors are displayed. These errors represent parcel lines that are not coincident with the boundaries of the parcel polygons, or those parcel polygons that do not contain a tax key point. You'll fix these errors using ArcMap in the next exercise.

26. Close ArcCatalog.

Find and fix errors in parcel polygon features

In exercise 1d you learned how to find and fix topology errors using the Error Inspector. In this exercise, you will use another ArcMap tool, the Fix Topology Error tool, to fix the errors in the parcel feature class. Then you will generate an error summary to make sure you've found all of the errors.

In this exercise you will perform the following tasks:
- Add the topology and its associated feature classes to a map document.
- Visually inspect errors and symbolize dirty areas.
- Fix the polygon error.
- Merge polygon features.
- Delete unnecessary lines.
- Mark the county park boundary line as an exception.
- Divide a parcel.
- Change parcel attribute values.
- Validate the topology.

⌑ Add the topology and its associated feature classes to a map document

1. Start ArcMap with a new, empty map.

2. Click the Add Data button, navigate to your **MyArcCity** folder, double-click the **Arc City** geodatabase, double-click the **ParcelBldg** feature data set, click the **Parcel-Bldg_Topology**, and click Add. When prompted, click Yes to add the feature classes participating in the topology.

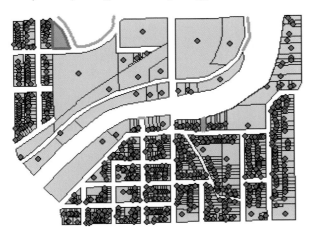

The topology layer and the three feature classes participating in the topology are added.

Visually inspect errors and symbolize dirty areas

There are several topology errors that you must fix. You'll begin with the polygon error in the northwest part of the city. To keep track of where you have made edits, you'll display the dirty areas.

3.   In the table of contents, right-click the **ParcelBldg_Topology** and choose Properties.

4.   In the Layer Properties dialog, click the Symbology tab. In the Show box, check Dirty Areas.

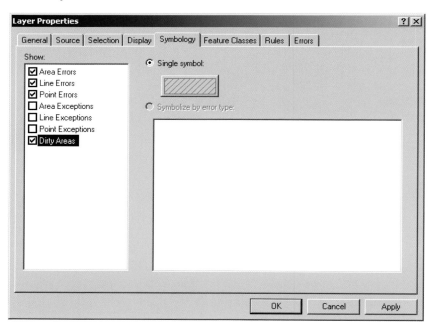

5.   Click OK. The symbology used for dirty areas is now shown in the ArcMap table of contents in the **ParcelBldg_Topology** legend.

Dirty areas represent areas in a topology that have been edited since the last time the topology was validated. As you fix the topology errors, the dirty areas will help you keep track of where you have made edits.

Fix the polygon error

The first error you will fix is associated with a polygon in the northwest part of the city. To help you determine what the problem is, you will find out what topology rule is being broken.

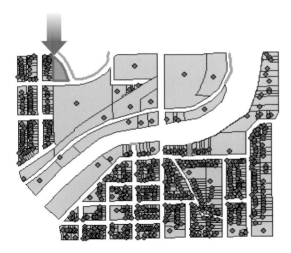

6. If necessary, open the Editor toolbar. Click the Editor menu and click Start Editing.

7. If necessary, open the Topology toolbar. On the Topology toolbar, click the Fix Topology Error tool.

8. In the northwest corner of the map display, right-click the polygon error and click Show Rule Description in the context menu.

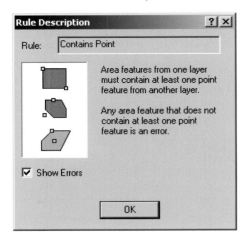

The Rule Description dialog tells you that the error is in the Contains Point rule. Notice on the map that the parcel you clicked does not contain a TaxKeyXY point.

There are several ways this error could have come about. For example, the information for this parcel may not have been entered in the TaxKeyXY table. Or, perhaps the CAD map was incorrect and this polygon is actually part of another parcel. You will begin investigating the problem by going back to the source—the CAD map.

9. Click OK to close the Rule Description.

10. Start ArcCatalog.

11. In the Catalog Tree, navigate to your **DigitalCity\SourceData** folder and preview the **354.DXF** CAD drawing (it's the one with the white icon). Zoom in to the parcel in question.

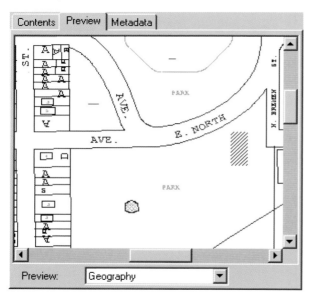

The CAD map shows park areas near the polygon in question. Because you are familiar with the area, you realize that this polygon is really a part of the park parcel on the south side of E. North Avenue. The third park area belongs to a county park and is outside the Arc City limits.

To correct the polygon error, you will merge the two city park polygons into one multi-part polygon feature so that they share the same tax key number (3540433111).

12. Close ArcCatalog.

Merge polygon features

13. To clear the map display of unneeded clutter, turn off the Topology layer.

14. On the Editor toolbar click the Edit tool.

15. While holding down the Shift key, click inside the two park parcels in the map display that are outlined in red in the graphic below.

16. From the Editor menu, choose Merge. In the Merge dialog, select Parcel_P-3540433111 as the feature with which the other feature will be merged.

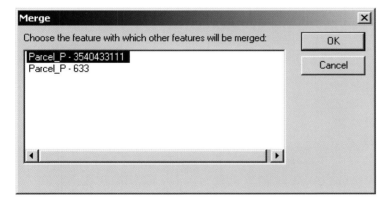

17. Click OK.

The polygons are merged to create a single, multipart feature, and the attributes from the parcel you chose in the merge dialog are retained.

18. From the Selection menu, click Clear Selected Features, then turn on the **Parcel-Bldg_Topology** layer.

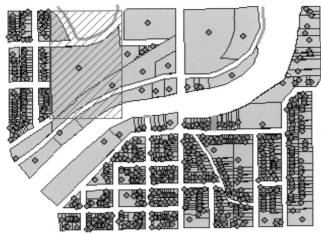

A dirty area covers the multipart polygon you just created.

◻ Delete unnecessary lines

Currently the topology shows several other errors that need to be fixed. Three of these errors are caused by the existence of a line where there is no parcel. To fix these three cases, you will delete the unnecessary line feature.

19. Zoom to the line error in the northeast corner of Arc City.

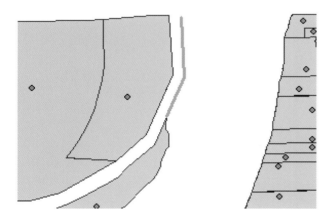

20. Click the Fix Topology Error tool, then, in the map display, drag a box around the line error.

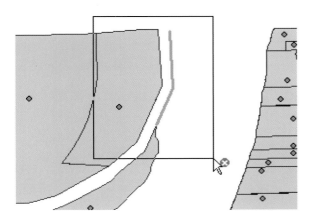

21. **Right-click in the Map display and choose Subtract.**

The Subtract command deletes the line feature from the Parcel_L feature class. Again, a dirty area is drawn around the area where you just made edits.

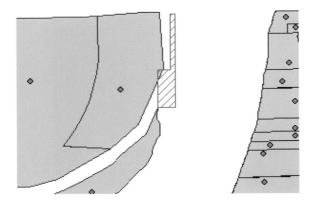

22. **Zoom to full extent.**

The next error you will fix is located near the center of Arc City.

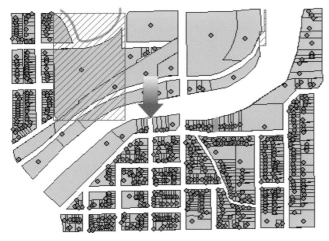

23. Zoom to the error indicated in the graphic above. Select the error with the Fix Topology Error tool, then right-click and choose Subtract.

24. Zoom to full extent.

There are two more sets of errors in the topology. There are also several dirty areas, one of which overlaps with an error you still need to fix. Before you fix the remaining errors, you will validate the topology to remove the dirty areas.

25. Zoom to full extent, then, on the Topology toolbar, click the Validate Entire Topology button. Click Yes on the warning message.

Having cleaned up the dirty areas, you will now fix the remaining topology errors, which include a large error in the northwest portion of the city and a smaller error near the center of Arc City.

Mark the county park boundary line as an exception

First you will address the error that's located in the northwest corner of Arc City. This error is actually the remnant of a park boundary that extends outside of the limits of Arc City. You do not want to delete this line, but you also do not want it marked as an error in your topology. To deal with situations like this, you can mark topology errors as exceptions.

26. Zoom in to the error that is located in the northwest portion of Arc City.

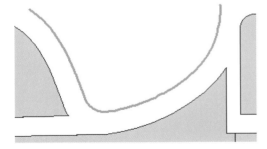

27. Click the Fix Topology Error tool, then drag a box around the entire line error to select it.

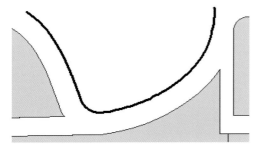

The error feature appears to be a single line, but it's actually made of several segments.

28. On the Topology toolbar, click the Error Inspector button.

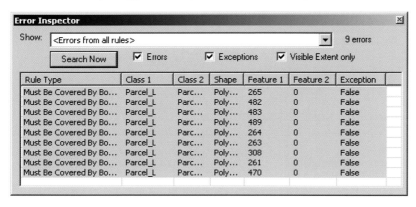

The error segments you selected are all listed in the Error Inspector.

29. Right-click anywhere in the list of errors and choose Mark as Exception.

30. Close the Error Inspector.

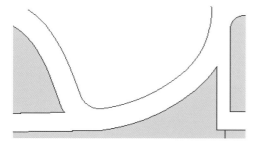

The underlying features that generated the errors still exist, but the topology errors they produced are now marked as exceptions and no longer appear in the topology layer.

(To turn exceptions back into errors, you can use the Error Inspector to search for and list all the exceptions in a topology. Once you have listed the exceptions of interest, you can then set their Exception status back to False.)

31. Zoom to full extent.

There is one more topology error to deal with.

Divide a parcel

32. Zoom in to the remaining error features located near the center of Arc City.

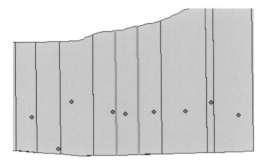

33. Turn off the topology layer so that you can see what is causing this error.

With the topology turned off, the cause of the errors is still unclear.

34. Toggle the Parcel_L layer on, off, then back on again.

By toggling the Parcel_L layer's visibility, you can see that a polygon (from the Parcel_P layer) exists where there should actually be three parcels. You may have also noticed three tax key points within that single parcel.

To fix these two error features, you will divide the single parcel polygon into three polygons based on the location of the two parcel lines that are currently marked as errors.

Before you begin digitizing the parcel boundaries, you'll need to set the snapping environment.

35. From the Editor menu, click Options. In the Editing Options dialog, click the General tab. Change the Snapping tolerance to **2** map units.

36. Click OK.

37. From the Editor menu, click Snapping. In the top part of the Snapping dialog, check End for Parcel_L.

Layer	Vertex	Edge	End
TaxKeyXY	☐	☐	☐
Parcel_L	☐	☐	☑
Parcel_P	☐	☐	☐

38. Close the Snapping Environment dialog.

When you digitize the lines to split the polygon, your cursor will now snap to the endpoints of the Parcel_L lines.

39. Click the Edit tool, then, in the map display, click the polygon that needs to be divided.

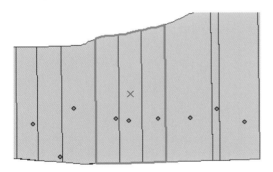

40. On the Editor toolbar, select Cut Polygon Features from the Task drop-down list, then click the Sketch tool.

With the current tool and task selected, you can split a polygon into two separate polygons at the location where you draw a line across it.

41. In the map display, click just above the north end of the line, then click the north end of the line along which you want to cut the parcel.

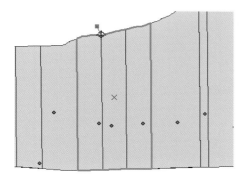

42. Place your cursor over the southern end of the same line you just clicked on and click again. Then, double-click just below the parcel (in the white area) you are going to split.

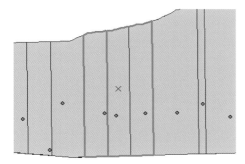

The line is struck across the polygon and the parcel is cut into two separate features. You now need to cut the parcel based on the location of the other parcel line that was causing the error.

43. Using the same process that you used in steps 41 and 42, cut the parcel along the other parcel line (shown below in red).

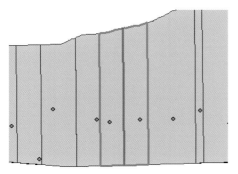

After you cut the parcel, there should be three parcels where there was previously one.

44. Clear all the selected features, then turn off the Parcel_L layer.

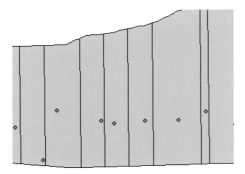

The parcel geometry is fixed, but you need to update the attribute values of the parcels you just split.

▢ Change parcel attribute values

The only attribute value you must update for the three new parcels is their tax key value, which should match the tax key value of the point each parcel contains.

45. In the table of contents, right-click TaxKeyXY and choose Label Features.

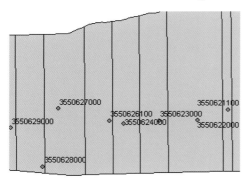

You'll begin with the easternmost parcel of the three you just created.

46. On the Editor toolbar, click the Edit tool, then click the parcel containing the TaxKeyXY point with a value of 3550623000.

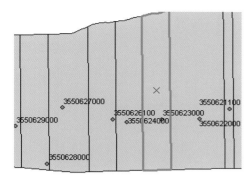

47. On the Editor toolbar, click the Attributes button.

48. In the right side of the Attributes dialog, click TKXY_TAXKE value, and type the label value of the TaxKeyXY point (**3550623000**) that is contained by the selected parcel, then press Enter. (Unless, of course, the value is already correct.)

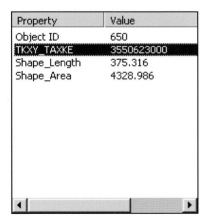

49. Repeat the process given in steps 46 through 48 to update the TKXY_TAXKE values for the two other new parcels. (From east to west their TKXY_TAXKE values are 3550624000 and 3550626100).

50. Close the Attributes dialog.

51. In the table of contents, right-click the TaxKeyXY layer and uncheck Label Features.

52. From the Selection menu, choose Clear Selected Features.

53. Zoom to the Full Extent.

Validate the topology

54. Turn on the Topology layer.

55. On the Topology toolbar, click the Validate Entire Topology button. When prompted about whether or not you want to validate, click Yes.

If you have fixed the errors correctly, the dirty areas are removed and no error features are displayed. If any errors do reappear, return to those areas and fix them.

At this point, it appears that all of the errors have been corrected or marked as exceptions. You cannot rely on visual inspection alone, however, because some errors may be too small to see unless you are zoomed in to them. You could use the Error Inspector to determine if there are any errors left (as you did in exercise 1d), or you could generate an error summary.

56. In the table of contents, right-click **ParcelBldg_Topology** and click Properties. In the Layer Properties dialog, click the Errors tab, then click Generate Summary.

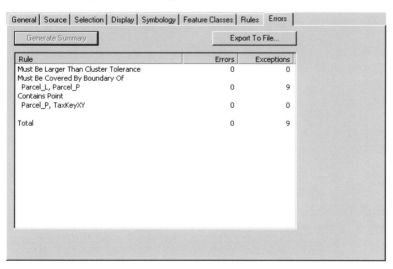

The error summary lists all the rules in your topology and how many errors and exceptions currently exist. The Must Be Larger Than Cluster Tolerance rule exists for every topology, because any feature smaller than the cluster tolerance is automatically considered an error. All errors have been fixed.

57. Click OK.

Save your edits

You've finished making the necessary edits to the parcel polygon features.

58. From the Editor menu, choose Stop Editing, then click Yes to save your changes.

59. From the File menu click Save. Name the map document **my_ex01f.mxd** and save it in your **MyArcCity** folder.

60. Close ArcMap.

Exercise 1g

Create building polygon features

In this exercise, you will create polygon features for buildings using the same process as you did for creating the parcel polygon features.

In this exercise you will perform the following tasks:
- Add a topology rule for the building line feature class.
- Validate the topology.
- List the errors using Error Inspector.
- Set the snapping environment.
- Fix the next set of errors.
- Fix the remaining errors.
- Create polygon features for buildings.

☐ Add a topology rule for the building line feature class

1. Start ArcCatalog.

2. In the Catalog Tree navigate to the **ParcelBldg** feature data set in your **Arc City** geodatabase.

3. Preview the Building_L feature class.

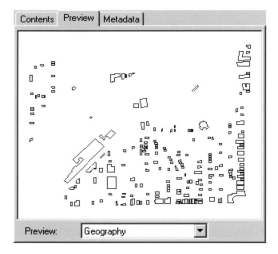

4. In the Catalog Tree, right-click **ParcelBldg_Topology**, and click Properties.

5. In the Topology Properties dialog, click the Feature Classes tab, then click the Add Class button.

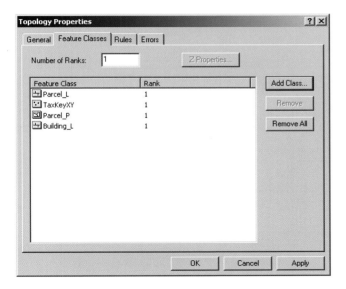

6. In the Add Class dialog, click Building_L, then click OK.

7. Click the Rules tab and click Remove All.

As with the case of the parcel polygons, you need to identify overshoots and undershoots. To do this, you can use the Must Not Have Dangles rule.

8. Click Add Rule. In the Add Rule dialog, specify that Building_L Must Not Have Dangles.

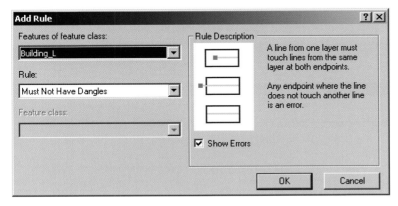

9. Click OK in the Add Rule dialog.

10. Click OK to close the Topology Properties dialog.

☐ Validate the topology

Now that you've added a feature class to the topology, you'll need to validate it. As you have seen before, the validation process will pick up any errors in the topology rule that you just defined.

11. Right-click **ParcelBldg_Topology** and choose Validate. When validation is complete, preview the updated topology. (Refresh from the View drop-down list.)

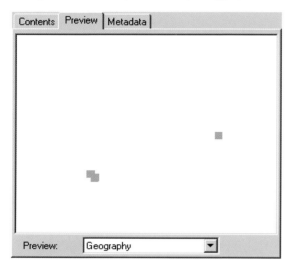

The validation process located all of the overshoots and undershoots (dangles) in the Building_L feature class. The good news is that it appears there are only a few errors.

12. Close ArcCatalog.

Start an edit session in ArcMap

13. Start ArcMap with a new empty map.

14. Add the **ParcelBldg_Topology** and its participating feature classes to ArcMap.

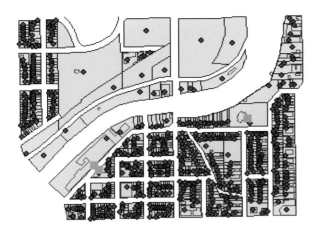

15. If necessary, load the Editor and the Topology toolbars.

16. Start an edit session. (From the Editor menu click Start Editing.)

☐ List the errors using the Error Inspector

Whether you use the Error Inspector, the Fix Topology Error tool, or a combination of the two depends on both your personal preference and the nature of the errors. In this case, you will use the Error Inspector.

17. Open the Error Inspector.

18. In the Error Inspector, uncheck Visible Extent only, then click Search Now.

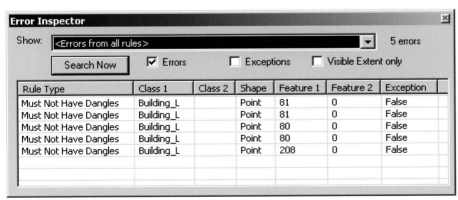

Rule Type	Class 1	Class 2	Shape	Feature 1	Feature 2	Exception
Must Not Have Dangles	Building_L		Point	81	0	False
Must Not Have Dangles	Building_L		Point	81	0	False
Must Not Have Dangles	Building_L		Point	80	0	False
Must Not Have Dangles	Building_L		Point	80	0	False
Must Not Have Dangles	Building_L		Point	208	0	False

A total of five errors are found. (Don't worry if the values in the Feature 1 column do not match the values shown in your dialog.)

19. In the Error Inspector, click the Feature 1 column header to sort the errors in ascending order, then right-click the first record in the list and choose Zoom To.

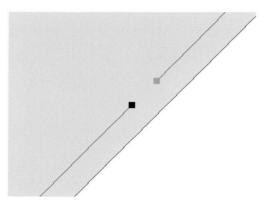

The endpoints of the building line feature do not meet, thus creating two topology errors from the same feature, one error at each endpoint. You cannot use the Extend, Snap, or Trim fixes because each of these fixes requires a second feature. Therefore, you will need to use the editing tools to correct the errors.

Set the snapping environment

20. On the Editor toolbar, click the Editor menu and click Options.

21. In the Editing Options dialog, click the General tab. Make sure the Snapping Tolerance is set to **2** map units. Then close the dialog.

22. From the Editor menu, choose Snapping. In the top part of the Snapping dialog, check End for Building_L.

Layer	Vertex	Edge	End	
TaxKeyXY	☐	☐	☐	
Building_L	☐	☐	☑	
Parcel_L	☐	☐	☐	
Parcel_P	☐	☐	☐	

23. Close the Snapping window.

Fix the first error

24. On the Editor toolbar, click the Edit tool. In the map display, double-click the building line feature containing the two errors.

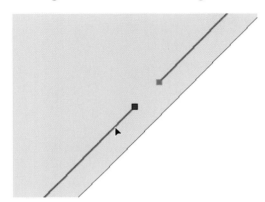

25. Place your cursor directly over one of the two endpoints. When the cursor changes to the box with four arrows, click and drag the endpoint directly over the other endpoint and release the mouse button.

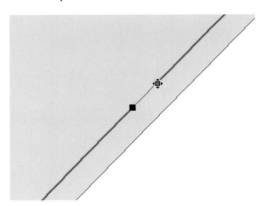

26. From the Selection menu, click Clear Selected Features.

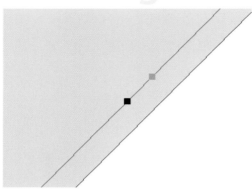

The line feature has been extended to form a complete loop, but you still must validate the data to remove the two errors from the topology.

27. **On the Topology toolbar, click the Validate Topology in Current Extent button.**

When the validation is complete, the error features no longer display. You will move on to another error.

Fix the next set of errors

28. **In the Error Inspector, click Search Now. The three remaining errors are listed.**

Your total error count has reduced from five to three. Two of the errors are associated with the same feature; most likely, this is the same type of error you just fixed.

29. **In the Error Inspector, right-click either of the errors that have the same Feature 1 value and choose Zoom To.**

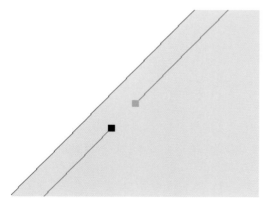

Just as you suspected, these two errors are also caused by a gap between the two endpoints of the same line feature.

30. Repeat the process you used in steps 24 through 27 to fix these two errors.

Fix the remaining error

31. In the Error Inspector, search for the remaining error, then zoom to it.

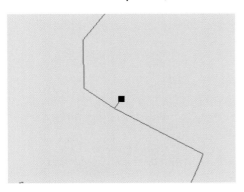

An extra line feature is causing this error. You will delete it.

32. Use the Edit tool to select the line, then press the Delete key.

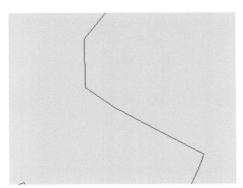

It seems that your editing task is complete, but before assuming that all the errors are repaired, you should validate the entire topology and check for errors one more time. (Sometimes new errors are introduced while editing.)

33. On the Topology toolbar, click the Validate Entire Topology button, and click Yes on the confirmation message.

34. In the Error Inspector, click the Search Now button.

If everything went according to plan, your building layer should be free from topology errors and ready for conversion to a polygon feature class.

35. Stop editing and save your edits.

36. Close ArcMap without saving the map document.

❏ Create polygon features for buildings

The procedure for converting the building lines is the same as the one you used for converting the parcel features, except that you will not be adding attributes from a point feature class.

37. Start ArcCatalog.

38. In the Catalog Tree, navigate to your **Arc City** geodatabase, right-click the **Parcel-Bldg** feature data set, point to New, then choose Polygon Feature Class From Lines.

39. In the Polygon Feature Class From Lines dialog, name the new feature class **Building_P**, then check Building_L as the feature class that will contribute lines.

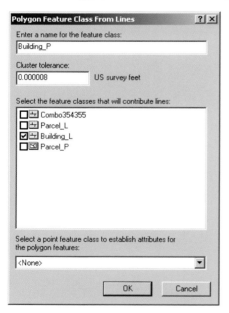

40. Click OK to create the new polygon feature class. Preview the new feature class after it's added to the feature data set.

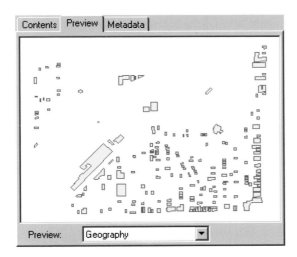

When you worked with the parcel features in exercise 1e, you used topology rules to compare the new polygon feature class to the line feature class it was created from. Normally, you would do the same with the new Building_P feature class. If you would like more practice working with a geodatabase topology, you can add Building_P and the appropriate rule to the topology, then check for errors. Otherwise, you can assume for the purpose of this exercise that there are no new errors.

41. If you are continuing to the next exercise leave ArcCatalog open, otherwise close ArcCatalog.

Exercise 1h

Create block features

Your Arc City spatial database now includes the completed parcel and building polygon features. The database design calls for two more feature classes: street centerlines and block polygons. You will add these two feature classes to the geodatabase in this exercise. Once this is done, all the necessary feature classes will be in your **Arc City** geodatabase.

In exercise 1a, you previewed the street feature classes given to you by the Arc City planning department. Now you will import that data into the **Arc City** geodatabase and build the block polygons from the street centerlines. Finally, you will add a field containing block identifiers to the new block feature class. The identifier field will be used later as the key field for linking to block attributes in other tables.

In this exercise you will perform the following tasks:
- Create a new feature data set to store streets and blocks.
- Import the streets shapefile into the geodatabase.
- Create block polygons from the street centerlines.
- Add a block number field to the block attribute table.
- Populate the new field.

Create a feature data set to store streets and blocks

In this task, you will create a new feature data set inside the **Arc City** geodatabase that will store the street and blocks data. The block polygons will be created from the street lines, and since these two feature classes are topologically related, it makes sense to group them together inside the same feature data set.

1. Start ArcCatalog if necessary.

2. In the Catalog Tree, right-click the **Arc City** geodatabase, point to New, and click Feature Dataset.

3. Name the new feature data set **StreetBlock**.

4. In the lower-right corner of the New Feature Dataset dialog, click the Edit button.

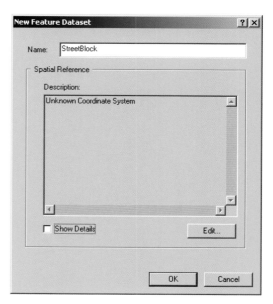

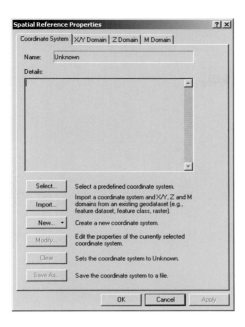

You will import the spatial reference from the **ParcelBldg** feature data set and assign it to the StreetBlock feature data set.

5. On the Spatial Reference Properties dialog, click Import. In the Browse for Dataset dialog, navigate to and select the **ParcelBldg** feature data set, then click Add.

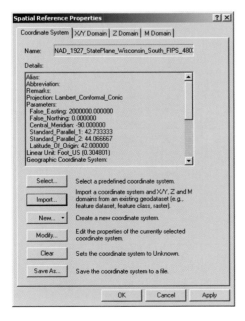

6. In the Spatial Reference Properties dialog, click OK, then click OK in the New Feature Dataset dialog.

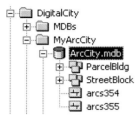

Now that the StreetBlock feature data set exists, you can import the street data into it.

Import the streets shapefile into the geodatabase

7. In the Catalog Tree, right-click the StreetBlock feature data set, point to Import, and choose Feature Class (single). For the Input Features, browse to your **SourceData** folder and select **STREETS.shp.** Name the output features class **Streets.** Do not change any of the optional settings in the dialog. Make sure your settings match the following graphic, click OK, then click Close when the process finishes.

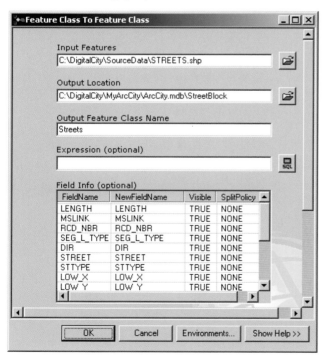

8. In the Catalog Tree, expand the **Arc City** geodatabase and the **StreetBlock** feature data set.

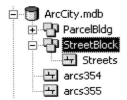

9. Preview the new Streets feature class.

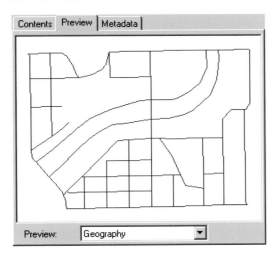

The streets are created. Now you will create the block polygons from the street centerlines.

⌐ Create block polygons from the street centerlines

10. In the Catalog Tree, right-click the **StreetBlock** feature data set, point to New, then click Polygon Feature Class From Lines.

11. In the dialog, name the new feature class **Blocks**. Change the cluster tolerance to **0.2**. Check Streets as the feature class that will contribute lines.

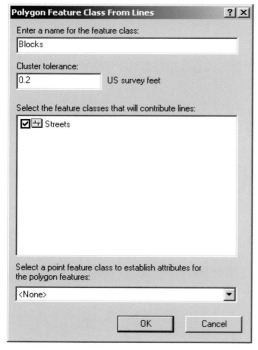

12. Click OK.

13. Preview the block features once they have been created.

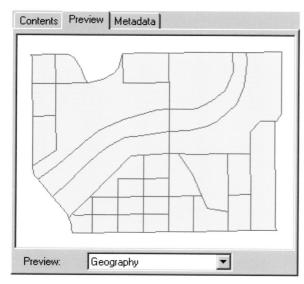

14. To make sure that all of the polygon features were created, compare the blocks with the streets by toggling between previews of the two feature classes.

Note: When you are working with a small data set like this one, a quick visual inspection is enough to see that the lines converted correctly to polygons. If the feature class contained many more features, you should use a topology to check the accuracy of the data conversion.

15. Close ArcCatalog.

Add a block number field to the block attribute table

Your final task for the Blocks data is to add a block number to each polygon feature. To do this, you will add a new field to the block attribute table and then manually enter the block numbers.

16. Start ArcMap with a new, empty map.

17. Click the Add Data button. Navigate to the **StreetBlock** feature data set in the **Arc City** geodatabase and add the Blocks feature class.

18. In the table of contents, right-click Blocks and click Open Attribute Table.

19. On the lower-right corner of the attribute table, click the Options button (you may need to widen the table window to see the button) and click Add Field.

20. In the Add Field dialog, enter **BlockID** for Name. Change the Type to Long Integer.

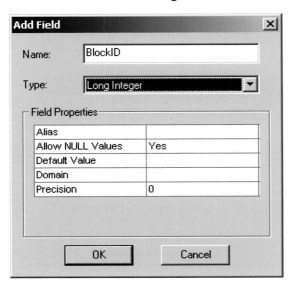

21. Click OK.

Attributes of Blocks

Object ID*	Shape*	Shape_Length	Shape_Area	BlockID
1	Polygon	1261.089402	96775.840390	<Null>
2	Polygon	1258.434026	96445.491638	<Null>
3	Polygon	1162.988661	82461.904828	<Null>
4	Polygon	1260.531058	96743.813778	<Null>
5	Polygon	949.495429	46248.675376	<Null>
6	Polygon	1261.246767	96866.941587	<Null>
7	Polygon	1258.433563	96482.153254	<Null>
8	Polygon	1258.875062	96528.595393	<Null>
9	Polygon	1754.521557	183896.416477	<Null>
10	Polygon	1943.619100	193662.468986	<Null>
11	Polygon	1717.382599	173118.371238	<Null>
12	Polygon	1258.294552	96484.077579	<Null>
13	Polygon	1256.485011	96182.151069	<Null>
14	Polygon	2436.773393	196415.368428	<Null>

Record: ◄◄ ◄ 30 ► ►◄ Show: All | Selected | Records (0 out of 30 Selected.)

The new field appears at the far right of the table. You will have to manually populate the values in this field.

22. Close the Attributes of Blocks table.

Populate the new field

To keep track of which block numbers you have added as you work, you'll set the feature labeling options so that the BlockID values will display as labels.

23. In the table of contents, right-click Blocks, choose Properties, then click the Labels tab.

24. From the Label Field drop-down list in the Text String box, choose BlockID.

Making this setting causes the software to use the BlockID values for labels.

25. In the Layer Properties dialog, click OK.

26. In the table of contents, right-click the Blocks layer and click Label Features.

Right now no labels appear, but as you enter each Block ID, the corresponding labels will appear.

27. If necessary, load the Editor toolbar.

28. From the Editor menu, choose Start editing.

29. Click the Edit tool and select the block feature that is in the northwest corner of Arc City.

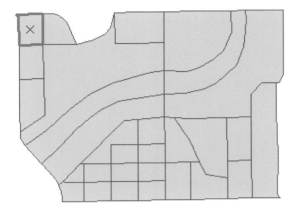

30. On the Editor toolbar, click the Attributes button. On the right side of the Attributes dialog, click the <Null> value for the BlockID, type 107000202, then press Enter.

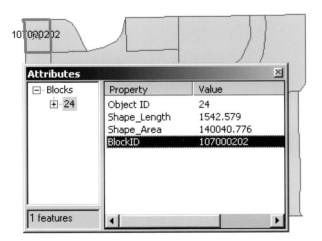

31. Attribute the rest of the blocks with their BlockID values.

Use the following map to determined which BlockID value to assign to each block.

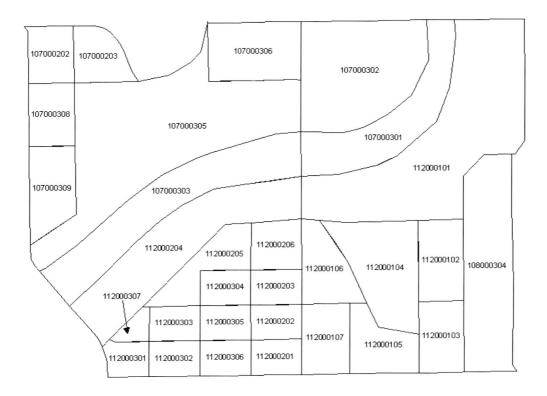

32. When you are finished adding all of the BlockID values, you can double-check your work by zooming to individual blocks to check their label values against the values shown on the reference map. (The labels will scale to fit within blocks when you zoom in close to them.)

33. When finished attributing the blocks, stop editing and save your changes.

34. From the File menu, click Save. Navigate to your **MyArcCity** folder, name the map document **My_ex01h.mxd**, then click Save.

35. Close ArcMap.

Exercise 1i

Review and clean up the database

It is always a good idea to review and tidy up your work at the end of a long process such as the work you have done in this chapter. Now that your geodatabase contains all the desired feature classes, you will make a backup copy of the geodatabase. Finally, you will remove the intermediate feature classes created during the conversion of the CAD data because you no longer need them.

In this exercise you will perform the following tasks:
- Make a backup copy of the geodatabase.
- Remove intermediate data.

◻ Make a backup copy of the geodatabase

1. Start ArcCatalog and navigate to your **Arc City** geodatabase.

2. In the Catalog Tree, right-click your **ArcCity.mdb** and click Copy.

3. In the Catalog Tree, right-click your **MyArcCity** folder and click Paste. This makes a copy of the geodatabase.

◻ Remove intermediate data
The table below shows the current contents of the **MyArcCity** geodatabase. Use the information in the table as a guide for the next steps.

Data	Status	Type	Purpose
Arcs354	Intermediate	Feature class—Line	Import CAD
Arcs355	Intermediate	Feature class—Line	Import CAD
Building_L	Intermediate	Feature class—Line	Extract building outlines
Building_P	Final	Feature class—Polygon	Final data
Combo354355	Intermediate	Feature class—Line	Combine quarter sections
ParcelBldg_Topology	Intermediate	Topology	Locate errors in feature data
Parcel_L	Intermediate	Feature class—Line	Extract parcel lines
Parcel_P	Final	Feature class—Polygon	Final data
TaxKeyXY	Final	Feature class—Point	Add parcel ID attribute

4. Expand your **Arc City** geodatabase. For each of the feature classes whose status is "Intermediate" in the table above, select the feature class, right-click, and then click Delete. Delete the **ParcelBldg_Topology** first because the feature classes that participate in a topology cannot be deleted unless they are removed from the topology or the topology they participate in is deleted.

5. If everything was successfully deleted, delete your backup copy of the **Arc City** geodatabase that you made in step 3.

Now the spatial data for Arc City is created. In the next chapter you will work more with the attribute data in the **Arc City** geodatabase.

Chapter 2

Using and geocoding attribute data

Creating a data model in a local government first requires identifying of the real world within which it operates. **People** move in, move out, are born, die, get educated, buy land, own dogs, drink water, commit crimes, etc. **Land** becomes developed, is bought and sold, increases and decreases in value, is subdivided and assembled, etc. Also, **buildings and facilities** are built, occupied (by people and businesses), age, get demolished, are repaired, are driven upon (streets) or used to provide water, remove sewage, etc. Finally, **businesses** occupy buildings, employ people, receive goods and revenues, use facilities, create and sell goods, etc. The government is involved in many of these activities as it organizes itself into functional units (departments, bureaus, offices, etc.) in order to divide up the work required to fulfill its responsibilities to its citizens (Huxhold and Levinsohn 1995). These functional units address many of the issues, problems, and day-to-day services related to the activities of the people, businesses, land, buildings, and facilities. Collecting data about those entities and their activities and maintaining those databases helps these organizational units perform their duties.

Legacy systems

Often, existing attribute databases are already in place in a local government before GIS is implemented. These are called legacy systems. For example, many local tax assessors have databases of parcel characteristics that are used to assist in the property assessment and reassessment process. Often, Computer-Assisted Mass Appraisal (CAMA) Systems are used to determine assessment values and these CAMA systems contain attribute data of the land and the buildings. The purpose of these files is to store information that is important to the assessed value of a parcel of land and its improvements (parcel number, address, owner name and address, number of dwelling units, style, assessed value, etc.) Likewise, many local governments collect and maintain building permit information to manage new development in their jurisdictions. These building permit legacy systems usually contain a data file used by the building inspection department. Their purpose is to keep track of all building permits for improvements to property so that inspectors can assure that the construction complies with local building codes. The data needed to do that includes property address, owner name and address, permit type, estimated cost, inspection status, and construction date.

Each of the files in these legacy systems is designed to serve its own purpose but individually cannot provide additional information that could be useful if the data were combined (such as determining the average value of two-family structures built in a certain year). That is why many local governments use relational database management software to combine and share the data among the departments.

Relational database management systems

Relational database management systems (RDBMS) provide a means to store, manage, update, query, and display attribute data through a series of independent tables that can be combined (related) when information from more than one table is needed. In GIS, these tables usually contain attribute data about features that can be mapped: parcel attributes (owner name and address, assessed value, land use, etc.) linked to parcel maps; census data (population totals by age, race, sex, etc.) linked to census tract or block maps; traffic accident records linked to street intersections or street segments. Often, there is so much attribute data collected about these features (parcels, blocks, intersections, etc.) that the data is organized into different RDBMS tables, each with its own theme or purpose and departments that manage them.

For example, a local government collects a variety of diverse data on the properties (land and buildings) within its jurisdictional boundaries: tax assessment data, building permit data, water consumption and billing data, licenses, crimes, etc. Each of these themes is often the responsibility of an office within the government (tax assessor, public works, building inspection, police department, etc.), and these offices often create computerized records to manage the data for that theme. If the organization is using an RDBMS, then the data for these themes is stored in separate tables and maintained separately by those offices.

When data from one office is needed by another office, the RDBMS allows the tables to be related. For example, when a new building is about to be built on a vacant lot, a building permit is applied for and a record in the building permit table is created. In the process of reviewing the application for the permit, employees in the building inspection office research existing information about the lot such as the current zoning. If zoning codes for lots are stored in the tax assessment table of the tax assessor's office, the two records (building permit record and the tax assessment record) need to be related in order to find the zoning for the lot. This can be done manually by querying the tax assessment table directly (usually by using the address or property number from the building permit to find the corresponding record in the tax assessment table), or it can be done by the RDBMS automatically through a "relational join" operation. This relational join combines data from two different tables that share a common identifier (property number, for example).

The advantage of using the RDBMS to perform the operation is that all of the records from the two tables are related and the data is virtually "moved" from one table to the other. The manual process produces only a single match of the two related records, and the data is only displayed on the screen. For example, the manual process does not result in the zoning code actually being added to the building permit record.

The key to relational databases is that all of the data necessary to do an analysis does not have to be on one table, thus allowing different departments to be in charge of different tables. Also, the number of records in each table does not have to be the same. For example, the Blocks table does not have to have as many records as the parcels in order to join them for the purpose of determining which parcels are in which blocks.

Unique identifiers

Whether a government already has legacy systems, whether it must create new digital attribute databases, or whether it obtains attribute data from other sources, both the attribute databases and the digital map records must contain unique identifiers that allow the relational database management software to join the attribute data to those map features. This means that to map parcel data, the parcel identifier must be in both the parcel map and the attribute table. To map census data, the census block number must be in both the block map and the census table.

Thus, a unique identifier is needed in each point, line, or polygon record of the spatial data so that those map objects can be linked to the attributes of the features they represent. Likewise, the attribute databases must contain the same unique identifier so that the attributes of each feature are associated with the correct map feature.

In this chapter, you will process the Arc City data so that the attribute databases contain unique identifiers and are joined to their parcels, street segments, blocks, and districts in the spatial data. This process is often called geocoding the attribute data.

About this chapter

In the previous chapter you created the geographic features for Arc City; however, the spatial database contains only the geometry of the features and the identifiers of the block and parcel features. None of the descriptive attributes of those features (e.g., owner name, number of bedrooms, assessed value, etc.) have yet been assigned to them.

In this chapter you will use the relational database management capabilities of the geodatabase to add tax assessment attributes to the parcel polygons you created in the previous chapter and geocode the parcels. This will allow you to query the attribute data by block or district and aggregate and display attribute data by parcel, street segment, block, and district.

Exercise 2a

Join tax assessment data to parcel features

The assessment database already contains the parcel identifier because it is part of a legacy system maintained by the tax assessor. The parcel features also have parcel identifiers (tax key numbers) because they were added from the coordinate file of parcel identifiers when the polygon features were created back in exercise 1c of chapter 1. Normally, when creating a GIS, you would be required to enter this information manually for each parcel; however, since there is already a unique identifier on both the attribute table and feature class, you can join the two. Recall that our goal here is to assign the attributes to the features so we can query our feature classes.

In this exercise you will perform the following tasks:
- Import the taxroll table.
- Review the tax assessment data and parcel attribute fields.
- Join the taxroll table to the parcel feature class.
- Save the joined data.

Before you begin

The exercises in this chapter assume you have completed chapter 1. If you did not successfully complete all the exercises in chapter 1, you must replace your **Arc City** geodatabase with the **ArcCity_Ch1results** geodatabase that is provided on the data CD included with this book. To update your **Arc City** geodatabase with the newer version, use the same method outlined in the first task of exercise 1e in chapter 1, except replace your **Arc City** geodatabase with the **ArcCity_Ch1results** geodatabase instead of the **ArcCity_ex01e** geodatabase.

Import the taxroll table

1. Start ArcCatalog.

2. Navigate to your **C:\DigitalCity\MyArcCity** folder.

3. In the Catalog Tree, right-click the **Arc City** geodatabase, point to Import and choose Table (single).

4. For the Input Table, navigate to your **C:\DigitalCity\SourceData** folder and add **taxroll.dbf**. Name the output table **taxroll**.

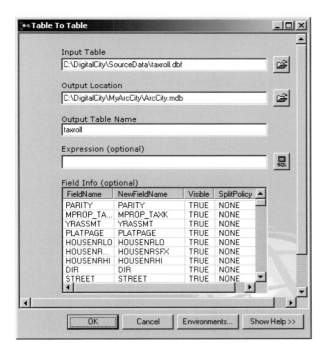

5. Click OK in the Table to Table dialog. Click Close when the process completes.

You'll review the new geodatabase table in ArcMap.

6. Close ArcCatalog.

Review the tax assessment data and parcel attribute fields

7. Start ArcMap with a new, empty map.

8. Click the Add Data button, navigate to your **C:\DigitalCity\MyArcCity** folder, double-click the **Arc City** geodatabase, then add the taxroll table. Click the Add Data button again, this time add the Parcel_P feature class from the **ParcelBldg** feature data set.

9. In the table of contents, right-click Parcel_P and choose Open Attribute Table.

Inside the Attributes of Parcel_P notice the TKXY_TAXKE field.

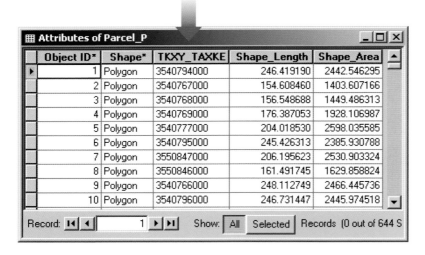

This field contains the tax key numbers that provide the unique identifiers for each parcel in Arc City.

10. Close the Attributes of Parcel_P.

11. In the table of contents, right-click the taxroll table and choose Open.

This table contains a field named MPROP_TAXK, which contains the tax key number for each record in the table.

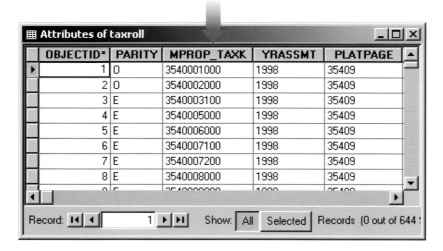

You may have noticed that each table contains 644 records. For each record in the Attributes of Parcel_P table, there is a corresponding record in the taxroll table that contains descriptive attributes. The way to tie these records together is through the common values stored in the TKXY_TAXKE and MPROP_TAXK field of the two respective tables.

Note: When joining data, the field names need not be the same, but the field types (e.g., text or short integer) must be the same.

12. Close the Attributes of taxroll table.

Join the taxroll table to parcel feature class

By joining the assessment data to the parcel data you will be able to access the assessors records for each parcel you select in the map. Since the taxroll table will be joined to the attributes of Parcel_P, you will initiate the join from the Parcel layer.

13. In the table of contents, right-click Parcel_P, point to Joins and Relates, and click Join.

14. At the top of the Join Data dialog you're asked what you want to join to the layer. If it's not already selected, choose Join attributes from a table.

15. In drop-down list number 1, choose the TKXY_TAXKE field.

Since the taxroll table is the only other table currently in ArcMap, it's automatically selected in drop-down list number 2.

16. In drop-down list number 3, choose the MPROP_TAXK field.

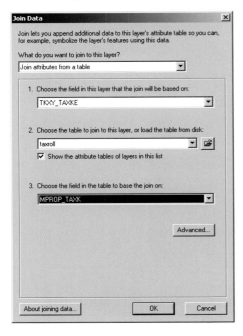

17. Double check to make sure your settings are correct, then click OK.

ArcMap joins the attributes in the taxroll table to the attributes of Parcel_P. Records from each table are matched by their tax key values, which are stored in the MPROP_TAXK field of the taxroll table and the TKXY_TAXKE field of the Parcel_P table.

18. To make sure the join was accomplished correctly, open the Attributes of Parcel_P and scroll horizontally in the table while reviewing its fields.

To help you keep track of which table the fields originated from, each field name now contains the title of its source table. (This is not true for the Object ID and Shape fields because they are generated by the software and are not user-defined fields.)

19. Close the Attributes of Parcel_P.

Save the joined data

Even though you can see all of the attributes from the taxroll table inside the Parcel_P table, the join is not permanent. It did not physically alter the original tables or create a new table. The table that you see is a virtual table that exists only inside the map document. If you save the map document, ArcMap will save the definition of how the tables inside it are joined together, not the actual data in the tables. Then, each time you open the map document, the latest versions of the source tables are rejoined.

Table joins are useful if, for example, you're working with parcel assessment data that changes often and accessing the most recent information is critical. But what if you want to create a permanent record from the results of a join that you can then use in other maps and projects? You can do this by exporting the joined data into a new feature class or table.

20. In the table of contents, right-click Parcel_P, point to Data, and click Export Data.

21. In the Export Data dialog, choose to export All features, then click the Browse button next to the Output shapefile or feature class box.

22. In the Saving Data dialog, make sure the Save as type drop-down list is set to Personal Geodatabase feature classes. Navigate to the **ParcelBldg** feature data set inside your **Arc City** geodatabase. Name the new feature class **ParcelData,** then click Save.

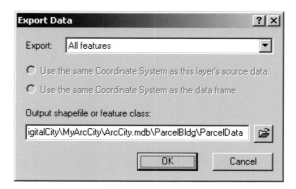

23. Click OK.

24. When prompted, click Yes to add the exported data to the map.

25. Open the Attributes of ParcelData layer and scroll horizontally across the table.

The attributes of the ParcelData feature class contain all of the fields from the taxroll table and the Parcel_P feature class.

26. Close the Attributes of ParcelData.

Save the map document

The Parcel_P layer and the taxroll table are no longer needed in this map.

27. In the table of contents, right-click Parcel_P and choose Remove. Remove the taxroll table using the same process.

28. From the File menu click Save.

29. In the Save As dialog, navigate to your **MyArcCity** folder, name the map document **my_ex02a.mxd**, then click Save.

30. If you are continuing on to the next exercise, leave ArcMap open. Otherwise, close ArcMap.

Joining the taxroll data to the Parcel_P data allowed you to create a new feature class from the parcels that included the attributes from both sets of data. You can now use this new feature class in your other projects.

Exercise 2b

Add census data to the blocks

In the last exercise you joined the taxroll data to the parcels and created a new feature class from the join. In this exercise, you will continue preparing the geodatabase by joining the block data with the census demographics. Like the original taxroll table, the census data is currently stored as a .dbf file and resides outside of the **Arc City** geodatabase. Before you join the two data sets, you will put the census data in the **Arc City** geodatabase using an export process from ArcMap. Then, once the census data is within the geodatabase, you will post process the table by adding a field to it and populate that field with the values necessary for joining it to the blocks data.

In this exercise, you will perform the following tasks:
- Import the census data.
- Create a new field to store the concatenation of Tract and Block IDs
- Populate the BlockID field.
- Join the census data to the Block features.

⌐ Add data to ArcMap

1. If necessary, start ArcMap with a new, empty map.

2. If you did not leave ArcMap open at the end of the last exercise, click the Add Data button.

3. Navigate to your **D:\DigitalCity\MyArcCity** folder, double-click the **ArcCity.mdb** to expand its contents. Inside the **Arc City** geodatabase, double-click the **ParcelBldg** feature data set, then click the ParcelData feature class, and click Add.

4. Click the Add Data button again. This time add the Blocks feature class from the **StreetBlock** feature data set in the **Arc City** geodatabase.

5. In the table of contents, drag the Blocks layer beneath the parcels layer. If you cannot change the order of the layers in the table of contents, make sure the Display tab is chosen at the bottom of the table of contents. (The color of your blocks and parcels layers may differ from the view result).

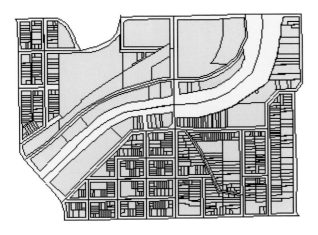

6. Click the Add Data button. In the Add Data dialog, navigate to your **C:\DigitalCity\ SourceData** folder and add the **CENSUSDATA.dbf**.

Export the census data table from ArcMap to the **Arc City** geodatabase.

In the previous exercise, you imported a table into the **Arc City** geodatabase using ArcCatalog. This time you'll use ArcMap's export functionality to put the census data table into the **Arc City** geodatabase.

7. In the ArcMap table of contents, right-click CENSUSDATA, point to Data and click Export.

8. Click the Browse button next to the Output table box. In the Saving Data dialog, make sure the Save as type drop-down list is set to Personal Geodatabase tables. Navigate to your **Arc City** geodatabase, then name the table **CensusData,** and click Save.

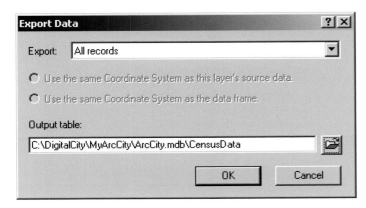

9. Click OK in the Export Data dialog. Then, when prompted, click Yes to add the new table to the current map.

10. In the ArcMap table of contents, right-click the original **CENSUSDATA.dbf** table and click Remove.

11. In the ArcMap table of contents, right-click CensusData and click Open.

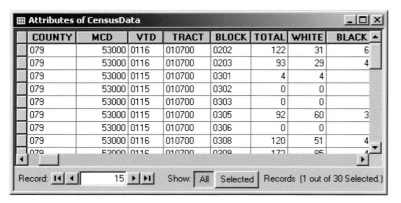

COUNTY	MCD	VTD	TRACT	BLOCK	TOTAL	WHITE	BLACK
079	53000	0116	010700	0202	122	31	6
079	53000	0116	010700	0203	93	29	4
079	53000	0115	010700	0301	4	4	
079	53000	0115	010700	0302	0	0	
079	53000	0115	010700	0303	0	0	
079	53000	0115	010700	0305	92	60	3
079	53000	0115	010700	0306	0	0	
079	53000	0116	010700	0308	120	51	4
079	53000	0116	010700	0309	172	85	4

Record: ⏮ ◀ [15] ▶ ⏭   Show: All | Selected   Records (1 out of 30 Selected.)

12. Scroll across the table and examine the fields in the Attributes of CensusData.

Within the table, there are several census geographic codes (COUNTY, MCD, VTD, TRACT, and BLOCK). The Census Bureau uses these codes to uniquely identify each block in the United States.

Create a new field to store the concatenation of Tract and Block IDs

The CensusData table now resides within the **Arc City** geodatabase, but it does not contain a field with the appropriate values needed to join it to the Blocks feature class. You will remedy this by creating a new field and populating it with the values you can use for the table join.

13. In the lower right-hand side of the Attributes of CensusData, click the Options button and choose Add Field. (If you cannot see the Options button, you may need to expand the size of the table.)

14. In the Add Field dialog, name the field **BlockID,** and set the Type drop-down list to Long Integer.

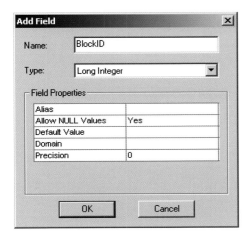

15. Click OK in the Add Field dialog.

16. The new field is added to the end of the table. To see it, scroll to the right end of the table.

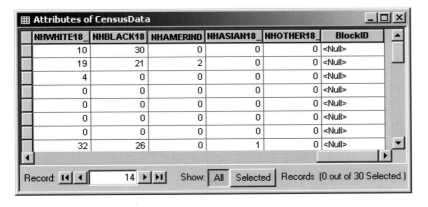

Your next task is to populate this field with the block identification values.

Populate the BlockID field

Your goal is to join the Census data attributes to the Blocks feature class. To do this, you will need a common attribute field in both data sets that you can use as the basis for the join.

The attributes of the Blocks feature class contains a BlockID field that is comprised of two components, the census tract number and the census block number. Within the Attributes of CensusData, there is a Tract field and a Block field, but a field containing a combination of these two attributes does not exist.

In this task, you will use the Field Calculator to concatenate the respective Tract and Block values in the Attributes of CensusData and place the results in the new BlockID field. Once the BlockID field is populated with the results of the concatenation, you can use it as a basis for the table join with the Attributes of Blocks.

17. In the CensusData table, right-click the BlockID field name, and choose Calculate Values. When prompted, click Yes on the warning message.

18. In the Fields list, click TRACT to add it to the expression box. Click the Plus Sign (+) button. In the Fields list, click BLOCK.

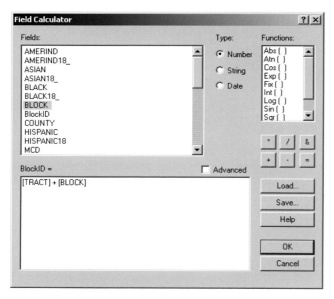

For each record in the table, this expression will take the value in the TRACT field and the value in the BLOCK field, concatenate them, then place the resultant value in the respective record of the BlockID field.

19. Click OK.

After a moment, the new attribute values are added.

NHASIAN18_	NHOTHER18_	BlockID
0	0	107000202
0	0	107000203
0	0	107000301
0	0	107000302
0	0	107000303
0	0	107000305
0	0	107000306

You can now use the BlockID values in the Attributes of CensusData to join to the BlockID values in Attributes of Blocks.

20. Close the Attributes of CensusData.

Join the census data to the Block features

To get to this point, you added a new field to the Attributes of Census Data and populated it with Block ID values that match the Block ID values in the Attributes of Blocks. With the preprocessing out of the way, you can now join the census attributes to the block features.

21. In the ArcMap table of contents, right-click the Blocks layer, point to Joins and Relates, and click Join.

22. If necessary, select Join Attributes from a table from the drop-down list at the top of the dialog. In drop-down list number 1, choose the BlockID field. In drop-down list number 2, choose CensusData. In drop-down list number 3, choose BlockID. (It's at the bottom of the list).

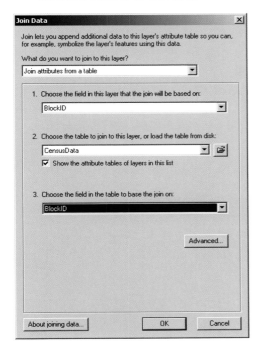

23. Make sure your settings are correct, then click OK.

24. Open the Attributes of Blocks. Scroll across the table to see that all of the census data attributes have been added to the table.

25. Close the Attributes of Blocks.

Another way to see the results of your join is to click the block features with the Identify tool.

26. On the Tools toolbar, click the Identify tool.

27. Click on any block feature in the map display.

28. In the Identify Results dialog, choose Blocks from the Layers drop-down list.

29. Click on other block features to see the attributes.

Because of the Join operation that you ran, you can access the CensusData attributes for any block feature you identify.

30. When finished browsing the data, close the Identify Results dialog.

Save the map document

31. From the File menu, click Save As.

32. In the Save As dialog, name your map document **my_ex02b.mxd** and save it in your **DigitalCity\MyArcCity** folder.

If you are continuing to the next exercise, leave ArcMap open. Otherwise, close ArcMap.

Exercise 2c

Create districts from blocks

Districts break a city into managerial units. For example, every district has its own fire station and police department; work crews for sewer, water, and streets are managed by district; and within the city commission, there is an elected representative from each district.

Districts are an important part of the daily work flow in Arc City and must exist as a feature class in the **Arc City** geodatabase. ArcCity consists of the three districts shown below.

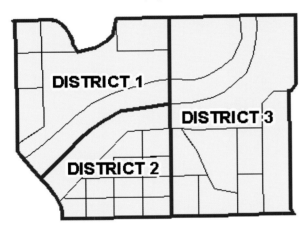

Each district consists of a group of blocks. You already have the blocks feature class in the **Arc City** geodatabase. Creating the districts, then, is a matter of combining the blocks into their respective districts. This will be done through the dissolve capability in ArcGIS because the borders of features that share the same values can be dissolved to make new features. Thus, adjacent blocks that have the same district numbers will have their common borders dissolved to create district features.

In this exercise you will perform the following tasks to create a district feature class:
- Add a DistrictID field to the attributes of Blocks.
- Populate the DistrictID field with each block's district number.
- Dissolve features based on an attribute.

Add data to ArcMap

1. If necessary, start ArcMap.

In this exercise, you will use the join between the Attributes of Block and the CensusData table that you made in the last exercise. If you still have your results open from the previous exercise you can skip step 2, otherwise you will need to open the map document you created in the last exercise.

2. From the File menu, click Open. In the Open dialog, navigate to your **C:\DigitalCity \MyArcCity** folder and open the **my_ex02b.mxd** map document that you created at the end of the last exercise.

Note: You need to finish exercise 2b before starting this exercise.

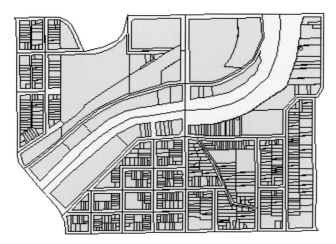

3. Open the Attribute of Blocks.

In the previous exercise, you joined the attributes from the CensusData table to the attributes of the Blocks feature class. When you saved the map document at the end of the exercise, the join was saved along with it, which means the table join is re-established whenever that map is re-opened.

In this exercise, you will dissolve the blocks and create a new feature class called Districts. Because of the join between the Blocks feature class and the CensusData table, the output from the dissolve operation will contain the attributes from both data sets.

First, however, you will need to assign district IDs to the blocks.

Add the DistrictID field to the Attributes of Blocks

4. In the Attributes of Blocks, click the Options button and click Add Field. Name the new field **DistrictID** and define its Type as Short Integer.

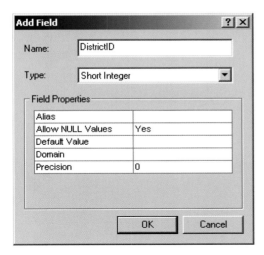

5. Click OK.

The new field is added to the Attributes of Blocks. This table currently is participating in a join, which is why the new field name appears in the table with the feature class name preceding it.

Blocks.BlockID	Blocks.DistrictID	OBJECTID	CensusData.COUNTY
112000302		24	079
112000306		28	079
112000301		23	079
112000201		18	079
112000307		29	079
112000303		25	079
112000305		27	079
112000202		19	079
112000107		17	079
112000105		15	079
112000103		13	079

Now that the field is in the table, you will manually add the district ID values for each block.

☐ Populate the District ID field with each block's district number
The three Arc City districts are shown on the next page. You'll select the blocks in each district and assign a district number to the selected features.

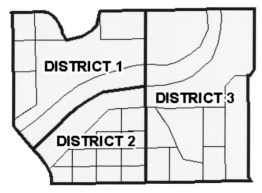

6. If necessary, move the attribute table to a location where you can see it and the map display.

7. In the ArcMap table of contents, uncheck the ParcelData layer.

8. From the Selection menu, choose Set Selectable Layers. In the Set Selectable Layers dialog, uncheck ParcelData.

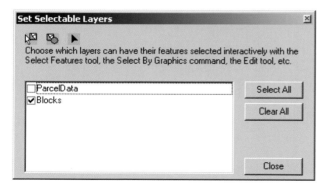

9. Click Close.

10. On the Tools toolbar, click the Select Features tool.

11. In the map display, click and drag a box, as shown in the graphic below, to select all the block features in District 1.

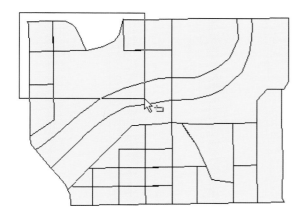

After the selection is made, your map display should match the following graphic.

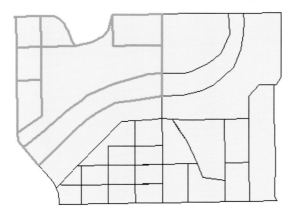

12. In the Attributes of Blocks, right-click the Blocks.DistrictID column heading and choose Calculate Values. When the Warning message appears, click Yes.

13. In the expression box of the Field Calculator, type **1.**

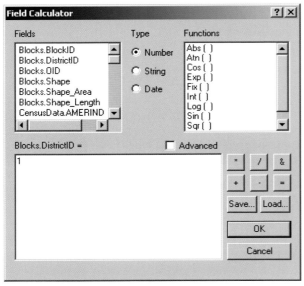

14. Click OK.

15. Scroll down in the Attribute of Blocks until you can see the selected rows, which now contain values in the Blocks.DistrictID field.

Blocks.BlockID	Blocks.DistrictID	OBJI
108000304		
107000309	1	
107000303	1	
107000308	1	
107000202	1	
107000203	1	
107000305	1	
107000306	1	
107000302		
107000301		

16. Use the same procedure to add district numbers to the blocks in district 2 and the blocks in district 3. (Use the graphic provided at the beginning of this task and on page 102 to determine which block belongs to which district.)

17. When you have finished assigning district numbers, close the Attributes of Blocks.

18. From the Selection menu, click Clear Selected Features.

⊔ Dissolve features based on an attribute

Now you can use the DistrictID field to dissolve the block features into the three districts that serve Arc City.

19. On the Standard toolbar, click the Show/Hide ArcToolbox™ Window button to open ArcToolbox.

20. Inside of ArcToolbox, expand the Data Management Tools toolbox, then expand the Generalization toolset.

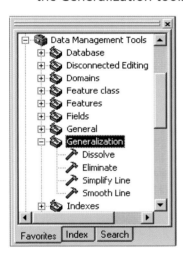

21. Inside the Generalization toolset, double-click the Dissolve tool.

22. In the Dissolve dialog, choose **Blocks** from the Input Features drop-down list. Name the Output Feature Class **Districts** and save it within the **StreetBlock** feature data set in your **Arc City** geodatabase. In the Dissolve_Field(s) list, check the box next to **Blocks.DistrictID**.

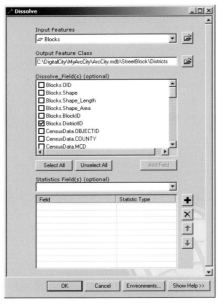

The Dissolve tool can summarize the attribute values of features that are dissolved and include the summary values in the output's attribute table. In this case, you want to sum the total population within each district.

23. In the lower half of the Dissolve dialog, choose **CensusData.Total** from the Statistics Field(s) drop-down list. (The red "x" will be removed when you choose a statistic type.) In the Statistic Type column, click the box to the right of the CensusData. Total field and choose **SUM**.

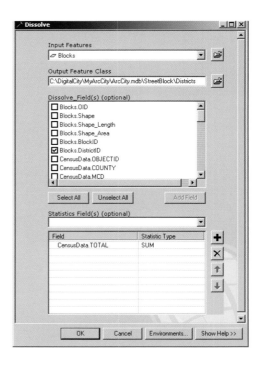

The CensusData.Total field stores each block's population. When the dissolve process runs, it will categorize all the block polygons into their respective districts, then create a total population value for each district by summing the values in the CensusData.Total field.

24. Click OK. When the process completes, click Close.

25. Close the ArcToolbox window.

When the dissolve process is completed, the Districts feature class is added to the map. (The color of your Districts feature class may differ from the graphic).

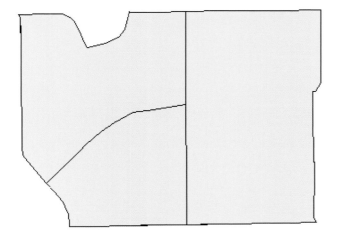

26. Open the Attributes of Districts. (Right-click the Districts layer in the table of contents and choose Open Attribute Table).

Blocks_DistrictID is the field on which the dissolve was based, so this field is automatically included in the output. Sum_CensusData_TOTAL is the Statistic Field you choose to add to the output and contains the total population in each district.

Blocks_DistrictID	SUM_CensusData_TOTAL	Shape_Length	Shape_Area
1	599	7818.248627	2772549.121733
2	810	5504.349644	1869654.640288
3	1963	8491.884678	4092811.065652

27. Close the Attributes of Districts.

□ Save the map document

28. From the File menu, click Save As. In the Save As dialog, name the map **my_ex02c. mxd** and save it in your **MyArcCity** folder.

29. If you are continuing on to the next exercise, leave ArcMap open. Otherwise, close ArcMap.

Exercise 2d

Calculate sales values

In exercise 2a you joined the assessor data to the parcel data, which resulted in a rich set of parcel attributes. One attribute that came with the assessor data is the conveyance fee. Using the conveyance fee along with a little background knowledge, you can calculate the sales value for the parcels in Arc City. Since certain folks in the city frequently ask for sales figures, you have decided to make this information a permanent part of the parcel data.

To create the sales figures and store them with the parcel attributes, you will perform the following tasks:
- Create a field to hold sales values.
- Select parcels by their conveyance dates.
- Calculate the sales values.

☐ Add data to ArcMap

1. If necessary, start ArcMap with a new, empty map.

2. If you did not leave ArcMap open at the end of the last exercise, click the Add Data button and add the **ParcelData** feature class from the **ParcelBldg** feature data set in the **Arc City** geodatabase.

☐ Create a field to hold sales values

3. Open the Attributes of ParcelData.

4. Scroll through the table until you see the CONVEYDATE and the CONVEYFEE fields.

CONVEYDATE	CONVEYTYPE	CONVEYFEE	CHGNR	
7907	WD	55	222222	
8009	WD	29.9	999999	
8606	QC	0	999999	
8810	LC	115.5	999999	
9802	QC	0	999999	
9506	QC	0	999999	

The CONVEYFEE field contains conveyance fee values. (A conveyance fee is the amount of money the seller pays the county to transfer, or convey, the property to a new owner.) The CONVEYDATE field contains the year and month of the last conveyance transaction. You will use the conveyance fee to calculate the property sales price. The fee is $1 per $1,000 of the sales price for conveyances dated through August 31, 1981. After that date, the fee is $3 per $1,000 sales prices.

Now you'll add a new field to hold the sales price values.

5. In the Attributes of ParcelData, click the Options button and click Add Field. Name the field **SalesPrice** and define its type as Long Integer.

6. Click OK.

Select parcels by their conveyance dates

To populate the SalesPrice field you will need to run two separate calculations, one for the parcels with conveyance dates on or before August 31, 1981, and another for the parcels with conveyance dates after August 31, 1981.

7. In the Attributes of ParcelData, click the Options button, then click Select by Attributes.

8. In the Select by Attributes dialog, make sure that the Method is Create a new selection. Scroll through the Fields list to find CONVEYDATE then double-click it. Click the Less Than or Equal To button (< =). Underneath the Unique Values list, click Get Unique Values, then scroll through the list of unique values to 8107. (This is the closest date to August 1981 without going beyond the date.) Double-click 8107 to complete your search criteria.

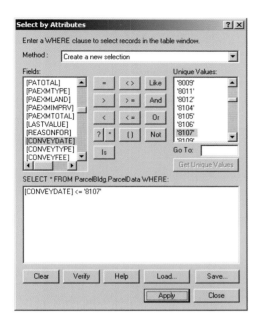

9. Click Apply. Then close the dialog.

A total of 155 properties are selected. (The number of records selected is reported at the bottom of the attribute table.) You'll calculate the sales price for the selected properties by dividing the conveyance fee by .001.

Calculate the sales values

10. Scroll horizontally to the end of the Attributes of ParcelData. Right-click on the SalesPrice field name and choose Calculate Values. When prompted, click Yes to continue.

11. In the Fields list, click CONVEYFEE to add it to the expression box. Click the divide (/) button. In the expression box, click at the end of the expression and type **.001**.

12. Click OK.

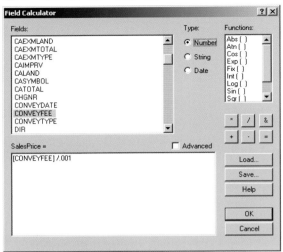

Only the selected records have their sales price calculated.

Now you'll select the properties with a conveyance date after August 1981. You could perform another attribute query, but you can achieve the same results simply by switching the selected records.

13. Click the Options button and click Switch Selection. Scroll through the table to verify that all of the selected records have a conveyance date that is larger than 8107.

All of the records that were selected are now unselected, while all the records that were not selected are now selected.

14. Open the Field Calculator for the SalesPrice field and change the value you divided by from .001 to **.003**.

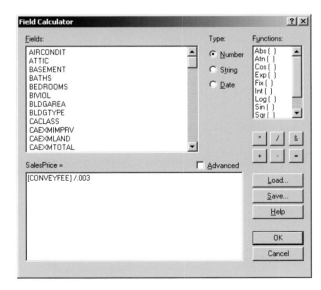

15. Click OK.

Notice that some records have a sales price of 0. If you scroll across to the CONVEYFEE field, you'll see that these properties also have a conveyance fee of 0. This means that the property has never been conveyed, or most likely, that the data is not available.

16. Click the Options button and choose Clear Selection.

17. Close the attribute table.

Save the map document

18. From the File menu, click Save As. In the Save As dialog, name the map document **my_ex02d.mxd** and save it in your **C:\DigitialCity\MyArcCity** folder.

19. If you are continuing on to the next exercise, leave ArcMap open. Otherwise, close ArcMap.

Exercise 2e

Query attribute files

You have already done some querying and table manipulation, but these exercises will help you become more comfortable with attribute querying and report generation.

In this exercise, after a general introduction about creating queries, you will perform the following tasks:
- Query for properties based on land use and sales price.
- Sort records for the parcel data.
- Refine the selection set.
- Query for commercial and industrial properties.
- Determine total industrial and commercial conveyance fees.
- Determine 1997 conveyance fees.

⌐ Creating an attribute query

Attribute queries are created using the Select By Attributes dialog in ArcMap. You can access this dialog from the Selection menu in ArcMap or through the Options menu on an open table. If the Select By Attributes dialog is opened from the Selection menu, you can only run queries on the layers in your map. To run queries on stand-alone tables in your map (tables not associated with a feature class), you must open the Select By Attribute dialog from the table's Options menu. (This method can also be used on a layer's attribute table.) Regardless of whether you're querying features through a layer's attribute table or the records in a stand-alone table, the method used to construct the query is the same.

The graphic on the following page shows the Select By Attributes dialog. In this case, you can see that it was opened from the Selection menu because the first drop-down list prompts you to choose a layer to base the query on. After picking the layer, you choose which query method you want to use, define the query statement, verify the syntax of your statement, then apply the query to select the features and records of interest.

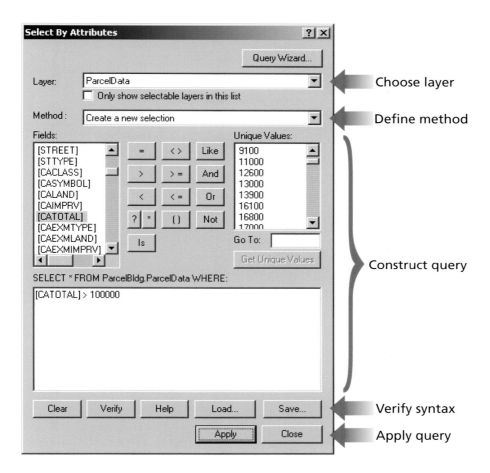

Choose layer

Define method

Construct query

Verify syntax

Apply query

The Method option defines how the selection is made. From the Method drop-down list, the following four options are available:

Create a new selection—This method selects a new subset of records from the table based upon the query criteria (e.g., a list of the single-family residences in the ParcelData layer attribute table). When this method is chosen, any records that were selected before the query was run are unselected if they do not fall within the selection parameters defined by the query. In other words, with this method a completely new selection set is made every time a query is run.

Add to current selection—This method adds additional records (with new query criteria) to those previously selected (e.g., all apartments in the ParcelData table in addition to the previously selected single-family residences).

Remove from current selection—This method removes records from the current selection that meet the query criteria (e.g., all properties that are either single-family

residences or apartments, but are tax delinquent, leaving non-tax-delinquent ones in the selection).

Select from current selection—This method selects records from the current selection that meet the query criteria (e.g., all properties that are single-family residences or apartments, are not tax delinquent, and are owner occupied).

Once a set of records is selected, you can use Switch Selection to see all the records that are the reverse of your selected set. For example, if all records with "residential" for land use were selected, to get all non-residential records, use Switch Selection in the Options menu at the bottom of the table.

How queries are structured

ArcGIS uses SQL (Standard Query Language) syntax to formulate a query on tables in your personal geodatabase. SQL syntax requires a field name, a logical operator, and a value for the item to create an expression. Complex queries can combine more than one expression by using a logical connector. As you make your field, operator, value, and connector selections, the expression is built in the box at the bottom of the dialog box.

1. Field name

The name of the field in the table that you want ArcGIS to use in searching for values that meet your criteria. A field name is required in order for the query to work. Double-click the field name in the "Fields" box of the Select by Attributes dialog box.

2. Logical operator

A symbol that you use to define the limits of the search, representing equal to (=), greater than (>), less than (<), greater than or equal to (>=), less than or equal to (<=), not equal to (<>), etc. A logical operator is also required for the query. Click the symbol desired to add it to the SQL statement.

3. Value for the item

A number or character string that you state in your query as the value, or criteria, to be used by ArcGIS in searching all of the records on the defined field. A field value is required. Unique values are listed in the box on the right side of the dialog box.

4. Logical connector (optional)

The logical connector is an optional element of the query that combines more than one expression.

Complex queries can be built by combining expressions together with the AND and OR operators. For example, to select all the houses that have more than fifteen hundred square feet and a garage for three or more cars in a layer, use this query:

[AREA] > 1500 AND [GARAGE] > 3

When you use the OR operator, at least one expression of the two expressions separated by the OR operator must be true for the record to be selected, for example:

[RAINFALL] < 20 OR [SLOPE] > 35

More on logical operators

NOT operator

Use the NOT operator at the beginning of an expression to find features or records that don't match the specified expression, for example:

NOT [STATE_NAME] ='Colorado'

NOT expressions can be combined using AND and OR. For example, to select all the New England states except Maine, use the query:

[SUB_REGION] ='New England'AND NOT [STATE_NAME] ='Maine'

IS NULL operator

You can use the IS NULL operator to select features and records that have null values for the specified field. For example, to find cities whose 1996 population hasn't been entered, you can use:

[POPULATION96] IS NULL

There is no"is null"operator button, so you are required to type that phrase in if you want to use it.

More on expressions

Expressions include partial string searches and wildcards.
    To build a partial string search, you use the LIKE operator (instead of the = operator) and include wildcards as follows:
        If you are querying personal geodatabase (Access) data:
        '?'indicates one character.
        '*'indicates any number of characters.

NOTE: If you are querying an ARC/INFO® coverage, shapefile, INFO™ table, dBASE table, or SDE data, use"_"for one character and"%"for any number of characters.
    These wildcard characters also appear as buttons on the dialog that you can click to enter the wildcard at the current cursor location in your expression.

Thus, the query that will find both Catherine Smith and Katherine Smith in a layer based on personal geodatabase looks like this:

[OWNER_NAME] LIKE '?atherine smith'

If you use a wildcard character in a string with the = operator, the character is treated as part of the string, not as a wildcard.

Click on the Help button in the Select by Attributes dialog box to see more information and options in building expressions for querying tables in ArcGIS.

◻ The table interface

Once the query has been structured, it is necessary to click on the Apply button in the dialog box so that ArcGIS can apply the query to the table you have selected. When the selection is complete, ArcGIS highlights the selected records in the table in a color and it also highlights in the same color the features of the selected records on the map. You should click on the Close button of the dialog box to see them.

In addition to the values of the items for the records, the table interface window has some options available at the bottom of the window. On the bottom left, you are given buttons that will allow you to move up and down among the records in the table. You are also given the choice of showing All of the records in the table or just the Selected records; the number of each is also given. The Options menu gives you additional features, some of which you have already used in previous exercises.

◻ Add data to ArcMap

1. If necessary, start ArcMap with a new, empty map.

2. If you did not leave ArcMap open at the end of the last exercise, click the Add Data button and add the ParcelData feature class from the **ParcelBldg** feature data set in the **Arc City** geodatabase.

◻ Query for properties based on land use and sales price

3. In the ArcMap table of contents, right-click the PacelData layer and click Open Attribute Table. Position the table so that it's not covering the map display.

You're interested in getting some basic information about the sales price for multifamily properties in Arc City. As you may recall from the previous exercise, not all of the properties have sales price information. You'll exclude these properties.

4. In the attribute table, click the Options button and click Select by Attributes.

5. In the Select by Attributes dialog, make sure the Method drop-down list is set to Create a new selection.

To construct the first part of your query, you'll select parcels with multifamily resi-dences. These parcels can be selected by querying for the "03" values within the LAN-DUSEGP field.

6. In the Fields list, double-click [LANDUSEGP]. Click the Less Than (<) operator. Click Get Unique Values, then in the Unique Values list double-click '03'.

Reminder: You can also construct the expression manually by typing it in the expression box.

7. From the set of operators, click the AND operator.

8. Construct the second part of the query statement using the following expression: [SalesPrice] > 0.

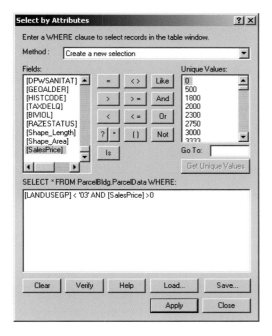

Using "AND" as a connector between the two expressions requires that both expressions be true for a record before it can be selected.

9. Click the Verify button to make sure that the expression is formatted correctly. (If the verification process returns an error message, fix the errors in the expression then verify it again.)

10. Click OK, then click Apply.

11. Close the Select by Attributes dialog.

Note: If the blocks feature class does not exist in your current map, your map will vary slightly vary from the graphic, but the set of selected parcels will match.

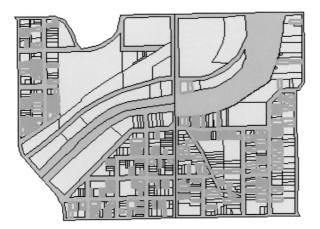

The query results in a selection of 230 parcels. (You can see the exact number of selected records by looking at the bottom of the attribute table to the right of the Show buttons.)

Sort records for the parcel data

To help examine the attributes of your current selection, you will sort the selected records by their sales price values.

12. At the bottom of the Attributes of ParcelData table, click the Selected button, then scroll horizontally to the end of the attribute table so you can see the SalesPrice field.

13. Right-click on the SalesPrice field name and choose Sort Descending.

RAZESTATUS	Shape_Length	Shape_Area	SalesPrice
9	334.293134	4919.655120	4333333
9	424.735635	9062.201006	166000
9	338.055727	5103.476580	160000
9	340.426358	5267.555479	132000
9	329.059698	5465.893178	125500
9	399.088462	9953.439798	125000
9	251.188502	2518.577118	122000
9	247.615357	2451.111173	111100
9	356.954982	6429.607558	105000
9	315.400946	3811.263295	105000
9	386.175057	6109.660787	100000
9	338.419100	5173.799602	99900

Record: [I] [◄] [0] [►] [►I]   Show: All | Selected   Records (230 out of 644 Selected.

Sorting the records can help you get a quick glance at the highest or lowest values in a field. Once the data is sorted, you can scan the range of values by scrolling down the table. Another way to look at the distribution of values within a field is through the Statistics command.

14. Right-click the SalePrice field name again and click Statistics.

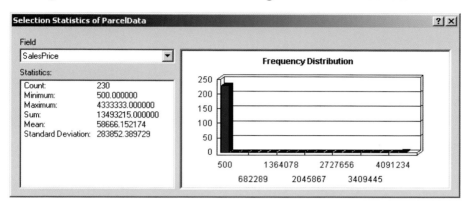

The dialog produced by the Statistic command contains basic statistics and a Frequency Distribution histogram for the selected values in the field you chose. (If you have not selected any records, the statistics are calculated for all the values in the field.) The histogram shows the range of values along the horizontal axis and the total number of values within a discrete value range along the vertical axis. The histogram is not precise; for example, you can only approximate how many values are within each range, but it does provide an accurate overview of the distribution of the selected values. In this case, the values fall mostly at the lower end of the full range, indicating that there are some extreme values (outliers) that are skewing the range away from a normal distribution.

? **Question:** What are the highest and lowest sales prices recorded for multifamily homes?

Highest price?

Lowest price?

15. Close the Selection Statistics dialog.

⌐ **Refine the selection set**

Based on the statistics you just generated, you know there are some high-priced properties within the city.

Your next query will determine where in Arc City the higher priced homes are located. You already have the residential properties selected. You can make use of your current selection by making another selection from it.

16. From the Selected Attributes of ParcelData, click the Options button and click Select by Attributes.

17. In the Select by Attributes dialog, change the Method to Select from current selection. Then construct the following expression:
    [SalesPrice] >= 100000

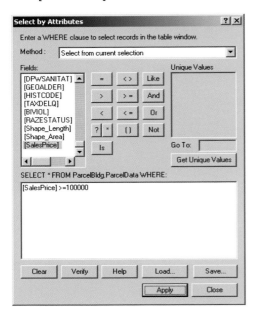

18. Click Apply, then close the dialog.

Eleven properties are selected.

Look at the selected features in the map display. Except for one cluster, the properties are distributed fairly evenly south of the river.

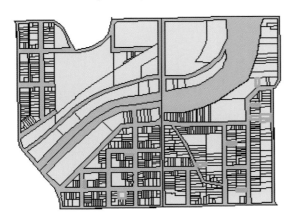

Query for industrial and commercial properties

The conveyance fees provide a source of revenue for Arc City, particularly the industrial and commercial properties that are assessed at a higher value than residential properties. During the next few tasks, you'll determine the total conveyance fees paid by industrial and commercial properties, then you'll determine the total for 1997 (the most recent year for which you have data).

First, you'll select all the commercial and industrial properties (land-use group codes 04 through 09) for which the city has received a conveyance fee.

19. Open the Select by Attributes dialog from the Options menu. From the Method drop-down list choose Create a new selection, then construct the following expression:
[LANDUSEGP] >= '04' AND [LANDUSEGP] <= '09' AND [CONVEYFEE] > 0

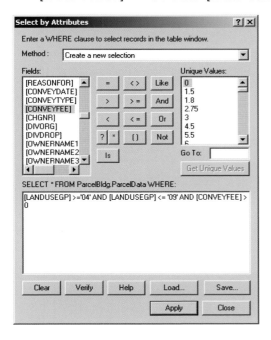

20. Verify the expression to check for errors, then click Apply.

After the query runs, there should be thirty-seven records selected.

21. If necessary, click the Selected button to show just the selected records in the attribute table.

With appropriate parcels selected, you can now determine the total amount of money they produced through conveyance fees.

Determine total industrial and commercial conveyance fees

22. Scroll across the table until you locate the CONVEYFEE field. When located, right-click on CONVEYFEE and choose Statistics.

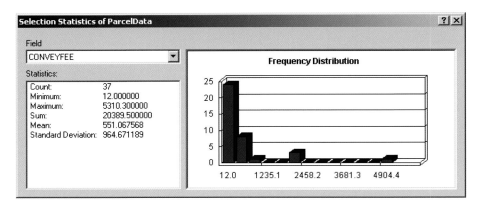

For the thirty-seven selected properties, Arc City has collected $20,389.50 in fees. This information was derived from the Sum value in the statistics dialog.

Note: This total reflects only the most recently paid fee. If a property has been sold more than once, those fees are not included.

23. Close the Statistics dialog.

Determine 1997 conveyance fees

Next, you'll determine the fees collected for commercial and industrial properties for the year 1997.

24. In the Select by Attributes dialog, change the Method to Select from current selection, then click the Clear button at the bottom of the dialog to clear the previous expression from the text box.

Your new query will need to select those properties that have a conveyance date in 1997.

25. In the fields list, click CONVEYDATE, then click Get Unique Values.

Notice that the date is a combination of year and month. Therefore, you will need to use wildcard characters in the query.

26. Construct the following query expression (you will have to type in everything to the right of the LIKE operator):
   [CONVEYDATE] LIKE '97??'

Note: When using wildcard characters, the Like operator must be used instead of a mathematical operator.

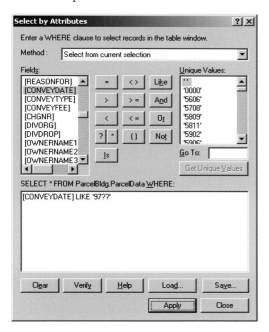

27. Verify the expression to check for errors. Click Apply, then close the Select by Attributes dialog.

After the query runs, there should be only four properties selected.

28. To find out how much revenue was generated from their conveyance fee, generate the statistics for the CONVEYFEE field.

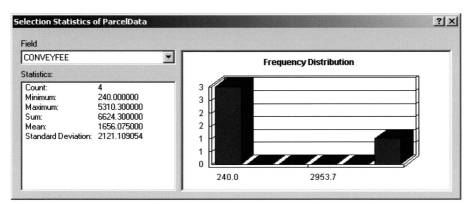

29. Close the Statistics dialog, then close the Attributes of ParcelData.

30. From the Selection menu, click Clear Selected Features.

Save the map document

31. From the File menu, click Save As. In the Save As dialog, name the map document **my_ex02e.mxd** and save it in your **C:\DigitalCity\MyArcCity** folder.

32. If you are continuing on to the next exercise, leave ArcMap open. Otherwise, close ArcMap.

Exercise 2f

Geocode parcels with blocks and districts

The objective of this exercise is to overlay the block feature class (Blocks) onto the parcel feature class (ParcelData) to create a new feature class (ParcelAll) that contains the correct block and district identifiers for each parcel in Arc City. This will geocode the parcel data with the attributes needed to produce the Arc City land-use report.

Overlays are used to integrate the attributes and geometry stored in separate feature classes. The output from an overlay is a new feature class that contains the attributes and geometry from the two input feature classes. There are several types of overlays, each is characterized by the way it combines the geometries contained in the input feature classes.

In this exercise you will use a Union overlay to combine the parcel feature class with the block feature class so that the block and district identifiers are added to each parcel. In ArcGIS terms, you will Union the Blocks feature class with the ParcelData feature class to create a new ParcelAll feature class that will then have polygon features representing every part of Arc City (parcels, blocks, districts, and rights-of-way). The new ParcelAll feature class will have in its Attribute Table all the parcel data from ParcelData plus the block and district identifiers from Blocks.

The resulting features will also be more realistic since rights-of-way and parcels are more evident.

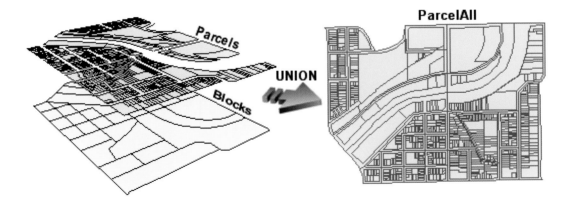

When this exercise is completed, the resulting ParcelAll feature class could be joined back to ParcelData to get just the BlockIDs and DistrictIDs.

In this exercise you will perform the following tasks:
- Perform the polygon union.
- Review the polygon attribute tables.

Polygon overlay using the Union command

When two maps containing different types of polygons (such as blocks and parcels) are overlaid, the result is a new map (or feature class) whose polygons have characteristics of both original sets of polygons. The polygon Union function creates new polygons wherever the boundaries of the polygons from the first feature class cut through the polygons of the second feature class. Graphically, this is represented as shown below:

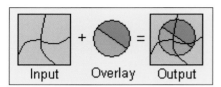

The new output data is reflected in the attribute table and the new polygons of the new feature class. In this exercise, you will Union the parcels and blocks, resulting in each parcel identifier having its corresponding block and district identifiers. Thus, the parcels will have been geocoded with block and district identifiers. Also, areas where there are no parcels (road rights-of-way or river) will be part of the output feature class, coded with blocks and districts.

☐ Add data to ArcMap

1. If necessary, start ArcMap with a new, empty map.

2. Unless they already exist in your map, click the Add Data button and add the ParcelData feature class from the **ParcelBldg** feature data set in your **Arc City** geodatabase. Then, click the Add Data button again and load the **Blocks** feature class from the **StreetBlock** feature data set.

☐ Perform the polygon Union

You'll use a geoprocessing tool stored in ArcToolbox to combine the ParcelAll and Blocks feature classes.

3. Open ArcToolbox. (On the Standard toolbar, click the Show/Hide ArcToolbox Window button.)

4. In ArcToolbox, expand the Analysis Tools toolbox, then expand the Overlay toolset.

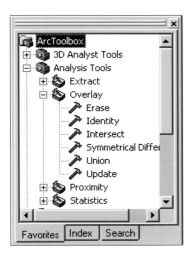

5. In the Overlay toolset, double-click the Union tool.

Inside this dialog you must specify which feature classes will participate in the overlay and the name of the output feature class. The remaining choices on this dialog are optional. (If you would like more detail about a particular option on this dialog, click the Show Help button in the dialog, then click on any of the options in the dialog to get more information about them).

6. In the Union dialog, click the Input Features drop-down arrow and choose Blocks. Click the Input Feature drop-down arrow again and choose ParcelData.

These are the two feature classes that you will overlay with one another.

7. In the Union dialog, click the Browse button that's to the right of the Output Feature Class box. In the Output Feature Class dialog, navigate to your **ParcelBldg** feature data set, name the new feature class **ParcelAll**, then click Save. Leave the remaining settings on the dialog set to their defaults.

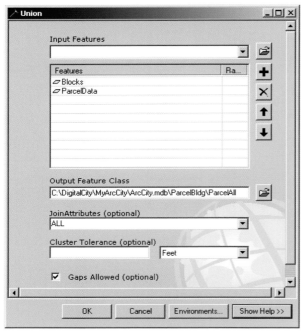

8. Make sure your settings match the above graphic, then click OK. Click Close when the process completes, then close ArcToolbox.

ParcelAll is a combination of the features from the two input feature classes as well as the attributes from both feature classes.

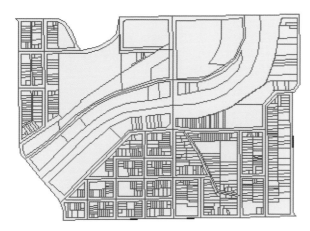

9. Turn off (uncheck) all the layers in the table of contents, then alternate turning ParcelData and ParcelAll on and off so you can see how their geometries differ.

Notice that ParcelAll contains a polygon for every square inch of Arc City (including right-of-way polygons).

Review the polygon attribute tables

10. Open the Attributes of ParcelAll. Scroll across the table and review its attribute fields.

The ParcelAll attribute table contains all of the attributes from the ParcelData feature class and the Blocks feature class. Near the end of the table you can see the block attributes such as the BlockID and DistrictID fields.

? **Question:** The number of records in the attribute table is greater than the number of parcels in Arc City. Why is this?

11. Close the Attributes of ParcelAll.

12. From the File menu, click Save as. In the Save As dialog, name the map document **My_ex02f.mxd** and save it in your **C:\DigitalCity\MyArcCity** folder.

13. Close ArcMap

The ParcelAll feature class contains all the attributes you need to produce the Arc CIty land-use report. These attributes include each parcel's block and district identification number, land use, and number of housing units. In the next chapter you will use ParcelAll along with Report Wizard in ArcMap to create that report.

Answers

◻ **Exercise 2e: Query attribute files**

What are the highest and lowest sales prices recorded for multifamily homes?

Highest price: $4,333,333.00
Lowest price: $500.00

How much revenue was generated by the sale of these properties?   **$6,624.30**

◻ **Exercise 2f: Geocode parcels with blocks and districts**

The number of records in the attribute table is greater than the number of parcels in Arc City. Why is this?   **Because during the overlay polygons were also created for the right-of-way features.**

Chapter *3*

Reporting and performing spatial analysis

Once the database is complete—the spatial data has been converted and registered on a continuous coordinate system and the feature attribute data has been geocoded and linked to their respective features—it is time to make use of the full capabilities of the geographic information system. This chapter contains exercises that are typical applications of GIS technology in local government of analyzing data and creating reports as well as performing spatial analysis.

Data analysis and display with GIS

While map retrieval and maintenance are the most-often used applications of GIS technology, spatial query and display applications are also often used. Spatial query is the simple process of asking questions about the spatial and attribute data. (Nyerges and Dueker 1988). Generally, GIS answers two types of questions:

❏ **What is at (a location)?**—This represents spatial access into the attribute data. The user identifies a feature on the map display (such as a land parcel) then receives attributes of that feature (such as the name of the parcel owner), displayed either on the map or in a report or table. The GIS software first identifies the feature being accessed, then obtains its unique identifier, goes to the attribute data to find the record with that same identifier, and retrieves the attributes requested. The system uses the map to access the attribute data.

❏ **Where is (an object)?**—This represents attribute access into the spatial data. The user defines a value for some particular attribute (such as an arson as a type of crime) and receives a map display of the features that have those attribute values (such as buildings where arsons occurred). The GIS software first reads through the attribute table and finds a record that contains the value (arson) for that attribute (type of crime). It then reads the unique identifier of that attribute record and finds the same identifier in the record of the spatial data of the desired feature type and highlights the feature (building). It then continues looking for more attribute records with that same value and highlights each feature whose associated (linked by a unique identifier) attribute record contains that value. The system uses the attribute value to display the map feature having that value.

Once the data has been accessed in either of these two manners, you can display the results of these queries using other methods. In addition to displaying the attribute values directly onto the map or highlighting the features having the desired attribute values, you can also display symbols representing attribute values or change the color or pattern of the features depending on the values.

A kind of symbol display is known as dot-density mapping. This capability displays incidents of a common attribute (such as water-main breaks) as dots, allowing the user to see any clustering of the incidents that could indicate a geographic tendency. Changing feature colors or patterns based on attribute values is known as choropleth mapping. This capability displays shaded or color-filled polygons (such as census tracts) based on an attribute statistic (such as average property value).

Spatial analysis with GIS

Yet it is the spatial analysis capability of GIS software that sets it apart from computer-aided mapping software. In spatial analysis, the software performs a spatial function, usually on the attributes of the spatial features. Spatial analysis functions create new data for the user. Thus, spatial analysis takes sets of data, analyzes them spatially, and creates new features with new information from that analysis. Buffering, polygon overlay, and network analysis are functions of spatial analysis.

Buffering—A buffer is a polygon feature that is created by the software. The shape of the polygon is determined by measuring an equal distance around another map feature (a point, a line, or a polygon). Use buffers when it is important to identify features within a certain distance of another feature (such as all properties within one thousand feet of a contaminated well). To do this, first generate the buffer around the well feature (a point). Then overlay the buffer polygon onto parcel polygons (or points representing parcels) using a polygon overlay function.

Polygon overlay—This function combines a polygon feature with another feature (a point, a line, or another polygon), creating a new feature that has attributes of both original features. Types of polygon overlays include:

❑ **Point-on-polygon**—This overlay adds polygon attributes to the attributes of point features. An example is wells (points) overlaid with counties (polygons) to identify which county each well lies within.

❑ **Line-on-polygon**—This overlay creates additional line segments wherever the polygons cross the lines, thus adding the polygon attributes to each new segment. An example is overlaying roads (lines) onto counties (polygons) to identify which portion of each road is in each county.

❑ **Polygon-on-polygon**—This overlay creates additional polygons wherever the original two types of polygons are not coincident. You use this when you overlay watershed districts onto counties to identify which portions of which watershed lie within each county.

Network analysis is a spatial analysis function that analyzes attribute data along a network of connected line segments (streets, sewer lines, water mains, etc.) and develops a particular path or route along the network based upon some optimization criteria (such as minimum travel time, shortest distance, etc.) The new information that network analysis creates is a route feature—a particular combination of connected line segments that have a specific characteristic such as optimum path.

Other spatial analysis capabilities that have been used in the previous chapters include Dissolve (features that share the same values can be dissolved to make new features such as creating districts from blocks in chapter 2, exercise 2c) and Merge (combining two or more features such as merging the two park polygons into one parcel in chapter 1, exercise 1f).

Reports and spatial analysis in Arc City

You now have created the data files and learned the commands necessary to create tables and perform spatial analysis on information about Arc City. In this chapter you will put these resources to work by completing five exercises that will produce GIS products for Arc City officials.

Produce the Arc City land-use report and map

The Arc City supervisors have requested a land-use report and map to provide them with a comprehensive overview of the city. The report provides statistics (counts, totals, and percents) on housing units and parcels by land-use group for each district. The map shows land use by parcel.

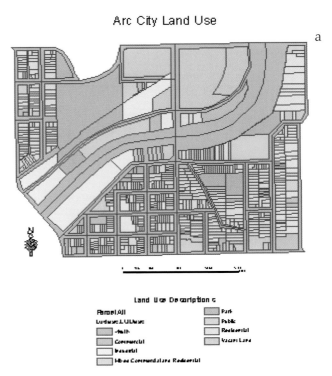

Arc City Land Use

Land Use Descriptions

District 1 Land Use

Description	Parcels	Housing Units
Commercial	5	6
Industrial	7	0
Mixed Commercial and Residential	2	5
Park	4	0
Public	4	10
Residential	103	196
Vacant Land	4	0

Cnt_LUDesc Sum
129
Sum_NRUNITS Sum
217

Produce a residential density report of the districts in Arc City

You will need to display on a report a summary of population and housing units by district, the computation of each district's residential density (population per housing unit).

Residential Density

District ID	Parcels	Housing Units	Population	Density
1	129	217	599	2.8
2	216	340	810	2.4
3	301	1478	1963	1.3

DistrictCount Cnt_DistrictID Sum
646
DistrictCount Sum_NRUNITS Sum
2035
Districts.SUM_CensusData_TOTAL Sum
3372

Perform an analysis of the floodplain

You will overlay the floodplain map with Arc City parcels to identify the parcels that are in the floodplain. Various departments in the city will use the floodplain map and analysis report to regulate, control, and restrict development in the floodplain. Their intention is to minimize the negative environmental, social, and economic impacts that may result from poorly planned developments should a hundred-year flood occur. The map will also be used to identify the parcels that may qualify for federal flood insurance and help the city office of emergency preparedness plan for emergencies.

ArcCity Flood Plain Map

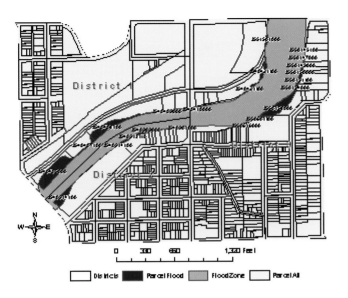

Legend: Districts | Parcel Flood | FloodZone | Parcel All

Scale: 0 330 660 1,320 Feet

Arc City Flood Plain

District	Tax Key	Address	# Units	Parcel Area	Flood Area	% Flood
1	3540405000	N 1890 COMMERCE ST	0	82164.11	55883.00	68.01
1	3540410000	N 2070 COMMERCE ST	0	27032.25	807.53	2.99
1	3540407100	N 1942 COMMERCE ST	0	45469.50	5176.03	11.38
1	3540408100	N 2000 COMMERCE ST	0	128146.23	38955.72	30.40
1	3540409000	N 2056 COMMERCE ST	0	26799.37	1375.52	5.13
1		0	0	294058.31	217350.29	73.91
2	3540914100	N 1781 WATER ST	0	247458.19	20758.81	8.39
2	3540913110	N 1887 WATER ST	0	42032.87	6496.66	15.46
2	3540909000	E 926 KANE PL	0	8144.22	1114.19	13.68
2	3540908000	E 930 KANE PL	0	5534.93	558.82	10.10
2	3540907000	E 936 KANE PL	0	5180.78	403.83	7.79
2	3540906000	E 1002 KANE PL	0	8244.40	308.75	3.74
2	3540905000	E 1008 KANE PL	0	8544.65	184.56	2.16
2	3540904000	E 1014 KANE PL	0	8662.02	133.63	1.54
2	3540903000	E 1020 KANE PL	0	5253.94	111.05	2.11
2	3540901000	N 1911 HUMBOLDT AV	0	21503.24	1352.92	6.29
2		0	0	279976.52	190266.37	67.96
3	3550158000	E 1354 BOYLSTON ST	0	71422.87	37082.89	51.92
3	3550616000	E 1222 KANE PL	3	5378.17	19.65	0.37
3	3550601100	E 1300 KANE PL	180	139872.57	4430.31	3.17
3	3550154000	N 2027 CAMBRIDGE AV	10	30470.67	2749.30	9.02

Prepare a mosquito analysis, map, and report

A chemical pesticide will soon be administered on the river to control the mosquito population in Arc City. Since an Arc City ordinance requires warning signs to be posted before pesticides are applied, the city is required to notify all property owners within 675 feet of the river prior to application. The supervisors want the Arc City GIS to produce a map of the properties affected and a list of their addresses so that the public works department will know how many signs to make, where they should be posted and where to mail notifications so that the property owners in the affected area can be informed of the pesticide application.

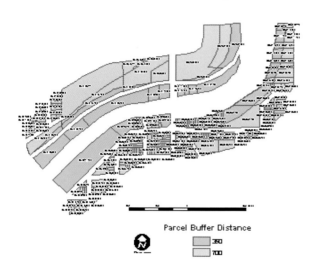

Mosquito Abatement
Parcel Notification Map

Parcel Buffer Distance

	350
	700

Mosquito Abatement: Parcel Notification Report

Tax Key	Owner	Address	Distance
3540914100	ANDREW JOHNSON	N 1781 WATER ST	350
3540626100	ARC CITY	E 925 KANE PL	350
3540625100	ARC CITY	N 1879 ASTOR ST	350
3540609000	ARC CITY	E 1001 KANE PL	350
3540608000	ARC CITY	E 1009 KANE PL	350
3550622000	ARC CITY	E 1152 KANE PL	350
3550621100	ARC CITY	E 1158 KANE PL	350
3540901000	ARC CITY	N 1911 HUMBOLDT AV	350
3540434100	ARC CITY METROPOLITAN	N 1983 COMMERCE ST	350
3540432000	ARC CITY METROPOLITAN	N 2029 COMMERCE ST	350
3540407100	ARC CITY REDEV AUTH	N 1942 COMMERCE ST	350
3540408100	ARC CITY REDEV AUTH	N 2000 COMMERCE ST	350
3550158000	ARC COUNTY	E 1354 BOYLSTON ST	350
3540416100	BENJAMIN B BLACK	N 2134 RIVERBOAT RD	350
3550154000	BIGGS LLC	N 2027 CAMBRIDGE AV	350
3551502000	BRYAN SIMON	N 2200 HUMBOLDT AV	350
3540421100	CHET T KNOWLES	N 2176 RIVERBOAT RD	350
3540435100	CITY METRO SEWERAGE DIST	E 401 GLOVER AV	350
3550632000	COLLEEN DURRELL	E 1118 KANE PL	350

Find possible drug houses near a playground

In spite of its small size, Arc City has some of the same problems as larger cities. One of these problems is children using drugs. The Arc City police department has observed that most of the sales of drugs to children have occurred in houses near playgrounds where children gather before and after school. Not having a large police force, the Arc City police chief has decided to use the city's GIS to identify the buildings that are most likely to be used by the drug pushers to make sales to the children. The GIS will be used to identify all single- and two-family homes within walking distance to the playground that are also not occupied by their owners and are tax delinquent. These characteristics indicate that the houses could be neglected and used by drug pushers. When you finish the exercise, your map will look like this:

Exercise 3a

Produce the Arc City land-use report

In this exercise you will produce the Arc City land-use report that summarizes the number of parcels and housing units by land use for each district in Arc City from the data contained in the ParcelAll layer.

The Arc City land-use report contains a statistical summary of the land use and housing unit information by district. These summary statistics can be obtained by using the Report function of ArcGIS. Reports in ArcMap can also be created with Crystal Reports®, but these exercises will use the simple report writer called Reports. The report capability of Crystal Reports provides much more flexibility and capabilities by using templates and the Crystal Reports Editor; however, the software also requires much more time to learn and is beyond the scope of this text.

The Report function in ArcGIS allows you to produce summaries of fields containing numeric values (e.g., number of housing units) and group them based on values in other fields (e.g., number of housing units in District 1). You can produce the following summaries:
- the minimum value found for the field
- the maximum value found for the field
- the sum of all values for the field
- the mean of all the values for the field
- the standard deviation of the values found for the field

In this exercise you will perform the following tasks:
- Create a table of the housing units and parcels per district.
- Create the district housing report.
- Modify the report's properties.
- Create a land-use description lookup table for the land-use group values.
- Create land-use summary tables.
- Create district land-use reports.
- Print the reports.
- Create a land-use map to accompany the reports.

☐ **Before you begin**

The exercises in this chapter assume you have completed chapters 1 and 2. If you did not successfully complete all the exercises in these chapters, you must replace your Arc City geodatabase with the **ArcCity_Ch2results** geodatabase that is provided on your data CD. To update your Arc City geodatabase with the newer version, use the same method outlined in the first task of exercise 1e in chapter 1, except replace your **Arc City** geodatabase with the **ArcCity_Ch2results** geodatabase instead of the **ArcCity_ex01e** geodatabase.

☐ **Start ArcMap and add data**

1. Start ArcMap with a new, empty map.

2. Click the Add Data button. Navigate to your **C:\DigitialCity\MyArcCity** folder. Double-click the **ArcCity.mdb**, double-click the **ParcelBldg** feature data set, then double-click the ParcelAll feature class to add it to the map.

(The color of the ParcelAll layer in your map will probably differ from the graphic.)

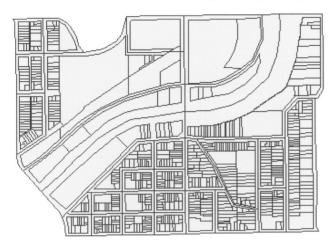

Using the attributes of this feature class, you will summarize the number of parcels and housing units found within each district.

Create a table of the housing units and parcels per district

The ParcelAll feature class contains parcels and rights-of-way. Before you summarize the number of parcels and housing units for each district, you must select the parcel features from ParcelAll.

3. Open the Attributes of ParcelAll. (Right-click the ParcelAll layer and click Open Attribute Table.)

4. From the Options menu in the Attributes of ParcelAll, click Select by Attributes.

Records in the ParcelAll feature class without a tax key value are right-of-way features. Records with a tax key value are parcels. Knowing this, you can select all of the parcels in ParcelAll by querying for records with a tax key value. You can do this in the Select By Attributes dialog by creating a query using the not equal to operator (< >) to look for values in the tax key field that are not empty strings.

When you query values stored in a text field, the strings you're querying for are contained within single quotes. For example, if you were querying for the state of Kansas in a United States feature class, your query would read, [State] = 'Kansas'. If you want to find records with empty values in a particular text field, you can set your query equal to two single quotes with nothing between them. For example, if you were looking for features with no value in the State field, your query would read, [State] = ''.

5. In the Select by Attributes dialog, double-click the [TKXY_TAXKE] in the fields list, click the Not Equal To operator (< >), then click the Get Unique Values button. At the top of the Unique Values list, double-click the two single quotes.

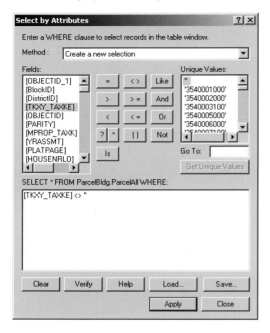

Translated to common language, this query means "find all the tax key records that do not contain empty values."

6. Click Apply, then close the Select By Attributes dialog. If necessary, move the table so you can see the selected parcels.

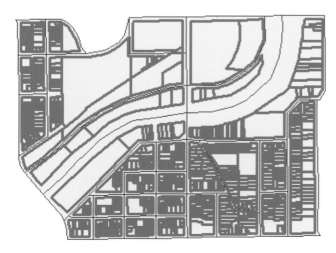

In the previous chapter, you combined the parcel data with the tax assessment table and the Districts feature class to produce the ParceAll feature class. As a result of these combinations, ParcelAll has several attribute fields including the DistrictID and NRUNITS fields.

For each parcel in ParcelAll, the DistrictID field contains its district number and the NRUNITS field contains the number of housing units on it. You will use these two fields to summarize information about the number of housing units in each Arc City district.

7. In the Attributes of ParcelAll, right-click the DistrictID field name, then click Summarize.

The summarize function categorizes tabular information based on the field you choose and calculates statistics for all the records that fall into each category. For example, you are going to use the summarize function to categorize the parcels by district then calculate the number of housing units within each district. To do this, you will use the DistrictID field to categorize the records and generate housing unit statistics from the NRUNITS field. The result of a summary operation is a new table.

8. In the Summarize dialog, verify that the field to summarize is DistrictID. For the second option, scroll through the list of fields until you find the NRUNITS field. Once located, click the plus sign (+) to the left of the field name to expand the list of available summary statistics, then check the options for Minimum, Maximum, Average, and Sum.

Based on these settings, the output table will indicate, for each district, the minimum number of units contained in a parcel, the maximum number of units contained in a parcel, the average number of units per parcel, and the district's total number of units.

9. For the output table, click the Browse button to the right of the text box. In the Saving Data dialog, set the Save as type drop-down list to Personal Geodatabase tables, then navigate to your **ArcCity.mdb**, and name the output table **DistrictCount**. Click Save.

10. At the bottom of the Summarize dialog, check the option to Summarize on the selected records only.

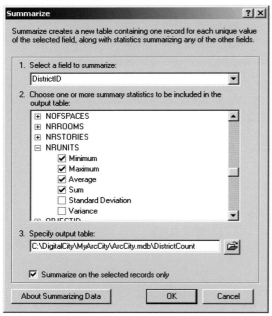

11. Click OK. When prompted, click Yes to add the table to the map document.

12. Close the Attributes of ParcelAll, then clear the selected features. (To clear the selected features, click the Selection menu and choose Clear Selected Features.)

13. Open the Attributes of DistrictCount and examine the attributes. (To open the table, right-click it in the table of contents and choose Open.)

Object ID*	DistrictID	Count_DistrictID	Minimum_NRUNITS	Maximum_NRUNITS	Average_NRUNITS	Sum_NRUNITS
1	1	129	0	6	1.682171	217
2	2	216	0	6	1.574074	340
3	3	301	0	180	4.910299	1478

The DistrictCount table contains one record for each district and all of the summary statistics you chose to include. The field naming convention generated from the summary function uses the field name from the origin table prefixed by the type of statistic that was performed on it.

By default, the summarize function counts all the records within each category and reports the counts. The results of these counts are placed in a field with a title that is prefixed by Count followed by the name of the field that was summarized. In this case, the field you summarized was the DistrictID field, so the record counts are contained in the Count_DistrictID field. And, since every record in the ParcelAll feature class is associated with a parcel, the counts in the Count_DistrictID field represent the number of parcels in each district.

The parcel counts per district range from 129 to 301. For every district, the minimum number of units found in any parcel was 0 (vacant lots and nonresidential land uses); the maximum number of units found in any parcel was 180.

? **Question:** Which district has the most housing units?
Which district has the fewest parcels?

14. Close the Attributes of DistrictCount.

Create the district housing report

With the statistics you need now compiled within the District table, you can begin to create the district housing report.

15. Click the Tools menu, point to Reports, and click **Create Report**.

On the Fields tab of the Report Properties, the Layer/Table drop-down list specifies the layer or table you will work with. The Available Fields scrolling box lets you choose the attributes to include in the report.

16. Click the Layer/Table drop-down arrow and click **DistrictCount**.

The fields in the DistrictCount table appear in the Available Fields list. In this case, you want your report to contain values from the DistrictID, Cnt_DistrictID, and Sum_NRUNITS fields.

17. In the Available Fields list, click DistrictID. Click the add fields button (right arrow) in the middle of the dialog to move the District ID field to the Report Fields list. Repeat this process to add the Cnt_DistrictID and the Sum_NRUNITS to the Report Fields list.

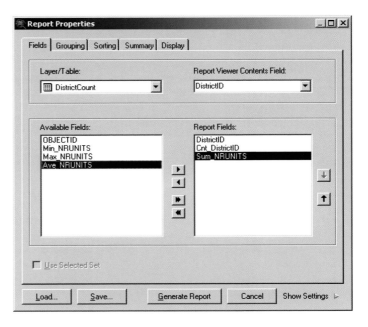

Next, you will use the Summary tab to place summary statistics at the bottom of the report.

18. Click the Summary tab.

The Available Sections drop-down list specifies where on the report the statistics will be placed. The Numeric Fields list includes all of the fields in your report that you can generate statistics for.

19. Make sure the Available Sections list is set to End of Report. In the Numeric Fields list, check the Sum column for the Cnt_DistricID and Sum_NRUNITS fields.

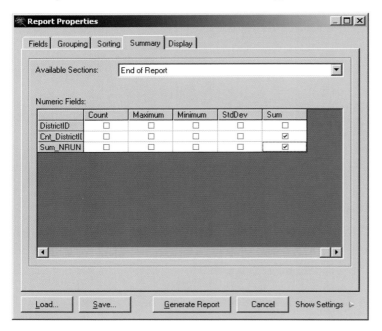

Based on these settings, the report will summarize the total number of parcels and units within the DistrictCount table and place the resultant statistics at the bottom of the report.

20. In the lower-right corner of the Report Properties dialog, click the Show Settings arrow.

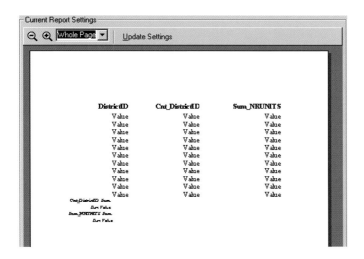

The Current Report Settings window allows you to see the overall layout of your report. You can keep it open while you create a report, and each time you change a report property you can click the Update Settings button at the top of the settings viewer to see how the changes you make affect the report's layout. What you can't see when you show the report settings are the values that will appear in the report; to see the values you must generate the report.

21. At the bottom of the Report Properties dialog, click the Hide Settings arrow, then click Generate Report.

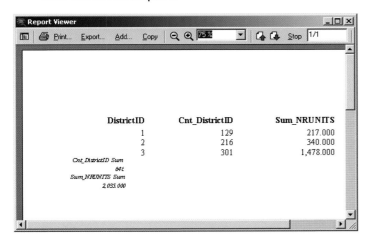

The size of your dialog will differ, but you probably can't see the whole report. The drop-down list at the top of the dialog lets you change the preview scale.

The report includes the information you wanted to show, but the formatting needs improvement. In the report's current form, the column headings are cryptic and the decimal places are not needed.

Next, you will change some of the report's display properties to make it easier to read.

☐ Modify the report's properties

22. Close the Report Viewer window.

23. In the Report Properties dialog, click the Display tab.

Report settings are grouped in categories (e.g., Report, Elements, and Background) in the Setting window on the left. Each setting has several properties. For example, the Field Names setting has properties for Border, Font, Height, and so on. Each property, in turn, has several possible values. For example, a font may be Times New Roman, Arial, Courier, or something else.

By default, the Elements category is expanded and the Field Names element checked, indicating that the report will display the names of the fields you added to the report.

First, you will add a title to the report.

24. Under Elements, check Title.

In the right-hand window, title properties and their values display.

25. Click the Report Title value. In the pop-up text box, replace the text with **Housing Units and Parcels by District**.

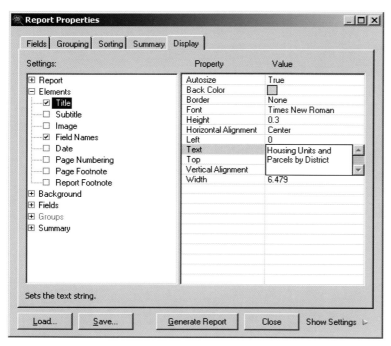

26. Press the Tab key to set the property's value.

After each of the following edits to an element's property values, press the Tab key to enter your setting.

27. In the Settings list, expand the Fields category. A list of all the fields in the current report appears underneath the category. Click the Cnt_DistrictID field.

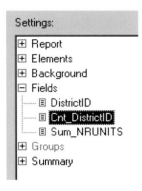

28. On the right-hand side of the dialog, click the Count_DistrictID value. Change the text to **Parcels**, then press the Tab key on your keyboard.

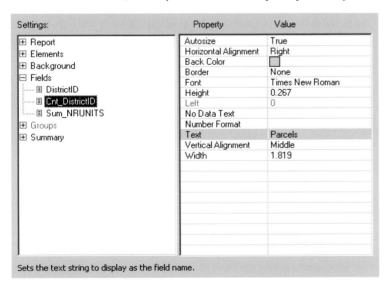

You just changed the Text property associated with the Cnt_DistrictID field in your report. Instead of appearing as Cnt_DistrictID, the heading for this field will appear as Parcels in the report. That should make it easier for Arc City employees to understand.

29. Click Show Settings to see how changing the field's text value affected the report.

Next, you will change the text for the Sum_NRUNITS field.

30. Change the Text property of the Sum_NRUNITS field to **Housing Units.**

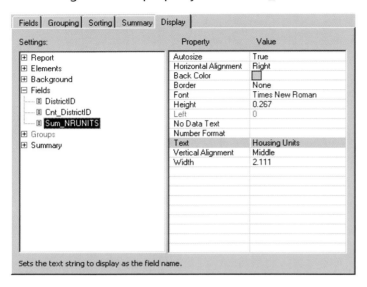

31. Update the Current Report Settings window. (To do this, click the Update Settings button located at the top of the Current Report Settings window.)

You should now see the settings that you changed; this includes the title you added and the two new field names.

In the next step, you will change the appearance of the housing unit values so that they do not contain decimal values.

32. On the right-hand side of the Report Properties dialog, click the Number Format property, then click the Ellipses button (...) that appears in the value column for this property.

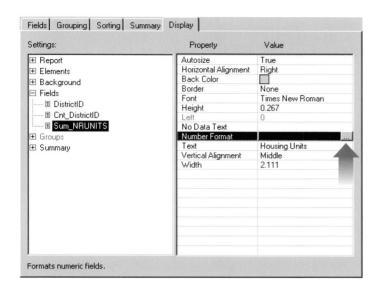

33. In the Number Format dialog, change the number of decimal places to **0**.

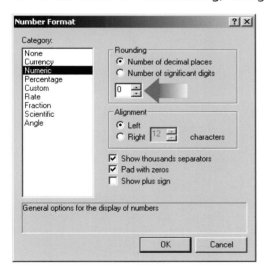

34. Click OK.

35. Click the Generate Report button.

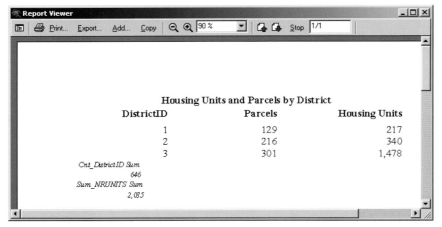

36. Close the Report Viewer window.

37. In the Report Properties dialog, click the Save button.

38. Save the report to your **C:\DigitalCity\MyArcCity** folder and name it **DistrictRep.rdf**.

You may want to print the report now or do it at the end of this exercise with all the other reports.

39. Close the Report Properties Dialog.

☐ Create a land-use description lookup table for the land-use group values

Currently, the land uses for the parcels in your ParcelAll attribute table are stored as two-digit numeric Land Use Group codes (01, 02, etc.). Aside from a few people in the GIS department, no one else in the city knows what type of land use each code represents. It would be better for people who read the report to see land-use descriptions (Residential, Industrial, etc.) instead of land-use codes.

To translate the land-use codes into meaningful text, you will create a lookup table that contains all of the coded values in one column and their respective descriptions in another column. To create the lookup table, you'll summarize the land-use codes in the attributes of ParcelAll. The result of this summary will be a new table containing a field with each unique land-use code. Once you have this table, you will add a field to it and populate that field with the land-use descriptions.

40. Open the Attributes of ParcelAll.

Before you summarize the land-use codes you need to select the parcels.

41. From the Options menu, click Select by Attributes. In the Select by Attributes dialog, construct a query to select all the parcels from ParcelAll. (Construct the same query you used in step 5.)

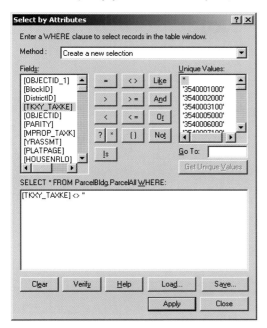

42. Apply the query, then close the Select by Attributes dialog.

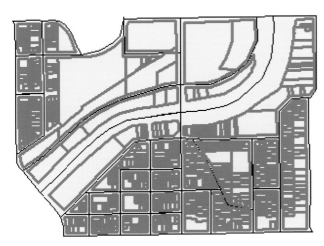

With the parcels selected, you can now summarize the land-use codes.

43. In the Attributes of ParcelAll, scroll to the right until you locate the LANDUSEGP field. (It's about three-quarters of the way to the right end of the table.) Right-click the LANDUSEGP field name, then choose Summarize.

44. In the Summarize dialog, verify that the field to summarize is LANDUSEGP. Skip the second option because, other than creating a table of unique land-use codes, no summary statistics are required. For the third option, save the output as a personal geodatabase table in your **ArcCity.mdb** and name the output **Ludesc**. At the bottom of the dialog, check the option to Summarize on the selected records only.

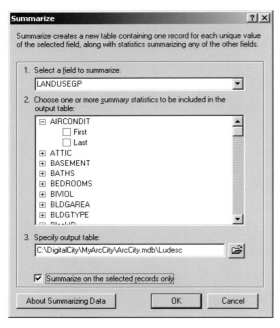

45. Click OK. When prompted, click Yes to add the new table to the map.

46. Close the Attributes of ParcelAll. Clear the selected features, then open the Ludesc table.

Object ID*	LANDUSEGP	Count_LANDUSEGP
1	00	2
2	01	165
3	02	220
4	03	124
5	04	34
6	05	8
7	06	7
8	07	4
9	08	9
10	09	12
11	11	11
12	12	20
13	13	30

The LANDUSEGP field contains the land-use codes; this was the field you chose to add to the summary table. Over the next few steps, you will add another field to the table and populate it with the land-use descriptions.

? Question: By default, the Count_LANDUSEGP field was added to the Attributes of Ludesc during the summarize process. What information is contained in the Count_LANDUSEGP field?

47. From the Options menu in the Attributes of Ludesc, click Add Field. In the Add Field dialog, name the new field LUDesc and set its type to Text.

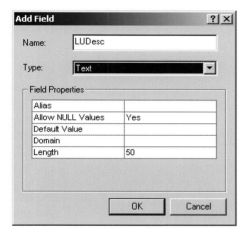

48. Click OK.

Your next step is to add the land-use code descriptions to the LUDesc field. The descriptions for these codes are as follows:

Land-use code	Land-use description
00, 01, 02, 03	Residential
04	Mixed commercial and residential
05, 06, 07	Commercial
08, 09	Industrial
11	Public
12	Park
13	Vacant land

To add these values, you will need to start an edit session in ArcMap.

49. On the Standard toolbar, click the Editor Toolbar button.

50. On the Editor toolbar, click the Editor menu and choose Start Editing.

51. In the Attributes of Ludesc, click the LUDesc cell with a LANDUSEGP of 00 and type **Residential.**

Object ID*	LANDUSEGP*	Count_LANDUSEGP	LUDesc
1	00	2	Residential
2	01	165	<Null>
3	02	220	<Null>
4	03	124	<Null>
5	04	34	<Null>
6	05	8	<Null>
7	06	7	<Null>
8	07	4	<Null>
9	08	9	<Null>
10	09	12	<Null>
11	11	11	<Null>
12	12	20	<Null>

Record: 1   Show: All | Selected   Records (0 out of 13 Selected.)   Options

52. Using the same method shown in step 51, add the correct land-use description to each record in the table.

Object ID*	LANDUSEGP*	Count_LANDUSEGP	LUDesc
1	00	2	Residential
2	01	165	Residential
3	02	220	Residential
4	03	124	Residential
5	04	34	Mixed Commercial and Residential
6	05	8	Commercial
7	06	7	Commercial
8	07	4	Commercial
9	08	9	Industrial
10	09	12	Industrial
11	11	11	Public
12	12	20	Park
13	13	30	Vacant Land

53. When you have finished entering the descriptions, click the Editor menu and choose Stop Editing. Click Yes to save your edits, then close the Attributes of Ludesc.

54. Close the Editor toolbar. (Click the same button you used to open it.)

Now that the land-use codes and their descriptions are contained in the Attributes of Ludesc, you can join this table to the Attributes of ParcelAll. Once this is done, the land-use descriptions will exist in the ParcelAll feature class.

? **Question:** Which field will be used to join the data from the Attributes of Ludesc to the Attributes of ParcelAll?

55. Right-click the ParcelAll layer in the table of contents, point to Joins and Relates, and click Join. In the Join Data dialog, set the "What do you want to join to this layer" option to "Join attributes from a table". From drop-down list number 1, choose the LANDUSEGP field. From drop-down list number 2, choose the Ludesc table. From drop-down list number 3, choose LANDUSEGP. Make sure your settings match the following graphic, then click OK.

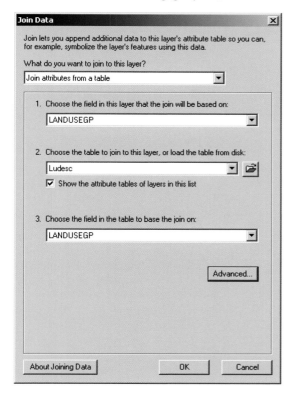

56. Open the Attributes of ParcelAll and scroll to the right end of the table to verify that the LUDesc values were appended to the table. (You may need to scroll down the table to see the parcel records, which have a land-use value assigned to them.)

LANDUSEGP	Count_LANDUSEGP	Ludesc.LUDesc
04	34	Mixed Commercial and Residential
00	2	Residential
03	124	Residential
04	34	Mixed Commercial and Residential
01	165	Residential
04	34	Mixed Commercial and Residential

Your next task is to summarize the land use in each district.

Create land-use summary tables

Now that you have land-use descriptions joined to the ParcelAll feature class, you will create land-use reports for each district. First, however, you'll need to create three summary tables from the ParcelAll feature class, one for each district that summarizes the number of parcels and number of housing units within each land-use category. Once these tables are generated, you can create the district land-use reports from them.

57. Open the Select by Attributes dialog from the Attributes of ParcelAll and construct the following query to select all the parcels in District 1:

ParcelAll.DistrictID = 1 AND ParcelAll.TKXY_TAXKE <> ''

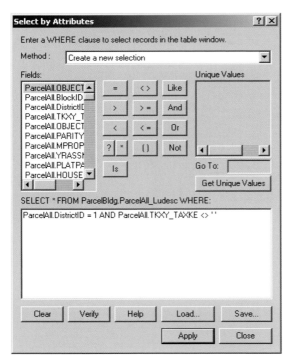

58. Click Apply, then close the Select by Attributes dialog.

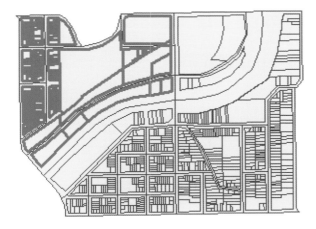

Next, you'll create a summary table for the selected records in ParcelAll.

59. In the Attributes of ParcelAll, right-click the Ludesc.LUDesc field name and choose Summarize.

60. In the Summarize dialog, verify that drop-down number 1 is set to summarize the Ludesc.LUDesc field. For option number 2, expand the ParcelAll.NRUNITS field and check the following summary statistics: Minimum, Maximum, Average, and Sum. For option number 3, save the output as a Personal Geodatabase Table within your Arc City geodatabase and name the new table **Dist1_LU.** At the bottom of the Summarize dialog, check the option to Summarize on the selected records only.

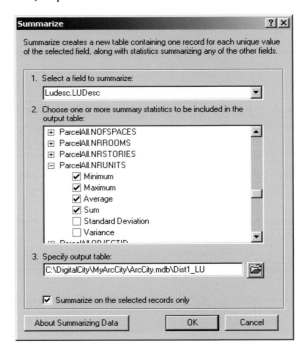

61. Make sure your settings match the previous graphic, then click OK. When prompted, click Yes to add the new table to the map document.

62. Open the Dist1_LU table.

OBJECTID*	LUDesc	Count_LUDesc	Minimum_NRUNITS	Maximum_NRUNITS	Average_NRUNITS	Sum_NRUNITS
1	Commercial	5	0	6	1.2	6
2	Industrial	7	0	0	0	0
3	Mixed Commercial and Residential	2	2	3	2.5	5
4	Park	4	0	0	0	0
5	Public	4	0	6	2.5	10
6	Residential	103	1	6	1.9029	196
7	Vacant Land	4	0	0	0	0

The Attributes of Dist1_LU table summarizes the land use in District 1. It also contains the number of parcels and statistics about the number of housing units within each land-use category. For example, you can tell that within District 1 there are 103 residential parcels or that the total number of housing units in District 1 with a commercial land use is 5.

You will use this table to produce a land-use report for District 1, but before you do, you should generate the same type of table for District 2 and District 3.

63. Summarize the land use for parcels in District 2 using the same process you did for District 1. To do this, repeat steps 57 through 61, but replace the query you used in step 57 with a query that selects the parcels in District 2 (ParcelAll.District = 2 and ParcelAll.TKXY_TAXKE <> ' '), then run the same summary routine that you set up in step 60, but name the output Dist2_LU.

The Attributes of Dist2_LU should look like the following graphic.

Object ID*	LUDesc	Count_LUDesc	Minimum_NRUNITS	Maximum_NRUNITS	Average_NRUNITS	Sum_NRUNITS
1	Commercial	8	0	1	0.125	1
2	Industrial	8	0	0	0	0
3	Mixed Commercial and Residential	14	0	5	1.857143	26
4	Park	8	0	0	0	0
5	Public	2	0	0	0	0
6	Residential	161	0	6	1.944099	313
7	Vacant Land	15	0	0	0	0

You have one more summary table to go.

64. Summarize the parcels for District 3, using the same process as you did for Districts 1 and 2. Name the output Dist3_LU.

Object ID*	LUDesc	Count_LUDesc	Minimum_NRUNITS	Maximum_NRUNITS	Average_NRUNITS	Sum_NRUNITS
1	Commercial	6	0	8	4.166667	25
2	Industrial	6	0	0	0	0
3	Mixed Commercial and Residential	18	1	8	2.944444	53
4	Park	8	0	1	0.125	1
5	Public	5	0	180	59.8	299
6	Residential	247	0	81	4.453441	1100
7	Vacant Land	11	0	0	0	0

65. Close all of your open attribute tables and clear the current selection. If necessary, close the Select by Attributes dialog.

You now have the three summary tables required to produce the land-use report for each district.

Create district land-use reports

In this task, you will make reports from the summary tables created in the previous task. Again you will use ArcMap's built-in report generator to produce three separate reports. To save time, you will create simple reports from the Report Properties dialog to produce the numbers you need for the land-use reports.

The three district land-use tables you created are **Dist1_LU**, **Dist2_LU**, and **Dist3_LU**. From these tables you will create three new reports: **Dist1LUR.rdf**, **Dist2LUR.rdf**, and **Dist3LUR.rdf** (.rdf is the file extension for ArcMap's Report writer).

66. From the Tools menu, point to Reports and choose Create Report.

67. In the Report Properties dialog, click the Layer/Table drop-down arrow and choose the Dist1_LU table.

68. In the Available Fields list, double-click the LUDesc field to add it to the Report Fields list. Do the same for the Cnt_LUDesc and Sum_NRUNITS fields.

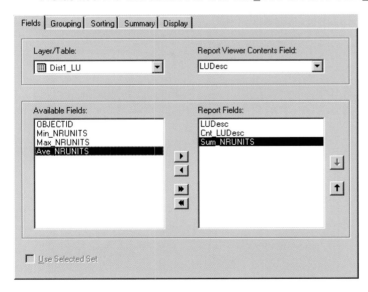

69. Click Show Settings to preview the layout of your report.

70. Click the Summary tab. Verify that the summary statistics will be placed at the end of the report, then check the Sum box for both fields.

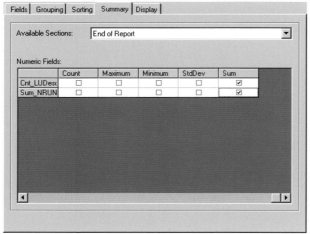

Next, you'll make formatting and heading changes.

71. Click the Display tab. Under the Elements category, check the Title option. On the right-hand side of the panel, click the Report Title value. In the pop-up box, type **District 1 Land Use,** then press the Tab key.

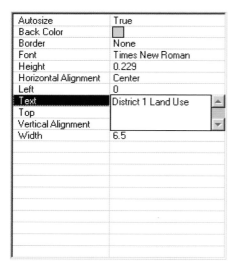

72. Update the settings in the Current Report Settings window.

73. In the Setting list, expand the Fields category. Within the Fields category, click the LUDesc field to display its properties. On the right-hand side of the dialog, click the text value and change the text to **Description**. Click the Width value and change the width to **3**. (This will make the column for this field wider.) Remember to press the Tab key after each text entry to make sure the change is entered.

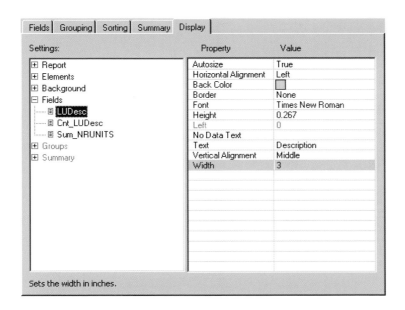

74. Update the Current Report Settings window.

Widening the LUDesc field has caused some alignment problems with the rows in the report. You will resolve this issue during the next few steps by making more changes to the field properties.

75. In the Fields category, click Cnt_LUDesc. Change the Text property to **Parcels** and its Width property to **.75**.

76. In the Fields category, click Sum_NRUNITS. Change the Text property to **Housing Units** and the width property to **1.5**. Click the Number Format property, then click the Ellipses button in the value column. In the Number Format dialog, change the number of decimal places to **0**, then click OK to close the Number Format dialog.

77. Update the Current Report Settings window.

The changes you made to the field properties put the report's rows back into alignment. You are now ready to generate the report.

78. Click Generate Report.

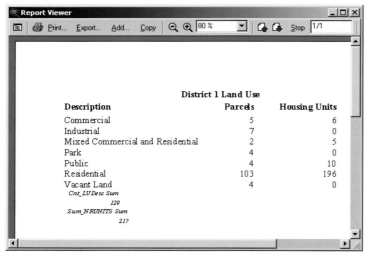

79. Close the Report Viewer window. In the Report Properties dialog, click Save. Save the report to your **C:\DigitialCity\MyArcCity** folder with the name **Dist1LUR.rdf**.

Before you print the report, you will create reports for the other two district summary tables.

80. In the Report Properties Dialog, click the Fields tab. From the Layer/Table drop-down list, click Dist2_LU.

81. Repeat the process you used in steps 68 through 78 to create a report for Districts 2. Name the District 2 land-use report **Dist2LUR.rdf** and save it in your **Arc City** folder.

82. Repeat the process again to create a land-use report for District 3. Name the report **Dist3LUR.rdf** and save it in your **Arc City** folder.

Print the reports

83. If the Report Properties dialog is closed, from the Tools menus, point to Reports, and choose Create Report.

84. In the Report Properties dialog, click the Load button. In the Load Report dialog, navigate to your **C:\DigitalCity\MyArcCity** folder and open the **Dist1LUR.rdf** report.

85. In the upper left corner of the Report Viewer, click Print. In the Print dialog, choose a printer that's available to you, then click Print.

86. Close the Report Viewer.

87. Print the District 2 and District 3 land-use reports. When finished, close the Report Properties dialog.

Create a land-use map to accompany the reports

The reports you created put the land-use figures into the hands of the city's personnel and elected officials. But the reports don't tell the complete story about land use in Arc City. In this task, you will map the land use so that, along with reading the land-use statistics, the decision makers can also visualize the distribution of land use in Arc City.

88. In the ArcMap table of contents, right-click ParcelAll and click Properties.

89. Click the Symbology tab. In the Show box, click Categories, then click Unique Values. Click the Value Field drop-down arrow and choose Ludesc.LUDesc. (It's at the bottom of the list.) Then click Add All Values. In the list of symbols, uncheck the symbol that represents all other values. (Since there are no features in this category, there is no reason to show this in the legend.) If you wish, you can choose a different Color Scheme.

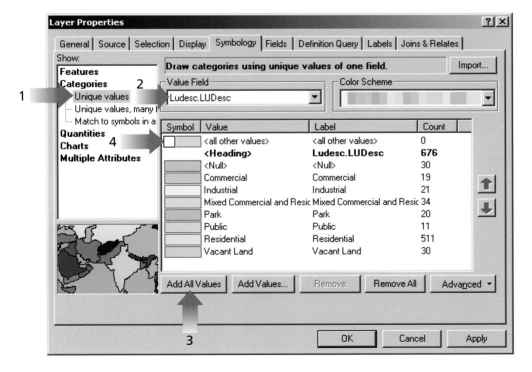

90. Click OK.

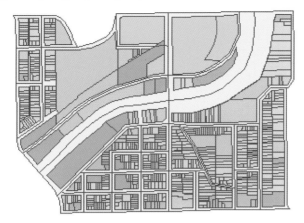

The parcels are now displayed according to their land use.

91. From the View menu, click Layout View.

Layout View is your design environment for creating maps. Unlike Data View, Layout View shows your map on a virtual page that reflects your current page settings (e.g., paper size and orientation). Within Layout View you can insert and arrange the position of map elements such as north arrows, legends, scale bars, and text.

92. From the Insert menu, click Title. In the text box that appears on the map layout, type **Arc City Land Use**. Press the Enter key and drag the title above the map body.

93. From the Insert menu, click Text. Type your name in the text box, and place it in the lower-right-hand corner of the layout.

94. From the Insert menu, click Legend.

The first panel of the Legend wizard prompts you to choose which layers you want to add to the legend. Since there is only one layer in your current map, that layer is your only choice.

95. In the first panel of the Legend wizard, change the Number of columns in your legend to **2,** then click Next. In the second panel of the Legend wizard, change the legend title to **Land Use Descriptions.** In the Title Justification box, click the option to center the title. (It's second from the left.) Click Next. Without making any changes, click Next on the remaining panels, then click Finish.

96. Once the legend is built and added to the layout, drag it below the map, and if necessary resize it so it fits on the layout page. (To resize the legend, select it with the Select Elements tool, then click and drag one of the four corner handles to expand or contract the legend's size.)

From this point you may want to add other map elements such as a north arrow, date, and scale bar. All of these can be added from the Insert menu. (To add the date, insert a text box and type the current date into it.)

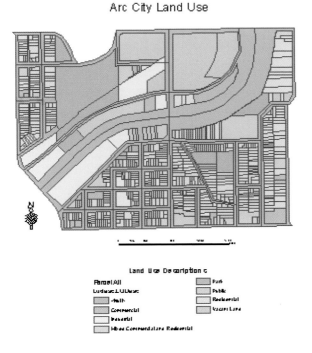

Arc City Land Use

The layout shown above is a simple example of how your layout could look. Every element on the layout has a host of properties controlling how it looks and where it's positioned on the layout. To access these properties, double-click any element on the layout using the Select Elements tool.

As an optional step, take a few minutes to open each element's Properties dialog and experiment with making changes to the properties.

97. When you're happy with the look of your layout, print the map. To print the map, click the File menu then click Print. (If you need to change the printer settings, click the Setup button in the Print dialog.) In the Print dialog, click OK.

Save your map and close ArcMap

98. From the File menu click Save As. Name your map **my_ex03a.mxd** and save it in your **C:\DigitalCity\MyArcCity** folder.

99. Close ArcMap.

Exercise 3b

Produce the Arc City residential density report

Normally you would be required to summarize the census data to get the population by
district. However, when you created the District layer, you also added the field for total
population. In this exercise, you will now use that field to calculate the residential population density. Also, when you created the housing unit reports, you created a summarized
table called DistrictCount that can be used to join to the District Table.

In this exercise you will perform the following tasks:
- Create a new field for residential density values.
- Join the district housing table to the attributes of Districts.
- Calculate the residential density values.
- Create the residential density report.

☐ Open ArcMap and add data

1. If necessary, start ArcMap with a new, empty map.

2. Click Add Data, navigate to your **C:\DigitalCity\MyArcCIty** folder, double-click
   the **ArcCity.mdb**, and add the Districts feature class from the **StreetBlock** feature
   data set.

☐ Create a new field for residential density values

3. Open the Attributes of Districts.

4. In the Attributes of Districts, click the
   Options button and choose Add Field.
   In the Add Field dialog, name the field
   Density and set its type as Double. Make
   sure your Add Field dialog matches the
   following graphic, then click OK.

5. Scroll across the Attributes of Districts to see the new field.

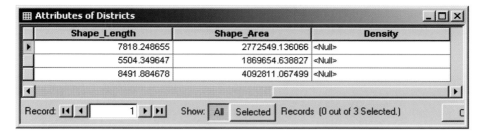

To determine the residential density, you must divide each district's total population by its total number of housing units. The Attributes of Districts contains the population in each district, but it does not contain the number of housing units. To bring the housing data into the table, you will join the DistrictCount table to the Attributes of Districts. Once the join is completed, you will be able to calculate the residential density values for the districts.

☐ Join the district housing table to the attributes of Districts

The DistrictCount layer contains the parcel and housing unit counts that you need to calculate the residential density values.

6. In the table of contents, right-click the Districts layer, point to Joins and Relates, and click Join. Make sure the drop-down list at the top of the Join Data dialog is set to Join attributes from a table. From drop-down list number 1, select Blocks_DistrictID. For drop-down list number 2, click the Browse button, navigate to your **Arc City** geodatabase and add the District-Count table. (This DistrictCount table was created in the last exercise. If you did not complete exercise 3a, you will need to do so before you can complete this exercise.) For drop-down list number 3, select DistrictID.

7. Click OK.

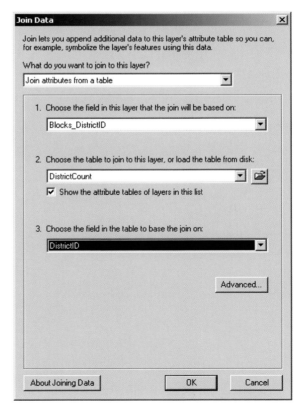

8. Scroll across the Attributes of Districts to verify that the join was successful.

Shape	Districts.Blocks_DistrictID	Districts.SUM_CensusData_TOTAL	Shape_Length
Polygon	1	599	7818.2486
Polygon	2	810	5504.3496
Polygon	3	1963	8491.8846

Record: 1 ▶ ▶| Show: All Selected Records (0 out of 3 Selected.) Options ▼

All of the data you need to calculate the residential density values are now in place within the Attributes of Districts.

Calculate the residential density values

9. Scroll across the table to find the new field. (Because the table is participating in a join, its name will appear as Districts.Density.) Right-click on the Districts.Density field name and choose Calculate Values. When prompted, click Yes to update values outside of an edit session.

To calculate density per district, you'll divide the total population in each district (the SUM_CensusData_TOTAL field in the Districts feature class) by the number of housing units in each district (the Sum_NRUNITS field in the DistrictCount table).

10. In the Field Calculator, construct the following expression:

[Districts.SUM_CensusData_TOTAL] / [DistrictCount.Sum_NRUNITS]

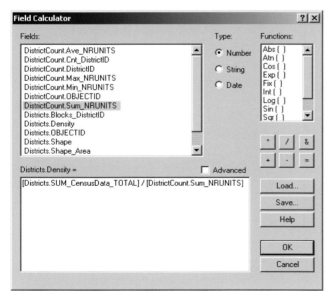

11. Click OK.

	Districts.Density
66	2.760369
27	2.382353
99	1.328146

Right now the Districts.Density field contains six decimal places. When you create the report, you will adjust its properties so that only one decimal place shows.

12. Close the Attributes of Districts.

Create the residential density report

With the data required now in the Attributes of Districts, you can begin to create the residential density report.

13. Open the Report Properties dialog. (From the Tools menu, point to Reports, then choose Create Report.)

In total, you will add five fields to the report. These five fields are listed in the table below.

Field name	Description
Districts.Blocks_DistrictID	District identifier
Districts.Sum_CensusData_TOTAL	District population
DistrictCount.Cnt_DistrictID	Count of parcels
DistrictCount.Sum_NRUNITS	Count of housing units
District.Density	Residential density values

14. On the Fields tab of the Report Properties dialog, add the following fields from the Available Fields list to the Report Fields list:

- Districts.Blocks_DistrictID
- DistrictCount.Cnt_DistrictID
- DistrictCount.Sum_NRUNITS
- Districts.Sum_CensusData_TOTAL
- Districts.Density

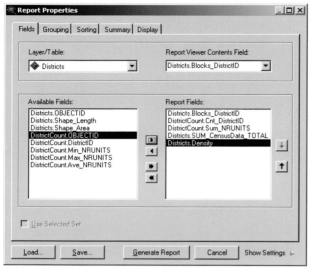

15. Click the Summary tab.

On the Summary tab, the Numeric Fields column is often too narrow to read the field name. To resolve this, you can increase the width of the column by clicking the right edge of the column's header and dragging it to a larger width.

16. Click the Sum option for the following fields:

- DistrictCount.Cnt_DistrictID
- DistrictCount.Sum_NRUNITS
- Districts.Sum_CensusData_TOTAL

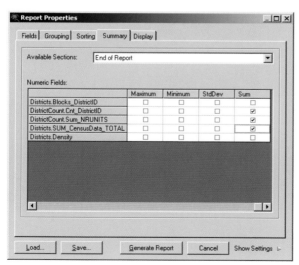

17. Click the Show Settings arrow to see how the current settings are affecting the report's layout.

The current layout looks sloppy. Over the next few steps you will improve the layout of the report.

18. Click the Display tab, then click the Report category. On the right-hand side of the dialog, click the Page Setup property, then click the Ellipses button in the Value column.

19. In the Orientation box of the Page Setup dialog, click Landscape.

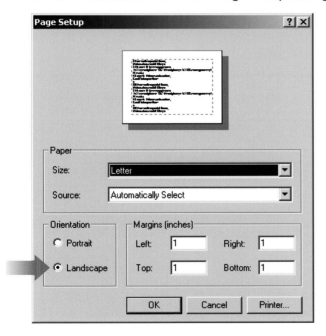

20. Click OK.

21. Update the Current Report Settings.

Changing the report's orientation to landscape created more space for the fields, but further formatting is still needed to make the report readable.

22. In the Settings list, click the Elements category and check the Title element. On the right-hand side of the dialog, enter **Residential Density** for the Text value.

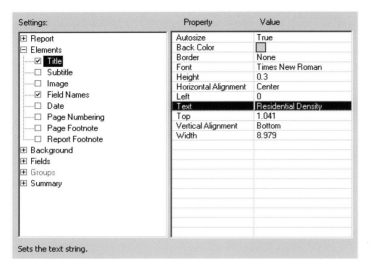

23. Update the Current Report Settings.

24. In the Settings list, click the Fields category. For each field listed below, set the Text and Width values as indicated in the following table:

Field	Text	Width
Districts.Blocks_DistrictID	District ID	1.1
DistrictCount.Cnt_DistrictID	Parcels	1.1
DistrictCount.Sum_NRUNITS	Housing Units	1.3
Districts.Sum_CensusData_TOTAL	Population	1.1
Districts.Density	Density	1.1

25. Update the Current Report Settings.

When you calculated the density values, several decimal places were generated, but in the report you only want to show one decimal place after the integer.

26. In the Fields list, click the Districts.Density field. On the right-hand side of the dialog, click the Number Format property, then click the Ellipses button that appears. In the Number Format dialog, change the Number of decimal places to **1**, then click OK.

27. Click Generate Report.

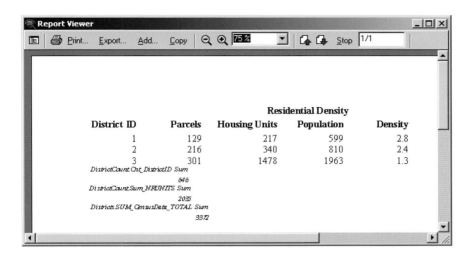

District ID	Parcels	Housing Units	Residential Density Population	Density
1	129	217	599	2.8
2	216	340	810	2.4
3	301	1478	1963	1.3

DistrictCount.Cnt_DistrictID Sum

646

DistrictCount.Sum_NRUNITS Sum

2035

Districts.SUM_CensusData_TOTAL Sum

3372

28. If you have a printer available, print the report, then close the Report Viewer.

29. On the Report Properties dialog, click Save. In the Save Report dialog, navigate to your **C:\DigitalCity\MyArcCity** folder, name the report **Residential_Density**, then click Save.

30. Close the Report Properties dialog.

☐ Save your map and close ArcMap

31. From the File menu click Save As. Name your map **my_ex03b.mxd** and save it in your **C:\DigitalCity\MyArcCity** folder.

32. Close ArcMap.

Exercise 3c

Produce the floodplain report and map

In this exercise you will generate a map and a report of the parcels and portions of parcels in Arc City within the floodplain of the river. The map and report will be used by various departments in Arc City to regulate, control, and restrict development in order to minimize negative environmental, social, and economic impacts resulting from poorly planned developments in these areas. The attribute data will be used to notify affected property owners of the availability of floodplain insurance and to place a replacement value on the improvements should a flood occur.

This exercise uses one of the more powerful capabilities of GIS software, the polygon overlay, which allows you to overlay the floodplain polygon onto the parcel polygons to create the desired map and attribute data.

In this exercise you will perform the following tasks:
- Import the floodplain feature class into the Arc City geodatabase.
- Add a field to store the original parcel area values.
- Overlay the parcels with the flood zone.
- Determine the percentage of each parcel in the floodplain.
- Add an address field.
- Produce the floodplain analysis report.
- Create the floodplain map.

Start ArcCatalog and import the floodplain feature class

The Federal Emergency Management Agency (FEMA) has published maps of floodplains on its Web site. The map for Arc City has been downloaded and stored in your SourceData folder as a shapefile named Floodzone.shp. You will now add the floodplain feature class to your geodatabase.

1. Start ArcCatalog.

2. In the Catalog Tree, navigate to your **C:\DigitalCity** folder and expand the **SourceData** folder.

3. In the **SourceData** folder, right-click **floodzone.shp**, point to Export, and click To Geodatabase (single).

4. For the Ouput Location, click the Browse button, navigate to your **C:\DigitalCity\ MyArcCity** folder and select the **ArcCity.mdb** and click Add. Name the output feature class FloodZone. You do not need to change any more settings for this conversion.

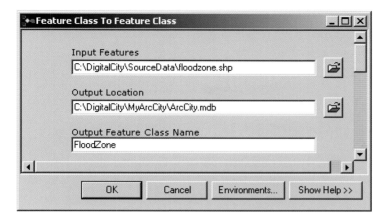

5.   Click OK, then click close when the operation completes.

6.   In the Catalog Tree, navigate to your **C:\DigitalCity\MyArcCity** folder, expand the **Arc City** geodatabase, then preview the FloodZone feature class.

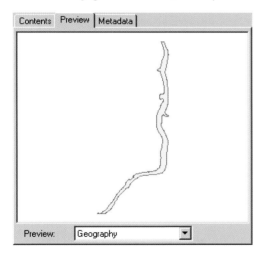

In upcoming steps you will overlay this feature class with the parcels in Arc City so you can determine which portions of the parcels lie within the flood zone.

7.   Close ArcCatalog.

Start ArcMap and add data

8.   Start ArcMap with a new, empty map.

9.   Add the following features classes from the **Arc City** geodatabase to your map:

- FloodZone
- ParcelAll (contained in the **ParcelBldg** feature data set)
- Districts (contained in the **StreetBlock** feature data set)

10. In the ArcMap table of contents, place the layers in the following order from top to bottom: FloodZone, ParcelAll, Districts.

11. Right-click the ParcelAll layer and choose Zoom To Layer.

(Your colors will probably differ from the graphic.)

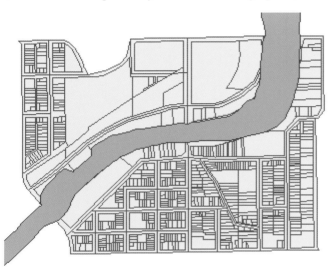

Looking at the map, you can get a rough idea of how a flood might impact Arc City. In the upcoming steps, you will get a better idea by generating the actual percentages of land area affected by the flood zone.

Add a field to store the original parcel area values

The floodplain report will show the total area of each parcel that is overlapped by the floodplain. The total area of each parcel is currently contained in the Shape_Area field of the ParcelAll feature class. However, when you overlay the parcels with the flood zone, the current values in the original Shape_Area field will be lost when the software recalculates the new area values. To preserve the original area values, you will create a new field and copy them into it.

12. In the table of contents, right-click the ParcelAll layer and click Open Attribute Table.

13. In the Attributes of ParcelAll, click Options and choose Add Field.

14. In the Add Field dialog, name the new field **ParcelArea** and set its Type as Double.

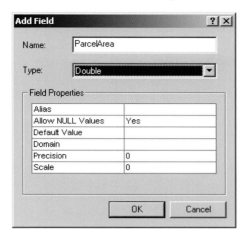

You defined the ParcelArea field type as Double because the values you are going to copy into it from the Shape_Area field are also stored as Double. ("Double" stands for double-precision floating point numbers.) To determine the field types in an existing feature class, open the feature class's properties in ArcCatalog and click the Fields tab. There you will find a complete list of all the fields in the feature class along with their types.

15. Click OK.

16. In the Attributes of ParcelAll, scroll horizontally to the end of the table, right-click the ParcelArea field name, and choose Calculate Values. Click Yes on the warning message when it appears.

17. In the Field Calculator, scroll through the Fields list, locate, then double-click the Shape_Area field to add it to the Expression box.

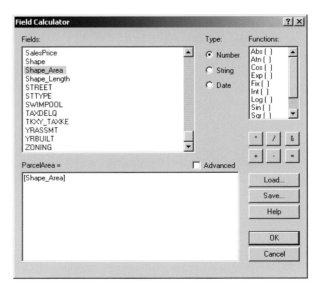

This expression will populate the ParcelArea field with the same values stored in the Shape_Area field.

18. Click OK.

Shape_Length	Shape_Area	ParcelArea
2253.060926	37838.726805	37838.726805
2250.896141	37423.072138	37423.072138
2039.593000	36028.050144	36028.050144
2253.480504	37636.911201	37636.911201
1615.387804	27366.649127	27366.649127
2253.503146	37866.651344	37866.651344
2249.995473	37523.131621	37523.131621
2249.351772	37711.631788	37711.631788
3243.652569	53954.730256	53954.730256

The Shape_Area field that you just made a copy of is created and populated by the software. When you create a polygon feature class, ArcCatalog automatically adds the Shape_Area field to it. When you edit a polygon feature class, ArcMap automatically calculates or recalculates the area values stored in the Shape_Area field. (The same relationship holds true for the Shape_Length field, which stores the perimeter of each polygon, and the lengths of line features.)

By creating the ParcelArea field and populating it with the values stored in the Shape_Area field, you have made a backup of each parcel's computer-generated area value. Because these values are now stored in a user-defined field, they will be preserved in the output from the overlay of the parcels and the flood zone.

19. Close the Attributes of ParcelAll.

Your next task is to overlay the parcels with the flood zone using the Intersect function.

Overlay the parcels with the flood zone

To find which parcels and how much of those parcels lie within the flood zone, you will use the Intersect command to overlay the parcels with the flood zone.

The Intersect overlay looks for overlapping areas in the input feature classes and places these overlapping areas in a new output feature class. While doing this, it splits each polygon boundary where it intersects the polygon boundary in the other feature class, thereby creating new features that contain the attributes from both input feature classes. This process works the same way as the Union overlay that you used in chapter 2, exercise 2f, except that only the areas of overlap are saved in the output.

The following graphic shows two overlapping feature classes on the left side of the arrow and the results of their Intersect on the right. One feature class consists of a circular area divided into two polygons, the other consists of a rectangular region broken into three separate features. After overlaying these two feature classes with Intersect, only the area of overlap was preserved and new features were formed based on where polygon boundaries overlapped. Although not shown here, the attributes of both input feature classes are appended to the output's attribute table.

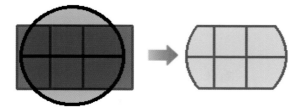

20. On the Standard toolbar, click the Show/Hide ArcToolbox button to show ArcToolbox. If necessary, click the Favorites tab at the bottom of ArcToolbox.

21. In the Toolbox window, expand the Analysis Tools toolbox, then expand the Overlay toolset and double-click the Intersect tool.

22. In the Intersect dialog, click the Input Features drop-down arrow and choose the ParcelAll layer to add it to the Features list. Repeat this process to add the FloodZone layer to the Features list. For the Output Feature Class, click the Browse button. In the Output Feature Class dialog, navigate to the **Arc City** geodatabase, name the output feature class **ParcelFlood,** and click Save. (Do not change any of the optional settings.)

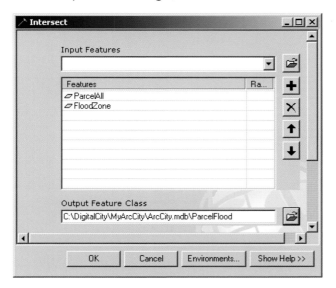

23. Click OK. When the Intersect process is finished, click Close.

24. On the Standard toolbar, click the Show/Hide ArcToolbox button to hide ArcToolbox.

25. In the table of contents, turn off the Flood Zone layer and, if necessary, change the color of the ParcelFlood layer so that it contrasts with the color of the parcels. (You

can quickly do this by right-clicking the color chip below the layer name in the table of contents and choosing another color from the palette.)

The output of the intersect process only contains features where the ParcelAll feature class and the FloodZone feature class overlapped.

26. **Open the Attributes of ParcelFlood and scroll across the table to see what fields it contains.**

The attribute table contains the original fields from both input layers and a couple of new fields (Shape_Area, and Shape_Length) that store the area and perimeter values of the new polygons.

Your next task is to determine what percentage of the parcels lie within the flood zone.

Determine the percentage of each parcel in the floodplain

Your first step in this task is to add a field to contain the percentage values.

27. **In the Attributes of ParcelFlood, click the Options button and choose Add Field.**

28. **In the Add Field dialog, name the field PctFlood and set its type as Double.**

29. **Click OK.**

To calculate the percentage values for the parcels, you'll divide the flood area (the Shape_Area field) by the total area (the ParcelArea field) and multiply the results by 100.

30. **Scroll horizontally to the end of the Attributes of ParcelFlood, right-click the PctFlood field name, and click Calculate Values. Click Yes on the warning message.**

31. In the Field Calculator, create the following expression to calculate the percentage of each parcel in the floodplain: **([Shape_Area] / [ParcelArea]) * 100.** (Use your keyboard to add the parenthesis.)

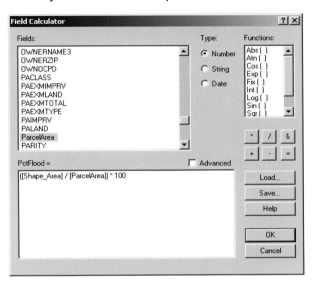

32. Click OK.

	PctFlood
32	67.958909
58	73.914011
47	6.729674
32	83.664907
52	72.683887
53	8.388813
54	3.167420
75	68.013885
32	11.383517

You are almost ready to create the report, but first you will reformat the address attributes so the complete address for each parcel exists within a single field. Right now the address attributes for each parcel are contained in four separate fields. Placing the full address in one field will save you time when you create your report because, instead of adding and formatting four fields, you only have to add and format one.

Add an address field

33. Open the Add Field dialog for the Attributes of ParcelFlood. (In the Attributes of ParcelFlood, click the Options button and choose Add Field.)

34. In the Add Field Dialog, name the new field **Address,** set its type as Text, and, in the lower portion of the dialog, change its Length property to **20.** Verify your settings with the following graphic, then click OK.

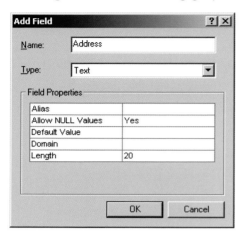

The address values for each parcel are contained within the DIR, HOUSENRLO, STREET, and STTYPE fields. DIR stands for direction and contains the street prefixes of N, S, E, or W. HOUSENRLO is the house number. STREET is the street name. And STTYPE is the street type, such as avenue or boulevard. Taken together these fields represent the full address for each parcel. In the next step, you will concatenate these into one address value.

To concatenate text values with the field calculator, you use the ampersand (&) operator. For example, the following expression "Louis" & "Graves" would produce the value LouisGraves. If you wanted to put a space between the two values you would do so by using quotation marks to delineate the spaces you want to add. For example, the expression "Louis" & " " & "Graves" would produce the value Louis Graves. Notice the one space between the two quotation marks. The field calculator treats whatever you place between the quotation marks as a string value, whether it's a space or a character value.

35. Open the Field Calculator for the Address field. (Right-click on the Address field name and choose Calculate Values). Click Yes on the warning message. In the Field Calculator, type the following expression (be sure to place a space between each pair of quotes):

[DIR] &" " & [HOUSENRLO] &" " & [STREET] &" " & [STTYPE]

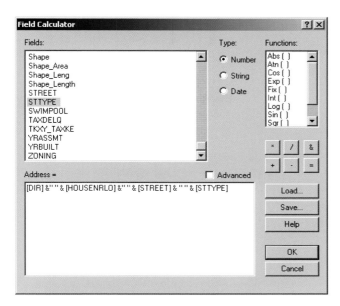

36. Click OK.

	Address
01	N 1890 COMMERCE ST
99	N 2070 COMMERCE ST
92	E 1354 BOYLSTON ST
39	N 1781 WATER ST
38	N 1942 COMMERCE ST
46	N 1887 WATER ST
68	E 926 KANE PL

Now that the full address for each parcel is contained in a single field, you can begin to create the floodplain analysis report. (Some of the records do not contain address values, which is okay because they are not parcels but street rights-of-way.)

37. Close the Attributes of ParcelFlood.

Produce the floodplain analysis report

38. Open the Report Properties dialog.

39. On the Fields tab, click the Layer/Table drop-down arrow and choose ParcelFlood, then add the fields listed in the table below to the report.

Field name	Field description
DistrictID	District number
TKXY_TAXKE	Tax key number
Address	Parcel address
NRUNITS	Number of units on property
ParcelArea	Area of parcel
Shape_Area	Area parcel within the flood zone
PctFlood	Percentage of parcel within the flood zone

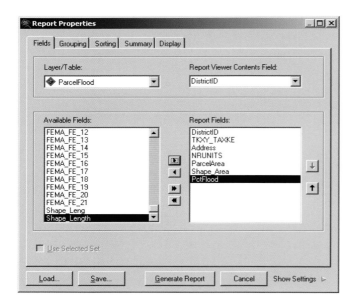

40. In the Report Properties dialog, click the Sorting Tab. In the Sort column, click the value associated with the DistrictID field, then choose Ascending.

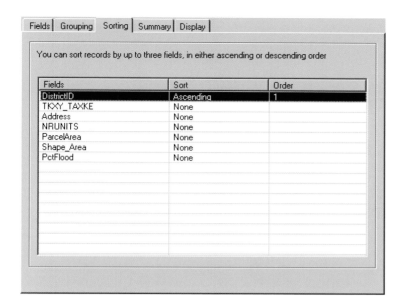

Based on this setting, the records shown in the report will be listed in ascending order by District. For example, all of the parcels in District 1 will be listed first, then all of the parcels in District 2, and finally all of the parcels in District 3.

41. **Click Show Settings.**

Right now, the report page is overcrowded and the formatting is sloppy. Over the next several steps, you will change the report's settings to improve its appearance. The settings you will make have been predetermined for you. Determining which report setting to make is a process of trial and error. One of the best ways to do this is to show and frequently update your report settings as you experiment with different settings.

Because you have already made several reports in this chapter, the amount of instruction in the following steps has been reduced based on the assumption that you already know from experience how to make many of the report settings.

42. **In the Report Properties dialog, click the Display tab.**

43. **In the Settings list, click Report. On the right-hand side of the dialog, use the Page Setup property to set the report's orientation to landscape, then change the Width property value to 6.6.**

44. **In the Settings list, expand the Elements category. Check the Title element. On the right-hand side of the dialog, change the Horizontal Alignment property to Left, the Left Property to 2, and the Text property to Arc City Flood Plain Report.**

These settings will add a title that is offset two inches from the left margin.

45. Under the Elements category, click Field Names. Change the font size to **10** (this is done by clicking the Font property, then clicking the Ellipses button to access the Font dialog), the Spacing property to **0,** and the Vertical Spacing property to **0.2**.

46. In the Elements category, check Page Numbering then check Page Footnote. You do not need to set any properties for the Page Numbering, but for Page Footnote, change its Text property value to **Arc City Flood Plain Report**.

Since the report will end up being more than a page long, it's a good idea to add page numbers and the title as a footnote to the report.

47. In the Settings list, expand the Fields category. For each field, define the Text and Width properties as indicated in the table.

Field	Text	Width
DistrictID	District	0.5
TKXY_TAXKE	Tax Key	0.75
Address	Address	1.5
NRUNITS	# Units	0.5
ParcelArea	Parcel Area	1
Shape_Area	Flood Area	1
PctFlood	% Flood	0.75

48. For the ParcelArea, Shape_Area, and PctFlood fields, use the Number Format property to set the number of decimal places to 2.

49. Update the Current Report Settings.

In the report settings, you can see that there are some formatting issues to fix. For example, the text in some of the fields is wrapping within the columns.

In the next step, you will improve the formatting of the report by standardizing the field properties.

50. For every field listed in the Fields category, set the Autosize property to False, Horizontal Alignment to Center, Back Color to Gray 10% (the color chip in the left-most column, second from the top), and the Font Size to **10**.

51. Update the Current Report Settings.

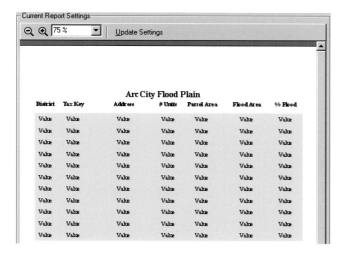

52. Click Generate Report. Then from the Report Viewer, print the report.

53. Close the Report Viewer. In the Report Properties dialog, click Save. Save the report in your **C:\DigitalCity\MyArcCity** folder and name it **FloodPlainReport**.

54. Close the Report Properties dialog.

☐ Create the floodplain analysis map

As a companion to the floodplain analysis report, you're going to create a map that shows which parcels are affected by the flood zone. The map will show all of Arc City, but must focus on the portions of the parcels that fall within the flood zone and their tax key numbers.

The following steps will guide you through the process of creating this map, but along the way feel free to choose your own styles and colors.

55. In the table of contents, re-order the layers from top to bottom in the following order: Districts, ParcelFlood, FloodZone, ParcelAll.

56. In the table of contents, click the color chip associated with the Districts layer to open the Symbol Selector. In the Options box on the right-hand side of the dialog, click the Fill Color drop-down arrow and choose No Color. Change the Outline Width to **2**. Click the Outline Color drop-down arrow and choose the black color chip located in the lower-left corner of the color palette.

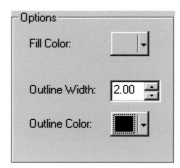

57. Click OK to close the Symbol Selector.

58. Right-click the color chip for the ParcelFlood Layer and choose Dark Umber from the color palette.

59. In the table of contents, click the FloodZone color chip to open the Symbol Selector. In the list of fill symbols on the left side of the dialog, click the Lake symbol, then click OK.

60. Open the Symbol Selector for the ParcelAll layer. In the list of fill symbols, choose the Yellow symbol.

61. Turn on all the layers in the table of contents if necessary.

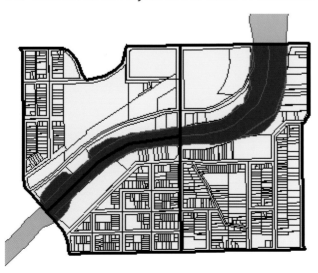

The objective of this map is to show which portions of the parcels fall within the flood zone. These features exist within the ParcelFlood layer, but right now the layer is showing both the parcel features and the flood zone features that exist in the right-of-way. Because you want the map to focus on the parcels in the flood zone, you will create a definition query for the ParcelFlood layer so that only the features with a tax key number are drawn in the map display.

62. Right-click the ParcelFlood layer and choose Properties. In the Layer Properties dialog, click the Definition Query tab.

63. On the Definition Query tab, click the Query Builder button. In the Query Builder, double-click the [TKXY_TAXKE] field in the fields list, click the Not Equal to (<>) operator, then use your keyboard to add two single quotes with no spaces between them.

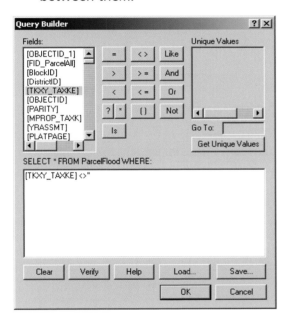

Translated, this query says, "Find all the parcels in the ParcelFlood layer that do not have an empty tax key value." The result of the query is that only features in the ParcelFlood layer with a tax key value are drawn in the map.

64. Click OK. Then click OK in the Layer Properties dialog.

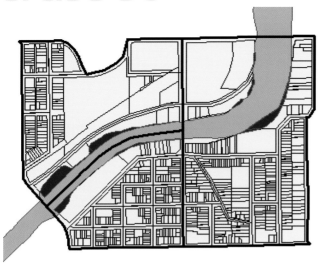

Because the map is intended to serve as a companion to the floodplain report, the reader must be able to cross-reference the parcels listed in the report with the parcels shown on the map. To make this possible, you will label the portions of the parcels that exist within the flood zone with their tax key values.

65. Open the Layer Properties dialog for the ParcelFlood layer and click the Labels tab. In the TextString box, click the Label Field drop-down arrow and choose Tax Key.

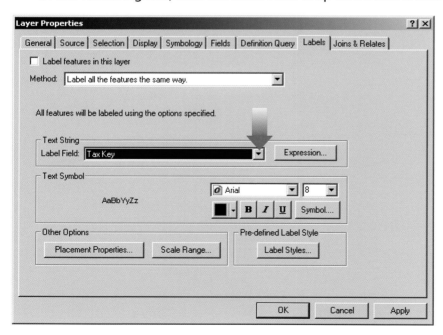

Based on this setting, ArcMap will label the features in the ParcelFlood layer with their tax key value.

To make the labels stand out in the map, you will add a halo around the label text.

66. On the Labels tab, click the Symbol button. In the Symbols Selector, click the Properties button. In the Editor dialog, click the Mask tab and in the Style box click the Halo option, then change the Size value to **1**.

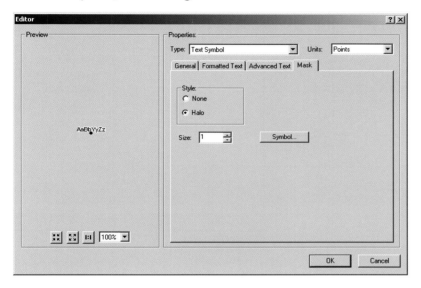

67. Click OK in the Editor dialog, the Symbol Selector, and the Layer Properties dialog.

68. In the ArcMap table of contents, right-click the ParcelFlood layer and choose Label Features.

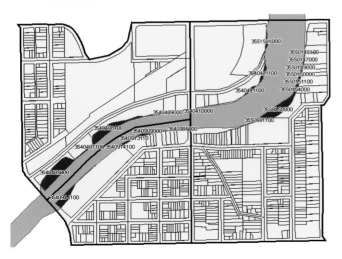

Next you will manually label the three districts.

69. On the Draw toolbar, click the New Text tool. (If the Draw toolbar is not visible, you will need to load it. To load the Draw toolbar, click the View menu, point to Toolbars, and click Draw.)

70. Click near the center of District 1 and type **District 1** in the text box, then press Enter on your keyboard. Repeat this process to add district labels for Districts 2 and 3.

The District labels that you just added are too small to see clearly on the map. To make them stand out better, you will change their style properties.

71. On the Drawing toolbar, click the Select Elements tool.

72. In the Map display, double-click the District 1 label. In the Properties dialog, click the Change Symbol button. In the Symbol Selector, select the Country 2 font style from the list of styles on the left-hand side of the dialog. On the right side of the dialog in the Options box, click the Bold button.

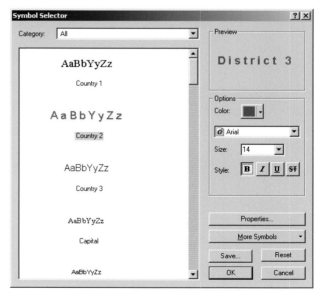

73. Click OK in the Symbol Selector, then click OK in the Properties dialog. Repeat the process you used in the previous step to define the same style for the District 2 and the District 3 labels.

Changing the style properties of the district labels may cause them to move a bit.

74. If necessary, use the Select Elements tool to reposition the district labels near the center of their respective districts.

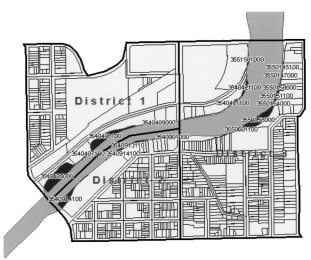

75. From the View menu, click Layout View.

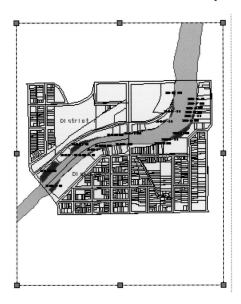

The extent of the Flood Zone layer is much larger than the extent of Arc City. To remove this excess, you will use a technique to clip the visible extent of the data frame to the extent of the Districts feature class.

76. In the table of contents, right-click the Data Frame title (Layers) and choose Properties. In the Data Frame Properties, click the Data Frame tab. In the Clip to Shape box, click Enable, then click Specify Shape. In the Data Frame Clipping dialog, select the Outline of Features option, then select Districts from the Layer drop-down list and All from the Features drop-down, list.

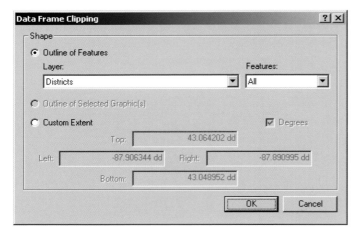

77. Click OK in the Data Frame Clipping dialog, then click OK in the Data Frame Properties dialog.

The body of the map is in place; now you can add the elements to the map, such as a title, legend, north arrow, and scale.

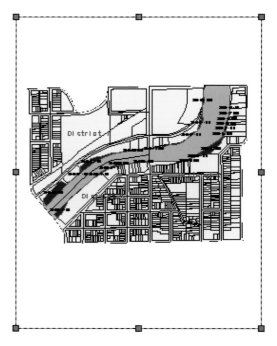

78. From the Insert Menu, click Legend. In the first panel, set the number of columns in your legend to 8.

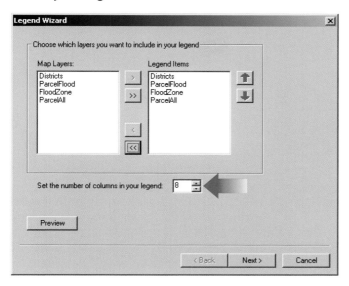

Changing the number of columns to 8 will spread your legend out horizontally because the symbol and text for each legend item will be placed in its own column.

79. Click Next. In the second panel, remove the text from the Legend Title box. (This legend will not have a title.) Click Next on the remaining panels and click Finish on the final panel.

It may take a few moments before the map legend is built and added to the map. Once it is added to the map, it will appear near the center of the data frame.

80. Drag the legend to a position just below the map.

81. From the Insert menu, click Title. In the text box that appears on the map type, **Arc City Flood Plain Map**, then center the title above the map.

82. From the Insert menu, choose Scale Bar. From the Scale Bar Selector, select Scale Line 1 from the list of available scale bar styles, then click OK. After the scale bar is placed on the map, drag it to a position that you like.

83. From the Insert menu, choose North Arrow. From the North Arrow Selector, select a north arrow of your choice then click OK. Drag the arrow to a position that suits your preference.

The look of your map may differ from the one on the following page.

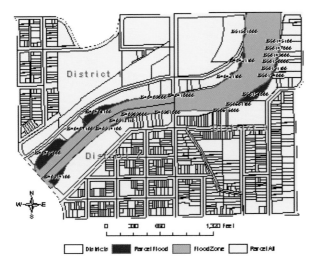

ArcCity Flood Plain Map

At this point, what you do with the map is up to you. You can use the Insert menu to add more text to the map such as your name and the date. You can also change the properties of any element on the map by double-clicking it with the Select Element tool. (You can also access the properties of an element by right-clicking the element with the Select Elements tool.) For example, if you wanted to give the legend a title or change the look of the scale bar, you could open their respective properties dialogs and make the necessary changes.

Print map and close ArcMap

84. If you have a printer available, from the File menu, choose Print.

85. From the file menu, click Save As. Save the map as **my_ex03c.mxd** in your **C:\Digital CIty\MyArcCity** folder. Close ArcMap.

Exercise 3d

Produce the mosquito analysis and report

A chemical pesticide will be administered on the river that runs through Arc City in order to control the mosquito population. Since an Arc City ordinance requires warning signs to be posted before pesticides are applied, the city must notify all property owners near the river before the chemical is applied.

This exercise involves using the Arc City GIS to produce a map of the properties affected and a list of their addresses so that the public works department knows how many signs to make, where they should be posted, and where to mail notifications so that property owners within 700 feet of the affected area can be informed of the pesticide application. Furthermore, those parcels within 350 feet of the river will be required to close their windows and bring all pets inside.

In this exercise you will perform the following tasks:
- Buffer the river centerline.
- Overlay the parcels and buffers.
- Symbolize ParcelBuffer by buffer zone.
- Create the mosquito abatement parcel notification map.
- Create the mosquito abatement parcel notification report.

Start ArcMap and add data

1. Start ArcMap with a new, empty map.

2. Click the Add Data button, navigate to your **Arc City** geodatabase and add the Streets feature class from **StreetBlock** feature data set. Click the Add Data button again and add the ParcelData feature class from the **ParcelBldg** feature data set.

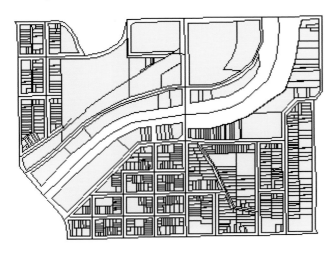

⌐ **Select the river centerline**

3. On the Tools toolbar, click the Select Features tool.

4. Hold down the Shift key and click each of the three line features that make up the centerline of the river in Arc City.

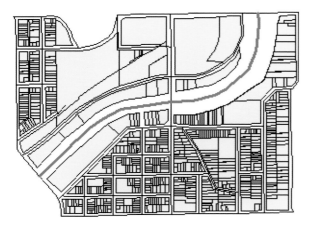

The centerline was drawn for the river and placed within the streets layer because barge traffic occurs on the river and city personnel consider the river part of the city's transportation network.

You will use the river centerline to create the buffers.

⌐ **Buffer the river centerline**

5. Open ArcToolbox.

6. In ArcToolbox, expand the Analysis Tools toolbox, then expand the Proximity toolset. Inside the Proximity toolset, double-click the Multiple Ring Buffer tool.

7. In the Multiple Ring Buffer dialog, choose streets from the Input Features drop-down list. Save the Output Feature class in your Arc City geodatabase and name it **RiverBuffer**. In the Distances text box, type **350** and click the plus sign to add it to the list of distances. Type **700** in the Distances text box and click the plus sign again.

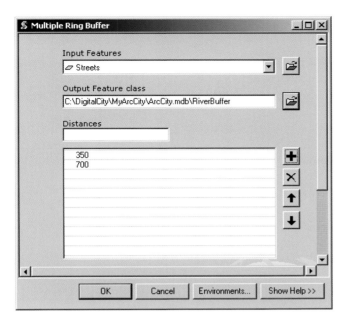

8. Click OK, then click Close when the process completes.

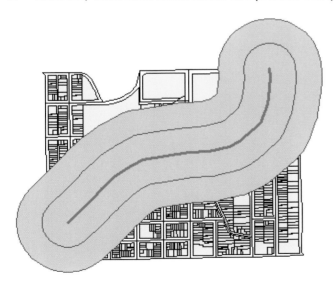

9. Open the Attributes of RiverBuffer.

OBJECTID*	Shape*	distance	Shape_Length	Shape_Area
1	Polygon	350	9951.225805	3099039.549797
2	Polygon	700	22094.097955	3865732.992466

Two records exist in this table, one for each buffer feature, and each record contains the distance value that was used to generate its associated feature. In an upcoming task, you will use the distance values to symbolize the parcels by the buffer zone in which they exist.

10. Close the Attributes of RiverBuffer.

Overlay the parcels and buffers

To determine which parcels exist within which buffer zone, you will overlay the ParcelData feature class with the RiverBuffer feature class using the Intersect function. The resultant feature class can then be used to map the notification extents and to generate a report that lists the owner names and addresses of the affected parcels.

11. In ArcToolbox, expand the Analysis toolbox (if necessary), then expand the Overlay toolset, and double-click the Intersect tool.

12. In the Intersect dialog, click the Input Features drop-down arrow and select the ParcelData layer. Repeat this process to add the RiverBuffer layer to the features list. Name the output feature class ParcelBuffer and save it within the **Arc City** geodatabase.

Do not change any of the optional settings.

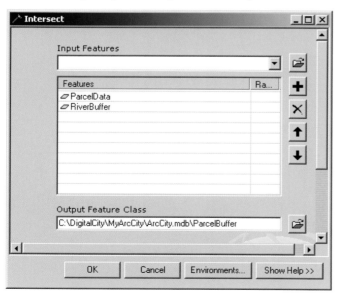

13. Click OK, then click Close when the process completes.

14. Turn off all of the layers except for ParcelBuffer. Close ArcToolbox.

The parcels in the ParcelBuffer feature class match the extent of the buffers they were intersected with. Although it's difficult to see in the current map display, two feature categories exist in this layer: those defined by the 350-foot buffer and those defined by the 700-foot buffer.

15. Open the Attributes of ParcelBuffer and scroll to the right end of the table.

ATUS	SalesPrice	FID_RiverBuffer	distance	Shape_Length	Shape_Area
	62000	2	700	317.353025	5977.413511
	140000	2	700	344.143339	7461.857270
	12500	2	700	146.749990	1206.226167
	0	2	700	477.714620	7253.866553
	75000	2	700	491.778405	7208.426005

The attributes of ParcelBuffer contain all of the fields from the ParcelData feature class and the distance field from the RiverBuffer feature class. You will use the distance field in the next task to symbolize ParcelBuffer, which will allow you to see which parcels fall within which buffer zone.

16. Close the Attributes of ParcelBuffer.

Symbolize ParcelBuffer by buffer zone

17. Open the properties of the ParcelBuffer layer and click the symbology tab. In the Show box, click Categories. Click the Value Field drop-down arrow and choose the

distance field. (It's near the end of the list.) Click Add All Values. In the Symbol column, uncheck the <all other values> symbol. In the Label column, click distance. When the cursor appears, delete the text in this field. (This will remove the distance label from the layer in the table of contents.)

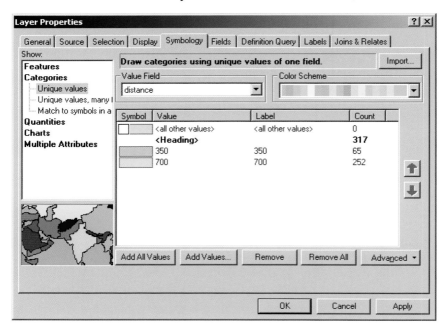

18. Click OK.

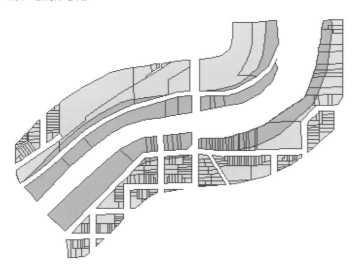

By symbolizing the ParcelBuffer layer based on the distance field, you can see which parcels are within which buffer zone. Notice that some parcels exist within both zones.

⌐ Create the mosquito abatement parcel notification map

Now that the analysis is complete, you can map the results and share this information with the public works department. The purpose of this map is to show which parcels are affected by the spraying and which notification zone the parcels fall within. The following steps guide you through the mapmaking process. Feel free to add your own style and effects to the map, yet just make sure the map meets its objective.

From here out, the amount of instruction given for creating maps and reports is minimal. If you have trouble completing a step, refer to earlier exercise tasks to review the method in question.

19. Open the properties of the ParcelBuffer layer. Click the Labels tab. Click the Label Field drop-down arrow and choose TKXY_TAXKE field from the list. In the Text Symbol frame, click in the Font Size text box and change the font size to **4**. Leave the Layer Properties dialog open.

20. Create text halos with a size of 1 around the labels in the ParcelBuffer layer, then close the Layer Properties dialog.

21. Turn on the labels for the ParcelBuffer layer.

22. Switch to Layout view.

23. Insert a legend.

24. Insert a north arrow.

25. Insert a scale bar.

26. Add a title to your map that reflects the theme of the map (e.g., **Mosquito Abatement Parcel Notification Map**).

27. Add any other elements to the map that you feel are necessary such as the date, your name, etc.

When completed, your map may look like the map on the following page.

Mosquito Abatement
Parcel Notification Map

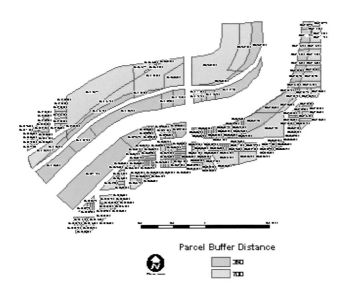

Parcel Buffer Distance

350

700

28. When you are finished with your map, print it.

The map shows all the parcels in the buffer zones with each parcel labeled with its tax key. Because of the map's scale and the size of the labels, for many parcels, it will be difficult for the reader to determine which label goes with which parcel. One way to get around this is to show the parcels by district, which allows you to show the map at a larger scale. This, in turn, creates more room for the labels.

The following graphic shows a notification map created for District 1.

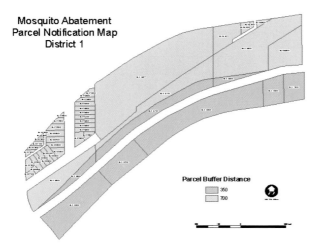

Mosquito Abatement
Parcel Notification Map
District 1

Parcel Buffer Distance

350

700

To create this map, a layer definition query was used in conjunction with the Clip to Shape option in the Data Frame Properties. First, the Districts layer was added to the map, then a definition query was applied to the Districts layer so that only District 1 feature would be drawn in it. Then the data frame properties dialog was used to clip the data frame to the extent of the visible features in the districts layer.

Create a mosquito abatement parcel notification report

Your final task is to create a report that lists all the parcels affected by the pesticide spraying. Like your previous task, this one has less instruction and relies on your past work.

Before you create the report, you will concatenate the address fields to create a single field containing the full address of each parcel. Once this field is created, you can add it to the report.

29. Add a text field to the Attributes of ParcelBuffer. Name the field **FullAddress** and set its length to **25**.

Shape_Length	Shape_Area	FullAddress
477.712530	7255.638934	<Null>
491.778445	7208.428590	<Null>
301.019518	5075.034848	<Null>
249.066785	2495.114845	<Null>

Record: 1   Show: All Selected   Records (0 out of 317 Selected.)

30. Populate the FullAddress field with the complete addresses by using the Field Calculator to concatenate the DIR, HOUSENRLO, STREET, and STTYPE fields. (The expression to use is **[DIR] &" " & [HOUSENRLO] &" " & [STREET] &" " & [STTYPE]**). When finished, close the Attributes of ParcelBuffer.

31. Create a new report based on the ParcelBuffer layer. Add the TKXY_TAXKE, OWNERNAME1, FullAddress, and distance field to the report.

32. Title the report **Mosquito Abatement: Parcel Notification Report**.

33. Set the Text property value of the TKXY_TAXKE field as **Tax Key,** the OWNER-NAME1 field as **Owner,** the Full Address field as **Address,** and the distance field as **Distance.**

34. Sort the records in the report in ascending order by the Distance field. As for the rest of the formatting, it's up to you to experiment with the report settings to get the look you're after. Once you have things the way you want them, generate the final report.

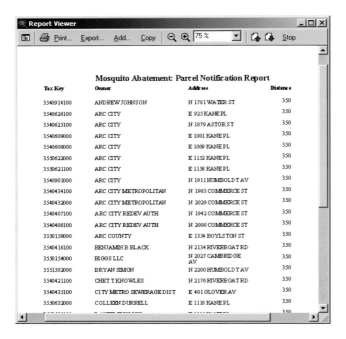

Mosquito Abatement: Parcel Notification Report

Tax Key	Owner	Address	Distance
3540914100	ANDREW JOHNSON	N 1781 WATER ST	350
3540626100	ARC CITY	E 925 KANE PL	350
3540625100	ARC CITY	N 1879 ASTOR ST	350
3540609000	ARC CITY	E 1001 KANE PL	350
3540608000	ARC CITY	E 1009 KANE PL	350
3550622000	ARC CITY	E 1152 KANE PL	350
3550621100	ARC CITY	E 1158 KANE PL	350
3540901000	ARC CITY	N 1911 HUMBOLDT AV	350
3540434100	ARC CITY METROPOLITAN	N 1983 COMMERCE ST	350
3540432000	ARC CITY METROPOLITAN	N 2029 COMMERCE ST	350
3540407100	ARC CITY REDEV AUTH	N 1942 COMMERCE ST	350
3540408100	ARC CITY REDEV AUTH	N 2000 COMMERCE ST	350
3550158000	ARC COUNTY	E 1354 BOYLSTON ST	350
3540416100	BENJAMIN B BLACK	N 2134 RIVERBOAT RD	350
3550154000	BIGGS LLC	N 2027 CAMBRIDGE AV	350
3551502000	BRYAN SIMON	N 2200 HUMBOLDT AV	350
3540421100	CHET T KNOWLES	N 2176 RIVERBOAT RD	350
3540435100	CITY METRO SEWERAGE DIST	E 401 GLOVER AV	350
3550632000	COLLEEN DURRELL	E 1118 KANE PL	350

(This report is just an example of how your report may look since the formatting you choose may be different.)

35. Save your report in your **C:\DigitalCity\MyArcCity** folder and name it **Mosquito Abatement.**

36. If they are still open, close the Report Properties dialog and the Attributes of ParcelBuffer.

☐ **Save your map and close ArcMap.**

37. From the File menu choose Save As. Name the map **my_ex03d.mxd** and save it in your **C:\DigitalCity\MyArcCity** folder, then close ArcMap.

Exercise 3e

Find possible drug houses near playgrounds

The Arc City police department has determined that the following property characteristics may be cause for concern and could indicate possible drug houses:
- They most likely are single- and two-family homes.
- They are most likely tax delinquent.
- They most likely have a raze order pending by the city. (A raze order means that the city has condemned the building and it should be razed or demolished.)
- They are within easy walking distance (a quarter of a mile) of a playground.
- They most likely are not owner-occupied.

In this exercise you will find properties with the above characteristics so that the Arc City police department can make appropriate investigations.

In this exercise you will perform the following tasks:
- Query the Arc City parcels to locate the playgrounds.
- Create a selection layer from the selected playgrounds.
- Select the properties with a potential for containing drug houses.
- Convert the selected parcels to a new feature class.
- Use a spatial query to find properties close to playgrounds.
- Determine potential drug houses that are not owner-occupied.

Add parcel data to a map document

1. Start ArcMap.

2. Click the Add Data button, navigate to your **Arc City** geodatabase, and add the ParcelAll feature class from the **ParcelBldg** feature data set.

Locate the playgrounds
To locate the playgrounds, you can query the parcel data by its land-use codes. The land-use code for playgrounds is 8860.

3. From the Selection menu, choose Select By Attributes.

4. In the Select By Attributes dialog, make sure the method is set to Create a new selection, then create the following query expression:

    [LANDUSE] = '8860'

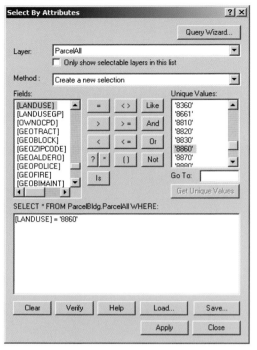

5.   Click Apply, then close the Select By Attributes dialog.

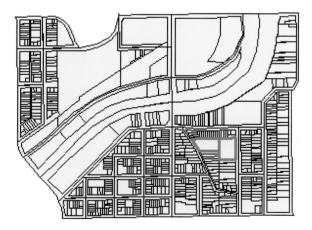

The two playgrounds selected will be used later in your analysis when you locate the potential drug houses within a one-quarter mile of them. At this point you need to preserve this selection.

Create a selection layer from the selected playgrounds

Selection layers are used to preserve a selected set of features, usually for some type of analysis, without creating a new feature class. These layers are only stored within the map document and cannot be shared between maps.

In the upcoming tasks, you will perform a series of queries on the ParcelAll feature class to locate potential drug houses. To preserve your initial selection of the two playgrounds, you will create a selection layer.

6. In the table of contents, right-click ParcelAll, point to Selection, then choose Create Layer From Selected Features.

The default name of the selection layer is ParcelAll selection.

7. In the table of contents, click the name of the ParcelAll selection layer once to highlight it, then click it again to activate the text cursor. (Do not double-click it.) When the cursor appears, change the layer name to **Playgrounds** and press Enter.

8. If necessary, change the color of the Playgrounds layer to make it contrast with the color of ParcelAll.

Selection layers are virtual layers, meaning that a permanent file is not produced when you create a selection layer. If you want to make the layer permanent, you can use the Export command to make a permanent feature class from it.

9. From the File menu, click Save As. Navigate to your **MyArcCity** folder and save the map document as **my_ex03e.mxd.**

The selection layer is now preserved within the map document.

Select the properties with a potential for containing drug houses

You'll begin by identifying all single- and two-family homes, the first characteristic identified by the police.

10. Open the Attributes of ParcelAll.

The land-use codes are stored in the LANDUSEGP field and the respective codes for single- and two-family homes are 01 and 02.

11. In the Attributes of ParcelAll, click Options and choose Select By Attributes. Use the following expression to query for single- and two-family homes:

[LANDUSEGP] = '01' OR [LANDUSEGP] = '02'

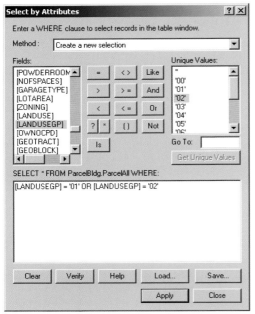

12. Click Apply, then close the Select By Attributes dialog. Move the attribute table to a location where it does not block the map display.

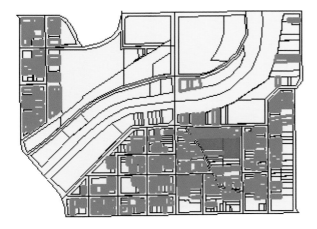

? Question: How many single- and two-family properties are there in the city?

The second characteristic of a potential drug house is a tax-delinquent status.

13. Taking care not to alter your current selection, scroll across the table and locate the TAXDELQ field. (It's near the right end of the table.)

LDER	HISTCODE	TAXDELQ	BIVIOL	RAZESTAT
		0	XXXX	9
		0	XXXX	1
	1	0	XXXX	0
	1	0	XXXX	9
	1	0	XXXX	9
	1	1	XXXX	9
		0	XXXX	9
	1	0	XXXX	9
		0	XXXX	9

This attribute field contains values for each record that indicate how many years a property has been tax delinquent. Notice that most properties are not tax delinquent (0 years), but some are one or more years delinquent.

You can sort the records to see which properties have the most years of tax delinquency.

14. Right-click the TAXDELQ field name and choose Sort Descending.

Question: What is the most number of years that a property has been tax delinquent?

The third characteristic identified by the Arc City police is that the property most likely has a raze order pending.

Two columns to the right of the TAXDELQ column, you'll see the RAZESTATUS field. (You may need to increase the width of the column to see its entire name). A raze status value of 9 means the property is normal and has no raze order.

From the current selection of one- and two-family homes, you will now select the houses that are tax delinquent or have a raze status.

15. From the Options menu, open the Select by Attributes dialog. Change the Method to Select from current selection and construct the following expression:

[TAXDELQ] > 0 OR [RAZESTATUS] <> '9'

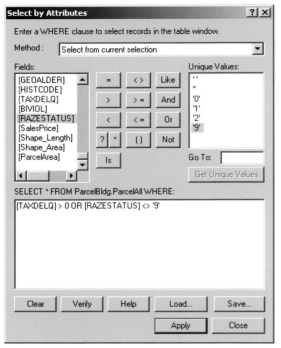

? **Question:** In the query statement you just constructed, why is the nine (9) in single quotes, while the zero (0) is not.

16. Click Apply, then close the Select by Attributes dialog.

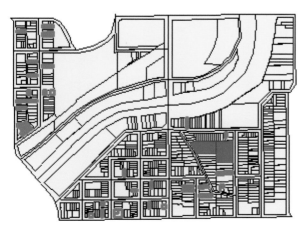

Only single- and two-family properties that are tax delinquent or have a raze order are now selected.

17. In the Attributes of ParcelAll, click the Selected button to see only the selected records.

? Question: How many single- and two-family properties in the city are tax delinquent or have a raze order not equal to 9?

Convert the selected parcels to a new feature class

In this step, you will export the selected features to a new feature class.

18. In the table of contents, right-click ParcelAll, point to Data, and choose Export Data.

19. In the Export Data dialog, make sure the Export drop-down list is set to Selected Features. Name the output feature class **DelinqRaze** and save it within the **Parcel-Bldg** feature data set of your **Arc City** geodatabase.

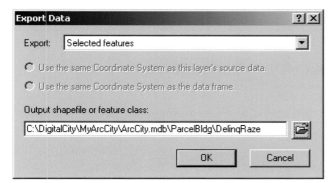

20. Click OK. When prompted, click Yes to add the new layer to ArcMap.

21. If necessary, change the color of the DelinqRaze layer so that it contrasts with the other layers in the map.

22. Clear the selected features in ParcelAll and close its attribute table.

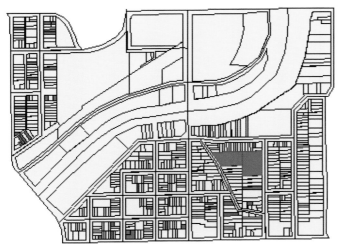

You now have a map showing the two playgrounds and all single- and two-family properties that are either tax-delinquent or have a raze order.

Use a spatial query to find properties close to playgrounds

The fourth concern for a potential drug house is that it is within easy walking distance, or one-quarter of a mile, of a playground.

To find the properties meeting this criterion, you'll use a spatial query instead of an attribute query.

23. From the Selection menu, choose Select By Location.

When constructing a spatial query with the Select By Location dialog, you can read through your settings as if they were one sentence. In this case your settings will read "I want to **select features from** the **DelinqRaze** layer that **are within a distance of** the **Playgrounds** layer that is **1320 feet.**"

24. In the Select By Location dialog, make sure that "select features from" is chosen from the first drop-down list in the dialog. In the list of layers, check the DelinqRaze layer. In the second drop-drop down list from the top, choose "are within a distance of." In the third drop-down list from the top, choose the Playgrounds layer. Check the Option to apply a buffer to the features in the Playgrounds layer, then enter a distance of **1320** in the text box, and choose feet as the distance units.

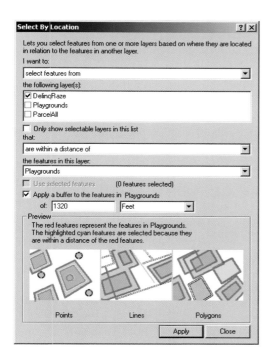

Read through the dialog and make sure your settings are correct.

25. Click Apply, then close the Select By Location dialog.

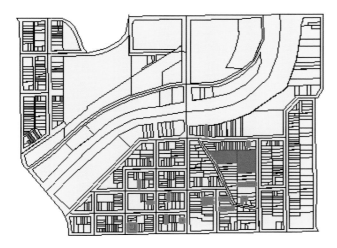

26. Open the Attributes of DelinqRaze.

27. In the Attributes of DelinqRaze, click the Selected button.

? Question: How many tax-delinquent single- and two-family properties with a raze order are within one-quarter mile of the playground?

⊐ Determine potential drug houses that are not owner-occupied

The final part of your analysis is to find the houses that, in addition to meeting all of the other criteria, are not owner-occupied.

28. Scroll across the Attributes of DelinqRaze and locate the OWNOCPD field.

iE	LANDUSEGP	OWNOCPD	GEOTRACT	GEC
	01		112	306
	01		112	306
	02	O	112	201
	01	O	112	201
	02	O	112	105

The values in this field indicate whether the property owner lives in the house or not. An "O" means that the home is owner-occupied and a blank indicates that the owner does not live in the house.

29. From the Options menu, choose Select By Attributes. In the Select By Attributes dialog, click the Method drop-down arrow, choose Select from current selection, then construct the following expression:

    [OWNOCPD] <> 'O'

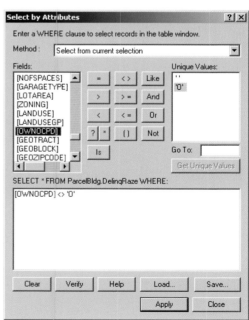

30. Click Apply then close the Select by Attributes dialog.

? **Question:** How many non-owner-occupied, tax-delinquent, raze-ordered, single- and two-family homes are within one-quarter mile of a playground?

31. Close the Attributes of DelinqRaze.

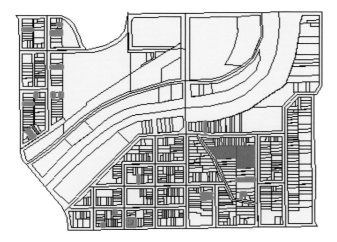

These properties may qualify as potential drug houses. To retain the results of your analysis, you could add a new attribute field to store a value for these potential sites. Instead, however, you will create a new feature class from your selection, which you can then use for further analysis.

32. In the table of contents, right-click DelinqRaze, point to Data, and choose Export Data.

33. In the Export Data dialog, make sure the Export drop-down list is set to Selected features. Name the output feature class **PotentialDrugHouses** and save it within the **ParcelBldg** feature data set in the **Arc City** geodatabase.

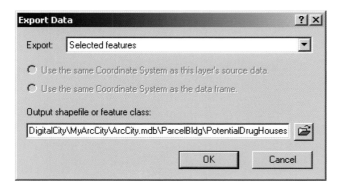

34. Click OK. When prompted, click Yes to add the new feature class to the map document.

35. From the Selection menu, choose Clear Selected Features.

36. If necessary, change the color of the PotentialDrugHouses layer to one that contrasts with the colors of the other four layers in your map.

37. In the table of contents, right-click PotentialDrugHouses and choose Zoom to Layer.

In the graphic below, the potential drug houses are shown in red. Look at the spatial distribution of the potential drug houses.

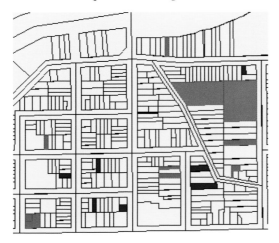

Assuming that property owners living outside of Arc City are less likely to know what is going on at their properties, it's worth your time to investigate the owners that live outside the city.

38. Open the Attributes of PotentialDrugHouses.

39. Scroll across the table and locate the OWNERCITY column. (It's near the middle of the table.)

40. Right-click on the OWNERCITY field name and choose Sort Ascending.

? **Question:** How many non-owner-occupied, tax-delinquent or raze-ordered, single- and two-family homes within one-quarter mile of the playgrounds have owners who live outside the city?
Where do they live?

41. Close the Attributes of PotentialDrugHouses.

Save the map and close ArcMap

42. From the File menu, click Save. Close ArcMap.

Answers

Exercise 4a: Produce the Arc City land-use report

Which district has the most housing units? **3**

Which district has the fewest parcels? **1**

By default, the CountLANDUSEGP field was added to the Attributes of Ludesc during the summarize process. What information is contained in the Count_LANDUSEGP field? **The number of parcels in each land-use category.**

Which field will be used to join the data from the Attributes of Ludesc to the Attributes of ParcelAll? **LANDUSEGP**

How do you know that the Count_LUDesc represents the number of parcels? **Because the summary table was generated from the selected parcels in the ParcelAll feature class. Therefore, the COUNT_LUDesc field represents the total record count found within each category, and the records in this case represent parcels.**

Exercise 4e: Find potential drug houses near a playground

How many single- and two-family properties are there in the city? **385**

What is the most number of years that a property has been tax delinquent? **13**

In the query statement you just constructed, why is the nine (9) in single quotes, while the zero (0) is not? **Because the RAZESTATUS field is a Text field, while the TAXDELQ field is an Integer field.**

How many single- and two-family properties in the city are tax delinquent or have a raze order equal to 9? **37**

How many tax-delinquent, single- and two-family properties with a raze order are within one-quarter mile of the playground? **15**

How many non-owner-occupied, tax-delinquent, raze-ordered, single- and two-family homes are there within one-quarter mile of the playground? **8**

How many non-owner-occupied, tax-delinquent or raze-ordered, single- and two-family homes within one-quarter mile of the playgrounds have owners who live outside the city? **8**

Where do they live?   **Brookfield, Massachusettes; Houston, Texas; Menomonee Falls, Wisconsin; Milwaukee, Wisconsin.**

Chapter 4

Updating spatial and attribute data

A geographic information system is of little value if its data is not up to date. One of the most daunting tasks in implementing GIS in local government is developing and adopting a data maintenance plan that will ensure that all of the digital data—spatial as well as attribute—is constantly kept current. This is because many different agencies are involved (due to data integration) and must coordinate and cooperate on an ongoing basis; because links between spatial data and attribute data must be maintained and coordinated at the same time; because new data is created and organizational responsibilities for their maintenance must be assigned; because it is important to maintain a historical record of changes over time; and because now that data is used in different ways, data errors that existed before can now be identified and must be corrected. While the cost and time to create the initial databases are very high, the ongoing data maintenance activities over time far exceed them. Therefore, it is important to ensure that the appropriate data responsibilities are assigned and procedural efficiencies put in place.

Subdivision plans

The automated mapping capabilities of GIS technology are a major efficiency in updating spatial data. Many local governments are experiencing a high rate of growth and that new development has created a plethora of new subdivision plans that must be reviewed and, eventually, adopted by the local governments. The associated tax assessment and building permit information has also increased because of this new development. This has placed a burden on those responsible for maintaining land records, and this is why so many local jurisdictions are rapidly adopting automated mapping capabilities.

Automated mapping alone, however, is often not enough to keep up with the volume of land records maintenance. Consider a subdivision plan submitted to the local authorities by a developer. It will have been drawn at a rather large scale (usually 1:1200-one inch to 100 feet-or larger) in order to show as much detail as possible. It will also contain some existing references (monuments) from which the measurements are made to give the subdivision an orientation to the existing land. If the plan does not have the State Plane coordinates or some other geodetic reference for those monuments, then it can be very difficult for the government to "fit" the subdivision in its basemap to update it. In addition, it is still rather time-consuming for the government to use a printed map submitted by a developer to update its basemap. This requires either digitizing the plan or scanning it into the GIS and converting it to a vector format and then registering the new subdivision to the basemap coordinate system. This process can be time-consuming and error-prone.

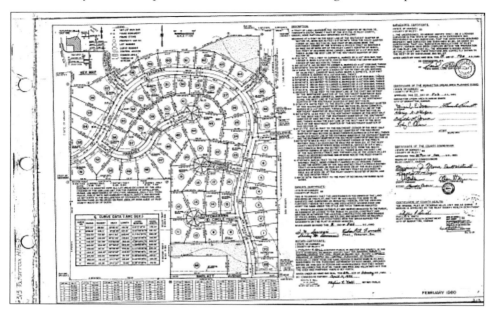

Conversion of hard-copy subdivision maps to GIS data is a time-consuming process. These maps are drawn at an extremely large scale, contain huge amounts of detailed information, and must be scanned or hand digitized to convert from hard copy to digital format.

That is why many jurisdictions now require that subdivision plans be submitted digitally. This makes sense, especially when the local government has automated mapping capabilities and when so many engineering and survey companies who create the plans are doing so with automated mapping software. Why redigitize? Why not just merge the digital file into the GIS database after the subdivision has been approved?

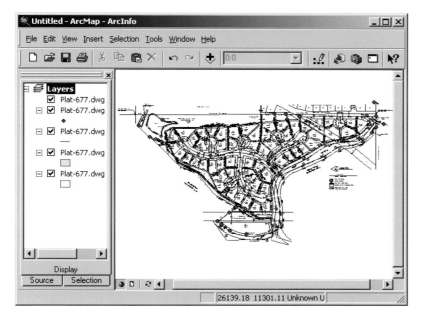

More and more, local jurisdictions and counties are requiring that engineering and surveying firms provide subdivision plans as digital drawing files.

Other spatial data

New subdivisions mean new streets. This means that the TIGER File or some type of street segment geographic base file (GBF) needs to be updated. This requires that the city create new records to store the new street information (name, address ranges, etc.), which has the effect of changing the topological relationships among the new features.

Take, for example, a simple block bounded by four streets. If the block is bisected north to south and east to west by two new streets, the four original streets will have to be split at their intersections with the new streets causing their number to double. This is shown in the following graphic.

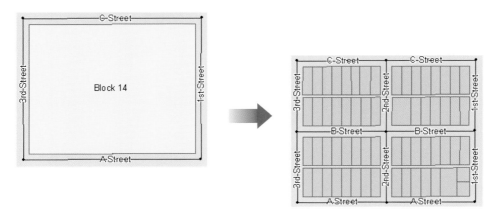

Attribute data

Maintaining attribute data by itself is not a difficult operation, but since a GIS contains links between the attribute data and the spatial data, careful coordination between those who update the map and those who update the attribute database is essential. For example, if someone in the engineering department updates the basemap with the new parcels in the subdivision plan before the tax assessor (or tax lister or register of deeds) creates the new records or updates the attributes of the records, then the data is not current. This may not be a large problem over a short period such as a day or a week, but major problems can be experienced if the attribute data is updated only when a new assessment is made, such as once a year or less.

Similarly, building permit information needs to be coordinated with tax assessment data and parcel maps when maintaining data in a GIS. The same holds true with any data the jurisdiction has chosen as part of the integrated GIS database. When all of these data maintenance activities are done in the same office or a small number of offices (which is often the case in small jurisdictions), the coordination problems are minimal; but when large governments with many departments and offices (and land parcels) adopt an integrated GIS database, serious data coordination problems can arise.

Updating Arc City with a new subdivision

During the time it took to build the spatial and attribute data for Arc City, some changes have taken place: a new subdivision has been approved that will divide an existing parcel of land into thirty-five new lots. The name of this subdivision is the Weil addition. The city engineer has received the digital plans of the Weil addition from the developer and must now update the parcel map of the city. The changes will affect the land-use report and the residential density report. In this chapter, you will update the **Arc City** geodatabase and produce a new land-use summary and land-use map that reflects these changes.

Exercise 4a

Convert CAD drawing of Weil addition to a geodatabase feature class

The farmer whose property is located at 909 North Avenue has decided to develop her land. Her surveyor has submitted a plan for the Weil addition along with several other maps to the Arc City engineer for certification. You have been asked to update the Arc City basemap to reflect the new properties.

In this exercise, you will convert the digital subdivision plan you received from the developer to a geodatabase feature class. The plan from the developer is a CAD file and its features are stored in page space rather than real-world coordinates. You will first transform the CAD data into real-world coordinates before converting it to a geodatabase feature class.

In this exercise you will perform the following tasks:
- Examine the coordinates of the GIS data and the CAD drawing.
- Transform the CAD drawing into real-world coordinates.
- Extract the parcel features and import them into the geodatabase.
- Create a topology to locate errors in parcel lines.
- Remove the dangles from the parcel lines.
- Create parcel polygons from the parcel lines.

❏ Before you begin
The exercises in this chapter assume you have completed chapters 1 through 3. If you did not successfully complete all the exercises in these chapters, you must replace your Arc City geodatabase with the **ArcCity_Ch3results** geodatabase that is provided on the data CD accompanying this book. To update your Arc City geodatabase with the newer version, use the same method outlined in the first task of exercise 1e in chapter 1, except replace your Arc City geodatabase with the **ArcCity_Ch3results** geodatabase (not the **ArcCity_ex01e** geodatabase).

❏ Start ArcMap and add data

1. Start ArcMap with a new empty map.

2. Click the Add Data button, navigate to your Arc City geodatabase and load the ParcelAll feature class from the ParcelBldg feature data set.

The first layer added to ArcMap defines the coordinate system of the data frame. After the coordinate system is defined for a data frame, any layer added to ArcMap that has a different coordinate system defined for it is projected to match the coordinate system of the data frame. This is referred to as on-the-fly projection and it allows data sets stored in different projections and coordinate systems to align within a map document.

3. Click the Add Data button. In the Add Data dialog, navigate to your **C:\DigitalCity\ SourceData** folder and double-click **SUBDIV.DWG**, then double-click the Polyline feature class.

The warning message appears because the CAD drawing has no coordinate system defined for it. Because of this, ArcMap cannot determine what the spatial reference of the data is and if an on-the-fly projection is required to align it with the other data in the map.

4. Click OK to close the warning message about the missing coordinate information.

Because the CAD drawing exists in a different coordinate space than the ParcelAll feature class and ArcMap cannot apply a projection to it, you do not see it within the current map extent.

Examine the coordinates of the GIS data and the CAD drawing

To get an idea about how the coordinates differ between the CAD data and the ParcelAll feature class, you will examine coordinates in these two layers at specific locations.

5. Place your mouse cursor over the southwest corner of Arc City and look at the coordinate values that appear in the status bar below the map display.

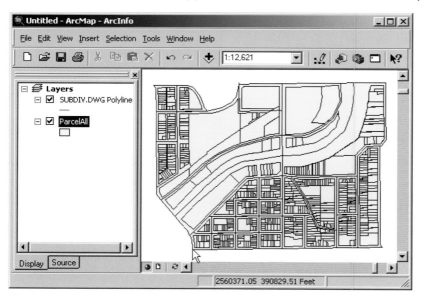

The approximate values of the *x* and *y* coordinates are 2,560,000 feet and 390,000 feet respectively. This means that Arc City is about 2,560,000 feet (or 485 miles) west of and about 390,000 feet (or 74 miles) north of the origin point for its local State Plane system.

6. In the table of contents, right-click the SUBDIV.DWG Polyline layer and click Zoom to Layer.

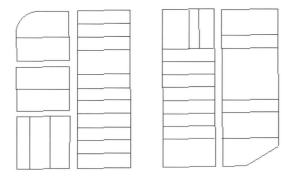

7. Place your mouse cursor over the southwest corner of the Weil addition and read the *x* and *y* coordinates in the status bar.

The *x, y* coordinates at the southwest corner of the CAD drawing are 0,0. If you check the *x, y* coordinates at the northeast corner, you will find they are approximately 580 feet and 365 feet. These ranges of coordinate values are common for CAD data that is not georeferenced because the lower left corner of the drawing is set as the starting point for the Cartesian plane on which the features are drawn.

In the next task, you will apply a coordinate transformation to the CAD drawing to bring it into alignment with the features in the ParcelAll feature class. First, you must locate the tract of land in the ParcelAll feature class that is being subdivided by the Weil addition.

The tax key number of the parcel that the farmer is subdividing is 3540539000. To locate this parcel, run a query for it.

8. From the Selection menu, click Select By Attributes. In the Select By Attributes dialog, create a query that will select the parcel in the ParcelAll feature class with a Tax Key value of 3540539000.

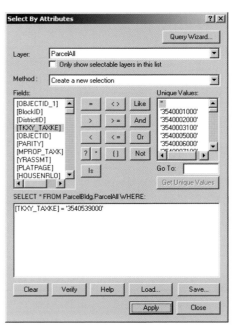

9. Click Apply, then close the Select By Attributes dialog.

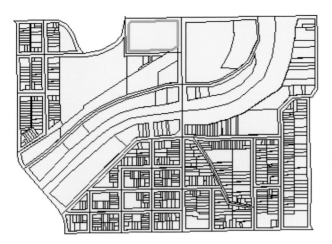

10. From the Selection menu, click Zoom to Selected Features.

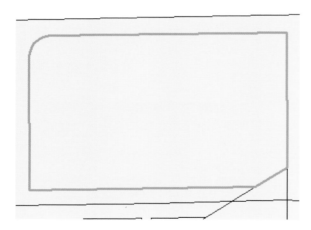

11. Examine the coordinate extent of this property by placing the cursor over its southwest corner and then over its northeast corner, each time reading the coordinates in the Status Bar.

Approximately, the *x,y* coordinates at the southwest corner of the parcel are 2561124.00 and 393070.00; at the northeast corner they are 2561703.00 and 393440.00.

Note: Here you are merely getting an approximation of the coordinates. In an upcoming task you will work with the exact coordinates. There are basically two ways the exact coordinates could be obtained: (1) in ArcMap, zoom in and snap to the corners during an edit session, and, (2) from a survey.

Transform the CAD drawing into real-world coordinates

To align the CAD data with the ParcelAll feature class, you will use a coordinate transformation. A coordinate transformation moves data from its original location in coordinate space to a new location. The transformation is based on the definition of "From" and "To" coordinate pairs. The "From" coordinates represent known point locations in the data you want to move. The "To" coordinates represent the known point locations to which you match the "From" points.

In this case, your "From" coordinates were taken from the southwest corner of the southwest parcel, and the northeast corner of the northeast parcel in the CAD drawing. The "To" coordinates pairs were taken from the southwest and northeast corner of the farmer's parcel.

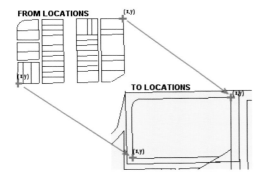

12. Open the Layer Properties of SUBDIV.DWG Polyline and click the Transformations tab. Check the Enable Transformations box, then click the Coordinates option.

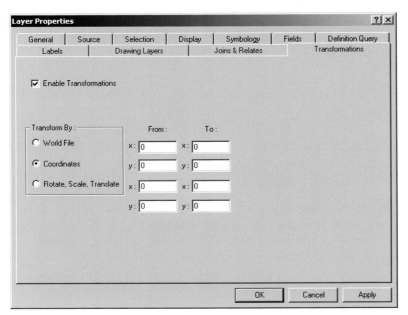

ArcMap allows you to perform either a one-point or a two-point transformation. A one-point coordinate transformation requires two pairs of *x,y* coordinate values. This transformation simply shifts the CAD layer to a new location in geographic space. A two-point coordinate transformation requires four pairs of *x,y* coordinates. The two-point transformation uses a transformation matrix that applies a coordinate offset, scale, and rotation uniformly to all coordinates read from the drawing source.

You'll use a two-point transformation.

13. Use the coordinate values provided in the table below to fill out the From and To text boxes on the Transformation tab.

x,y	From	To
x	0	2561124.3
y	0	393070.52
x	579.45	2561703.76
y	370.17	393440.65

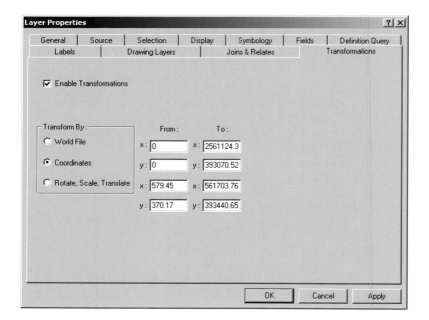

14. Click OK.

ArcMap uses the From and To values you defined to place the subdivision plan within the correct coordinate space.

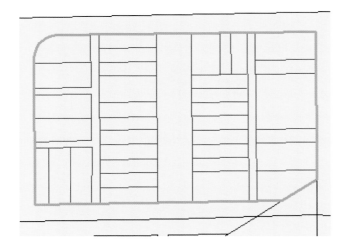

The result of this transformation is temporary, that is, ArcMap did not alter the underlying data, and the coordinate transformation only exists within the map document. Your next task is to make this transformation permanent.

Extract the parcel features and import them into the geodatabase

The transformation you have just completed is not permanent—it has been applied to the layer in the map document, not to the data. In this step you will make it permanent by extracting the parcel lines from the CAD file and exporting them as a feature class to the **Arc City** geodatabase.

15. In the table of contents, right-click SUBDIV.DWG Polyline, point to Data, and click Export Data.

16. In the Export Data dialog, set the Export drop-down list to All features. Click the Browse button. In the Saving Data dialog, name the output **Parcel_SL** and save it as a Personal Geodatabase feature class within the **ParcelBldg** feature data set of the **Arc City** geodatabase.

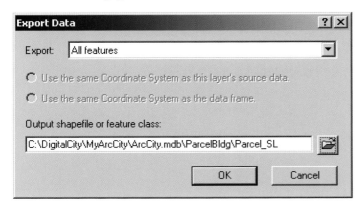

17. Click OK, then click Yes to add the exported data to the map.

You may remember from chapter 2 that the spatial reference defined for a feature data set is automatically applied to any new feature class that is added to it. So, in this case, the coordinate system of the **ParcelBldg** feature data set was automatically defined for the Parcel_SL layer when it was exported from the CAD drawing and placed in the **ParcelBldg** feature data set.

18. Clear the selected features in ParcelAll and remove the SUBDIV.DWG Polyline layer from the map.

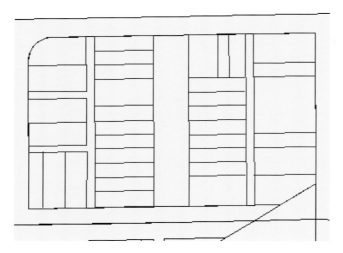

The parcel lines for the subdivision now exist within their own feature class. The data fits well with the existing data but, like most CAD data brought into a GIS, you will need to do some work on the data before it can become a functioning part of your existing geodatabase.

19. Close ArcMap without saving the map document.

Create a topology to locate errors in the parcel lines

In chapter 1 you created a topology to fix undershoots and overshoots, also called dangles. Over the next steps you will create a topology to catch any dangles that may exist in the Parcel_SL feature class.

20. Start ArcCatalog.

21. In the Catalog Tree, navigate to your **C:\DigitalCity\MyArcCity** folder. Expand the **Arc City** geodatabase. Right-click the **ParcelBldg** feature data set, point to New, and choose Topology.

22. On the first panel of the New Topology wizard, click Next. On the Second Panel, accept the default name and cluster tolerance and click Next. From the list of feature classes to participate in the topology, check Parcel_SL and click Next. Accept the default rank assigned to the Parcel_SL feature class and click Next.

23. Click Add Rule. In the Add Rule dialog, click the Rule drop-down arrow and select Must Not Have Dangles from the list. Read the Rule Description.

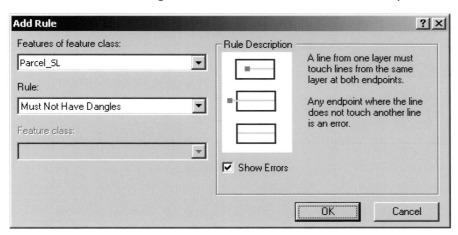

24. Click OK, then click Next and verify that your Summary panel matches the graphic.

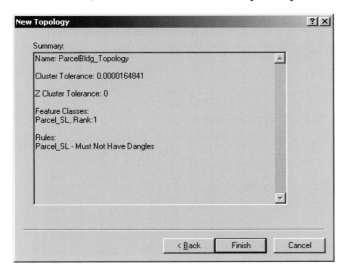

25. Click Finish. When the message appears, click Yes to Validate the topology.

26. If necessary, expand the **ParcelBldg** feature data set in the Catalog Tree. Click the **ParcelBldg_Topology**, then click the Preview tab above the Catalog Display.

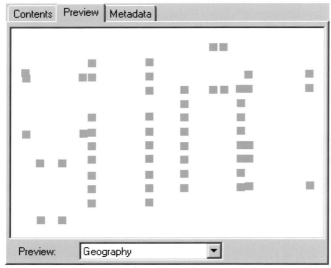

All of the red squares that you see represent an overshoot or an undershoot in the Parcel_SL feature class. In the next task, you will use ArcMap to fix these errors.

27. Close ArcCatalog.

Remove the dangles from the parcel lines

Instead of fixing the dangles one at a time, you will use an automated method to fix the undershoots all at once and then the overshoots all at once.

28. Start ArcMap with a new, empty map.

29. Click the Add Data button and add the **ParcelBldg_Topology** from the **ParcelBldg** feature data set of your **Arc City** geodatabase. When prompted, click Yes to add all the features classes that participate in the topology.

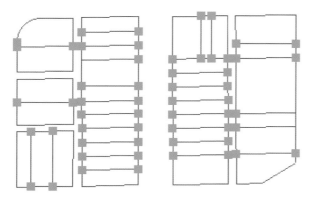

30. From the View menu, point to Toolbars and check Editor. Repeat this process to load the Topology toolbar.

31. Start an edit session. (From the Editor menu on the Editor toolbar, choose Start Editing.)

32. Open the Error Inspector. (On the Topology toolbar, click the Error Inspector button.) Position the Error Inspector so that it is not blocking the map display.

33. In the Error Inspector, click the Show drop-down list and choose <Errors from all rules>. For the remaining search options, check Errors and uncheck Exceptions and Visible Extent only. Click Search Now.

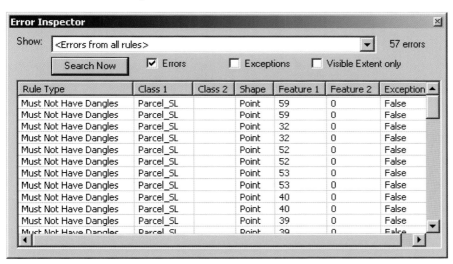

34. If necessary, scroll to the top of the list of errors in the Error Inspector. Click the first record in the list. Scroll to the bottom of the list. While holding down the Shift key on your keyboard, click the last record in the list.

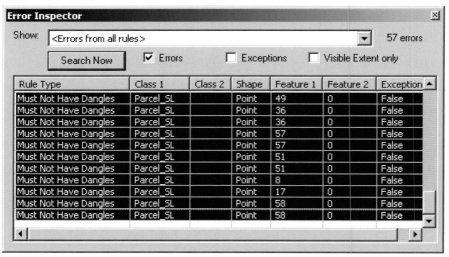

35. Right-click in the list of errors and choose Extend. Enter **0.6** in the Maximum Distance text box and press Enter on your keyboard.

Note: All of the dangles were previously examined using the Fix Topology Error tool. They were also measured with the Measure tool to determine an acceptable distance value for you to use. To prevent unwanted errors from occurring, always do this type of work before fixing errors with predefined fixes from the Error Inspector.

The remaining thirty errors are overshoots. You will fix these with the Trim command.

36. Right-click in the list of errors and choose Trim. Set the maximum distance to 0.6 and press Enter on your keyboard.

All of the original dangles have been repaired. You should validate the topology once more to check for any errors that may have been missed with the first pass.

37. On the topology toolbar, click the Validate Entire Topology button and, when prompted, click Yes on the verification message.

Now that the dangles are repaired, you can convert the Parcel_SL feature class to polygons.

38. Close the Error Inspector. From the Editor menu, choose Stop Editing. Click Yes to Save your Edits.

39. Turn off the Topology and the Editor toolbars, then close ArcMap. You do not need to save your map document.

Create parcel polygons from the parcel lines

In chapter 1 when you created the parcel polygons, you also added the tax key numbers from a point feature class. This time, however, the tax assessor's office has not yet provided you with this data. Therefore, you'll go ahead and create the parcel polygons without tax key numbers.

40. Start ArcCatalog.

41. In the Catalog Tree, navigate to the **ParcelBldg** feature data set in the **Arc City** geodatabase.

42. Right-click the **ParcelBldg** feature data set, point to New, and choose Polygon Feature Class From Lines.

43. In the Polygon Feature Class From Lines dialog, change the name of the new feature class to **Parcel_SP**. Accept the default cluster tolerance. In the list of feature classes that will contribute lines, check Parcel_SL. Leave the drop-down list for choosing a point feature class to establish attributes set to <None>.

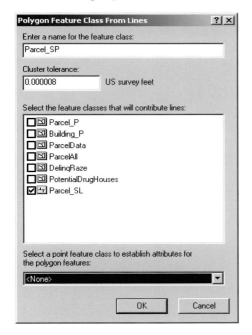

44. Click OK.

The new polygon feature class is created in the **ParcelBldg** feature data set.

45. Preview the geography of the Parcel_SP feature class in ArcCatalog.

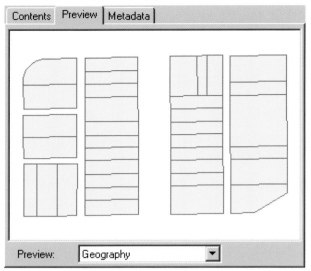

46. Preview the Attributes of Parcel_SP. (Set the Preview drop-down list to Table.)

OID*	Shape*	Shape_Length	Shape_Area
22	Polygon	288.75416410313	3383.37398224729
23	Polygon	346.972174360378	6576.46260803249
24	Polygon	288.66736580726	3381.7567998754
25	Polygon	485.19971972955	14702.9027841655
26	Polygon	341.782104887354	6312.61746439327
27	Polygon	295.155438570854	3528.69762333739
28	Polygon	309.883685739197	3772.74291357444
29	Polygon	0.827019329638073	1.17659010109203E-04
30	Polygon	294.054176409358	3461.81074751132
31	Polygon	331.35064143533	6416.40770706589
32	Polygon	296.549046396639	3606.16720056338
33	Polygon	300.477320349895	5399.21855641413
34	Polygon	224.927535656794	1962.32673547365

Record: ◄◄ ◄ 1 ► ►◄ Show: All Selected Records (of 36)

Preview: Table

The table only contains the attributes that were automatically created by ArcGIS.

While looking over the attributes, you may have noticed a value in the Shape_Area field that is extremely small.

OID*	Shape*	Shape_Length	Shape_Area
22	Polygon	288.75416410313	3383.37398224729
23	Polygon	346.972174360378	6576.46260803249
24	Polygon	288.66736580726	3381.7567998754
25	Polygon	485.19971972955	14702.9027841655
26	Polygon	341.782104887354	6312.61746439327
27	Polygon	295.155438570854	3528.69762333739
28	Polygon	309.883685739197	3772.74291357444
29	Polygon	0.827019329638073	1.17659010109203E-04 ←
30	Polygon	294.054176409358	3461.81074751132

This value indicates the presence of a sliver polygon. Slivers are very small and unwanted polygons created from positional errors that exist in input data used in overlays and line-to-polygon conversions. They are called slivers, because they are usually long and narrow.

With the sliver in question, there might have been a line that self-intersected, causing a loop near its end.

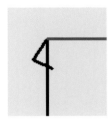

Or, the end points of two lines that were supposed to connect, failed to snap together, and ended up extending past and intersecting one another.

Regardless of its cause, when the lines were converted to polygons, the software recognized the geometric error as a polygon and created a feature from it while it was constructing polygons from the lines. Keep in mind that the errors that lead to slivers are often unnoticeable unless you zoom in extremely close, and even when you do, they can still be undetectable.

47. Close ArcCatalog, and start ArcMap with a new, empty map.

48. Add the Parcel_SP feature class to ArcMap.

49. Open the Attributes of Parcel_SP. Scroll down the attribute table and locate the record with a Shape_Area value of 0.000118. Once located, select this record in the table by clicking the box that's to the left of the record in the table.

Object ID*	Shape*	Shape_Length	Shape_Area
26	Polygon	341.782105	6312.617464
27	Polygon	295.155439	3528.697623
28	Polygon	309.883686	3772.742914
29	Polygon	0.827019	0.000118
30	Polygon	294.054176	3461.810748
31	Polygon	331.350641	6416.407707
32	Polygon	296.549046	3606.167201
33	Polygon	300.477320	5399.218556
34	Polygon	224.927536	1962.326735
35	Polygon	249.351729	3066.322436
36	Polygon	369.696792	7481.828243

When you select a record in a table, the associated record is also selected in the map, but you may have trouble seeing the sliver in the map because it is very small.

50. Right-click the Parcel_SP layer, point to Selection, and click Zoom to Selected Features.

As its name implies, the sliver is long and skinny.

51. On the Tools toolbar, click the Fixed Zoom Out button until you can see which parcel feature the sliver is associated with.

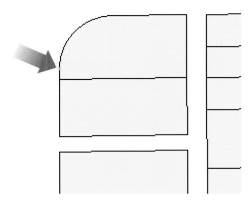

It is not always necessary to look so closely at a sliver, but in this case, we wanted to familiarize you with what they are and how small they can be. If you need to remove many slivers from a feature class, you can use the Eliminate tool. Inside of ArcToolbox, the Eliminate tool is within the Generalization toolset of the Data Management Tools toolbox. (The Eliminate tool is only available to ArcGIS users with an ArcInfo® license.)

52. Open the Editor toolbar and start an edit session.

53. Make sure the sliver polygon is the only selected feature, then press the Delete key.

54. Scroll through the table to make sure the record that was associated with the sliver polygon no longer exists.

55. Stop editing and save your edit.

56. Close the Editor toolbar.

57. From the File menu, click Save As. Name the map **my_ex04a.mxd** and save it in your **C:\DigitalCity\MyArcCity** folder.

58. Close ArcMap.

In a perfect world, bringing CAD data into your GIS would be a matter of copying the features from the CAD data and pasting them in the GIS data. But, as you just experienced, before you can integrate CAD data with your GIS, you usually must post-process the CAD data; that often includes coordinate transformations and data editing to fix digitizing errors.

Exercise 4b

Update the Arc City parcel data with new parcels in the Weil addition

In the last exercise, your work was devoted to converting the CAD data to a geodatabase feature class, then preparing and cleaning up the geometry of the new parcels so that they could fit seamlessly within the ParcelAll feature class.

In this exercise you will continue to work on the new parcels in the Weil addition. The assessor's office has delivered the tax key numbers of the new parcels and the engineering office has delivered their addresses. It's now up to you to create attributes for the parcels in the Weil addition using the information you have received. You will also add the district and block identification numbers to the new parcels and append them to the ParcelAll feature class. Since the Weil addition affects the land use in District 1, you will also update the land-use statistics for this district and produce an updated land-use map.

In this exercise you will perform the following tasks:
- Display the assessor's tax data as an event layer.
- Join the assessor data to the parcels in the Weil addition.
- Update the geometry of the blocks.
- Add block and district numbers to the new parcels.
- Prepare ParcelAll for the new parcels.
- Append the parcels in the Weil addition to the ParcelAll feature class.
- Update the attributes for the new parcels.
- Print a new land-use map.

Start ArcMap and add data

1. Start ArcMap with a new, empty map.

2. Click the Add Data button. Navigate to the your **Arc City** geodatabase and add the Blocks feature class from the **StreetBlock** feature data set. Click the Add Data button again and add the ParcelAll and Parcel_SP feature classes from the **Parcel-Bldg** feature data set.

3. In the table of contents, place the layers in the following order from top to bottom:
   - Parcel_SP
   - ParcelAll
   - Blocks

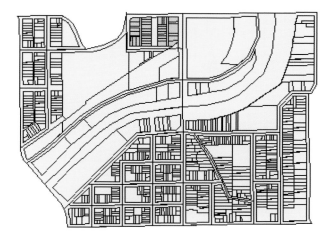

Display the assessor's tax data as an event layer

The tax key numbers assigned to the new parcels were delivered to you from the assessor's office in tabular form. Each record in the table contains an *x,y* coordinate pair along with the Tax Key number. The coordinate pair in each record defines a point that lies within the parcel to which the tax key number in the record corresponds.

In this task, you will display the points stored in the table that you received as an event layer. This will allow you to assign the tax key values to their respective parcel features in an upcoming task.

4. Click the Add Data button. Navigate to your **C:\DigitalCity\SourceData** folder and add the **Subdiv_xy.dbf** table.

5. Open the Attributes of Subdiv_xy.

OID	TKXY_TAXKE	X_ORIGIN	Y_ORIGIN
0	3540501000	2561613	393414
1	3540502000	2561590	393365
2	3540505100	2561601	393267
3	3540506000	2561588	393215
4	3540507000	2561616	393164
5	3540508100	2561602	393132
6	3540510100	2561494	393102
7	3540512000	2561455	393160
8	3540513000	2561455	393182
9	3540514000	2561455	393212
10	3540515000	2561454	393240

The X_ORIGIN and Y_ORIGIN fields contain the coordinate values you will use to display this table as an event layer.

6. Close the table.

7. In the table of contents, right-click **Subdiv_xy.dbf** and choose Display XY Data. In the dialog, make sure that the X Field and Y Field drop-down lists are set to X_ORIGIN and Y_ORIGIN respectively.

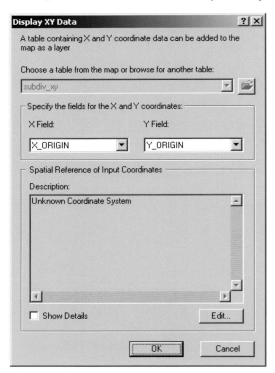

If you click OK now, the event layer would display in the correct location, but its spatial reference would not be defined and it could not participate in some types of analysis. Because of this, you will define its spatial reference.

This event layer has the same spatial reference as the rest of your Arc City data, so you can import the definition of its spatial reference from the **ParcelBldg** feature data set.

8. In the Spatial Reference of Input Coordinates frame, click the Edit button, then, in the Spatial Reference Properties dialog, click the Import button. Navigate to the **Arc City** geodatabase, click the **ParcelBldg** feature data set, then click Add. Click OK in the Spatial Reference Properties dialog.

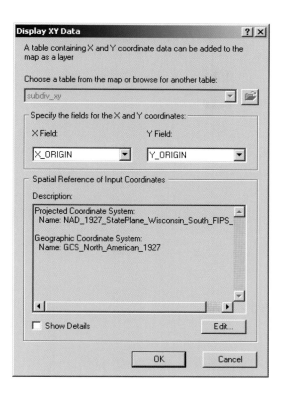

9. In the Display XY Data dialog, click OK.

10. Zoom to the Extent of the Parcel_SP layer.

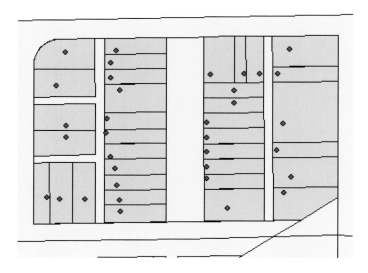

Each point in the event layer contains the tax key number for the parcel it lies within. Using a spatial join, you can assign the attributes of the Subdiv_xy events layer to the attributes of Parcel_SP.

☐ Join the assessor data to the parcels in the Weil addition

11. In the table of contents, right-click Parcel_SP, point to Joins and Relates, and click Join.

You have made several table joins in earlier exercises, this time you will perform a spatial join. Spatial joins combine attribute data based on the relative locations of the features in two feature classes. For example, using a spatial join, you can join the attributes of a point to the polygon that contains it, or join the attributes of a line to the point it intersects or to which it is closest. You can make several other types of feature class combinations with spatial joins.

In this case, the attributes of the points in the subdiv_xy layer will be joined to the attributes of the parcels in the Parcel_SP layer that they are contained by. Neither of the input feature classes will be altered because the output will be a new polygon feature class.

12. From the drop-down list at the top of the Join Data dialog, select Join data from another layer based on spatial location.

Once this option is chosen, the options on the dialog change to reflect settings for a spatial join.

13. For step 1, choose subdiv_xy Events from the drop-down list. For step 2, choose the option "Each polygon will be given all the attributes of the point that is closest to its boundary, and a distance field showing how close the point is (in the units of the target layer)". For step 3, name the output **SubdivTax** and save it within the **ParcelBldg** feature data set of the **Arc City** geodatabase.

14. Click OK.

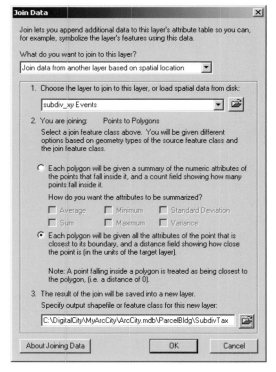

After the spatial join concludes, the SubdivTax layer is automatically added to the map.

15. Turn off the subdiv_xy Events and the Parcel_SP layers.

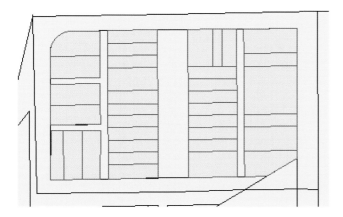

16. Open the Attributes of SubdivTax and review its contents.

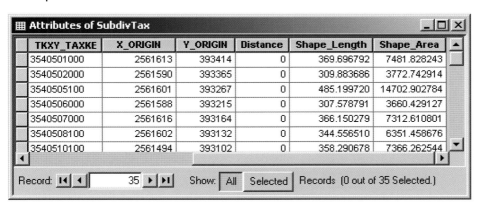

TKXY_TAXKE	X_ORIGIN	Y_ORIGIN	Distance	Shape_Length	Shape_Area
3540501000	2561613	393414	0	369.696792	7481.828243
3540502000	2561590	393365	0	309.883686	3772.742914
3540505100	2561601	393267	0	485.199720	14702.902784
3540506000	2561588	393215	0	307.578791	3660.429127
3540507000	2561616	393164	0	366.150279	7312.610801
3540508100	2561602	393132	0	344.556510	6351.458676
3540510100	2561494	393102	0	358.290678	7366.262544

Record: 35   Show: All Selected   Records (0 out of 35 Selected.)

Attributes of SubdivTax contains the fields from both of the input layers. The Distance field was automatically added by ArcMap and contains distance values representing how far each point is from the polygon that received its attributes. Since all of the points in this join were inside the polygons, the distance values are all zero.

17. Close the Attributes of SubdivTax.

18. If necessary, click the Source tab at the bottom of the table of contents. Remove the Subdiv_xy, Subdiv_xy Events, and Parcel_SP from the map.

Your new parcel data is coming together. What was once a CAD layer consisting of lines is now a parcel feature class with tax key attributes.

☐ Update the geometry of the blocks

The north-south street that runs through the center of the Weil subdivision splits the existing block into two new blocks. In an upcoming task, you will union the SubdivTax feature class with the Blocks feature class, which will assign the block and district IDs to the new parcels. Before you do this, you must split the block that contains the Weil addition along the centerline of the new street.

19. In the table of contents, turn off the ParcelAll layer, but leave the SubdivTax and Blocks layers on.

20. Open the Editor toolbar and start an edit session.

21. On the Editor toolbar, click the Task drop-down arrow and choose Cut Polygon Features, then click the Target drop-down arrow and choose Blocks.

22. On the Editor toolbar, click the Edit tool, then, in the Map Display, click the block that contains the new parcels.

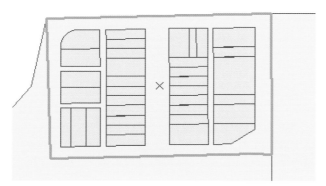

You will cut this block down the center of the subdivision, along what will eventually become North Weil Street. When you cut the polygon, try to follow as closely down the center of the street right-of-way as possible, but your cut does not have to be exact. The following graphic shows the line (drawn in red) along which you will cut the selected block.

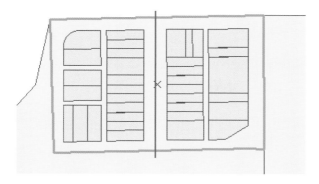

23. On the Editor toolbar, click the Sketch tool. Use the sketch tool to strike a line down the middle of the street right-of-way as shown in the above graphic. (To draw the line, click just above the block's northern boundary, then double-click just below its southern boundary).

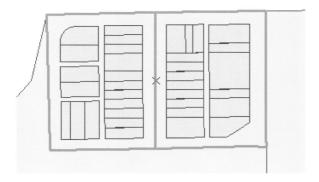

Along with the address information and tax key data, the assessor's office also provided you the new block identification values for the Weil addition. Of the two new blocks, the western block kept the original ID value of 107000306, while the ID value of the eastern block has changed to 107000304.

24. On the Editor toolbar, click the Attributes button.

On the left-hand side of the Attributes dialog, the two selected blocks are listed. You can determine which record in the dialog corresponds to which block feature by clicking the values in the left-hand side of the dialog, while watching to see which feature flashes in the map display.

25. Select the western (left) block in the Attributes dialog, and, if necessary, change its BlockID value to **107000306**. (To change the value, click the BlockID value in the right-hand side of the dialog, then type in the new value).

26. Select the eastern (right) block in the Attributes dialog, change its BlockID value to **107000304**, then close the Attributes dialog.

27. From the Editor menu, choose Stop Editing and click Yes to save your edits.

28. Clear the selected features (if necessary).

Add block and district numbers to the new parcels

To add the Block IDs, District IDs, and the right-of-way features to the new parcels, you'll union them with the blocks feature layer.

The spatial extent of SubdivTax is much smaller than the Blocks feature class, and when you union these two feature classes together you only want to union the SubdivTax features with the two new blocks. To control which blocks participate in the union, you will apply a definition query to the Blocks feature class.

29. Open the Properties of the Blocks Layer, click the Definition Query tab, then click the Query Builder button.

30. In the Query Builder dialog, construct a query that selects the block with a BlockID of 107000306 or 107000304.

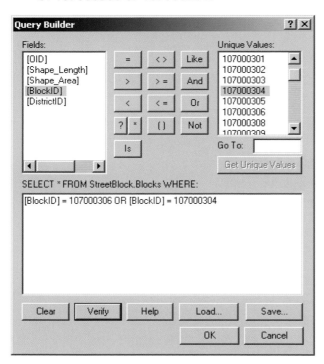

31. Click OK, then click OK in the Layer Properties dialog.

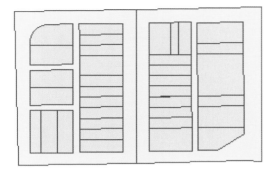

Now you can union the Blocks layer with the SubdivTax layer and only the two blocks containing the Weil addition will participate in the overlay.

32. Open ArcToolbox.

33. Inside ArcToolbox, expand the Analysis Tools toolbox, then expand the Overlay toolset. Inside the Overlay toolset, double-click Union.

34. In the Union dialog, use the Input Features drop-down list to add the SubdivTax feature class and the Blocks feature class to the Features list. Name the Output Feature Class **SubdivAll** and save it in the **ParcelBldg** feature data set of the **Arc City** geodatabase. Do not change any other settings.

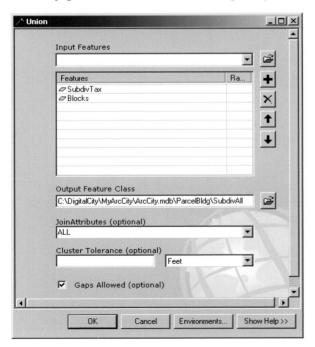

35. Click OK, then click close when the process completes.

36. Close ArcToolbox.

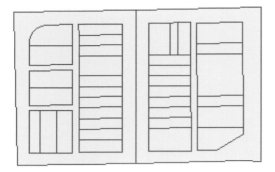

37. Open the Attributes of SubdivAll and review the table's contents.

SubdivAll now has the tax key, block, and district identifiers.

38. Close the Attributes of SubdivAll.

39. Remove SubdivTax from ArcMap.

Prepare ParcelAll for the new parcels

Up to now, you have been preparing the new parcels for their addition to the ParcelAll feature class. Now it's time to get the ParcelAll feature class ready to accept the new parcels. To do this, you will delete the parcels and right-of-way features from ParcelAll that will be replaced by the parcels in the Weil addition.

40. In the table of contents, turn off all the layers except ParcelAll.

The following graphics shows the features you will delete.

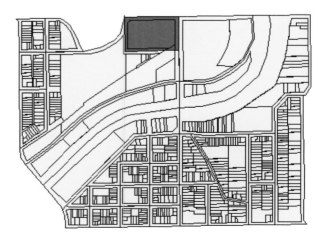

41. If necessary, zoom in to the parcels that will be deleted from ParcelAll.

42. Open the Editor toolbar (if necessary), and start an edit session.

43. On the Editor toolbar, click the Edit tool. Use the Edit tool to select all of the parcels shown selected in the graphic below.

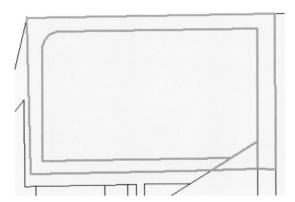

44. Press the Delete key on your keyboard.

At this point you could keep the edit session open and copy and paste the features from the SubdivAll features class into the ParcelAll feature class. However, when you copy and paste features from one feature class to another, the attributes for the features you copy and paste are lost. To preserve your attributes, you will use a geoprocessing function to append the SubdivAll features and their attributes to the ParcelAll feature class.

45. From the Editor menu, click Stop Editing. Click Yes to save your edits.

46. Close the Editor toolbar.

Append the parcels in the Weil addition to the ParcelAll feature class

The Append tool takes the features and attributes in one or more input feature classes and attaches them to the features in an existing feature class. You will use the Append tool to add the parcels in SubdivAll to the ParcelAll feature class.

47. Open ArcToolbox.

48. In ArcToolbox, expand the Data Management Tools toolbox, then expand the General toolset. In the General toolset, double-click Append.

49. In the Append dialog, click the Input Features drop-down list and choose SubdivAll. Click the Output Features drop-down arrow and choose ParcelAll. Make sure the Schema Type option is set to TEST.

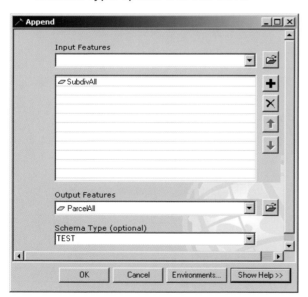

When the Schema Type option in the Append dialog is set to TEST, attributes are only appended from one feature class to another if they exist in fields with the same schema.

For example, SubdivAll and ParcelAll both have a TKXY_TAXKE field that holds text values, but only SubdivAll has a Distance field. During the append, the values in the TKXY_TAXKE field will be carried over from SubdivAll to ParcelAll, but the values in the Distance field will not be appended.

50. Click OK, then click Close when the process completes.

51. Use the Select Features tool to select the features that were appended to the ParcelAll layer.

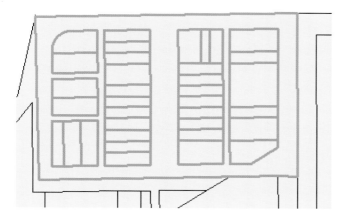

52. Open the Attributes of ParcelAll, and click the Selected button at the bottom of the table.

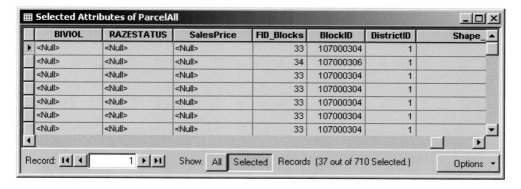

The new parcels and their attributes were appended to the ParcelAll feature class. Although the new parcels have their Block ID and tax key values, they do not have any other assessor data at this time.

You may have noticed in your table that there are two features that do not have a tax key value. This is because they are right-of-way features and not parcels.

53. In the Attributes of ParcelAll, click the All button, then clear the selected features.

? **Question:** How many parcels are there now in Arc City?

54. Close the Attributes of ParcelAll.

55. Remove the Blocks layer and the SubdivAll layer from your map.

Update the attributes for the new parcels

The new parcels already have the tax key numbers, block IDs, and district IDs assigned to them. At this point you will add the owner name, addresses, and land-use values to each of the parcels.

The subdivision is still in development—no parcels have been sold and no houses have been built. Because of this, the owner for every parcel is still the development company (Weil Development LLC) and the land use for each parcel is vacant (Land Use Group 13). While the owner names and land use are the same for every parcel, they do have unique addresses assigned to them.

56. From the Selection Menu, open the Select By Attributes dialog. In the dialog, construct the following query to select the parcels in the Weil addition. (Be sure to place the parenthesis around the OR statement):

([BlockID] = 107000304 OR [BlockID] = 107000306) AND [TKXY_TAXKE] <> ''

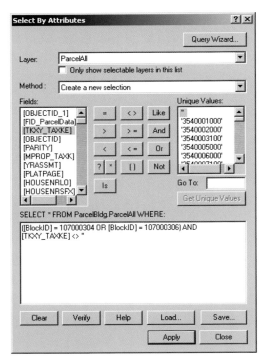

57. Click apply, then close the Select By Attributes dialog.

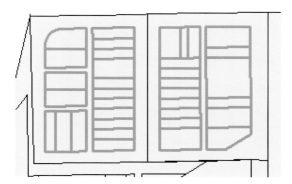

58. Open the Attributes of ParcelAll and click the Selected button.

59. Open the Field Calculator for the OWNERNAME1 Field. (Scroll across the table and locate the OWNERNAME1 field, then right-click on its name and choose Calculate Values. Click Yes on the warning message.) In the Field Calculator, set the OWNER-NAME1 field equal to **"Weil Development LLC"**.

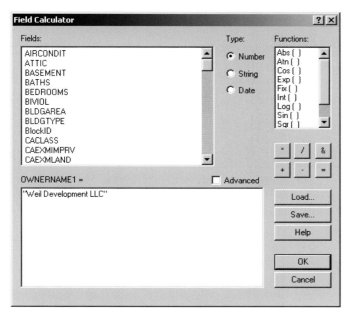

60. Click OK.

OWNERNAME1
Weil Development LLC
Weil Development LLC
Weil Development LLC
Weil Development LLC
Weil Development LLC
Weil Development LLC
Weil Development LLC
Weil Development LLC
Weil Development LLC

61. Open the Field Calculator for the LANDUSEGP field and create an expression that will set the land-use group value of the selected records to **13**.

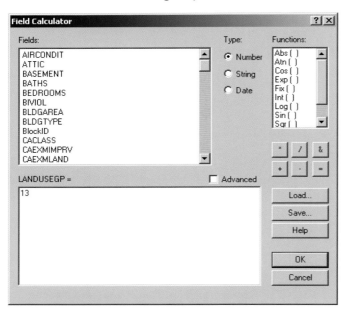

62. Click OK.

LANDUSEGP
13
13
13
13
13
13

Now that the ownership and land-use values are in place, you need to attribute the new parcels with their address numbers. To do this, you must start an edit session and manually add the address numbers to each parcel.

The following map shows the address number of each parcel and the street names.

The way to determine which street a parcel is addressed from is by its assigned address number. Parcels with a number in the 900 or 1000 range are associated with the east-west streets. Parcels with a number in the 2000 range correspond to the north-south streets. For example, the northwest parcel in the subdivision has a 909 address number, which means it was addressed from E. North Ave.

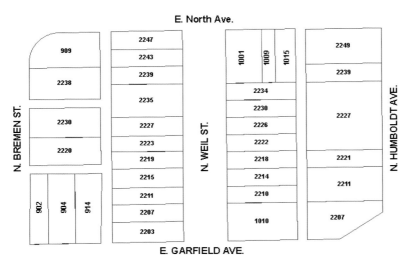

63. Clear the selected features and close the Attributes of ParcelAll.

64. Open the Editor toolbar and start an edit session.

65. On the Editor toolbar, click the Edit tool, then click the parcel in the northwest corner of the Weil addition.

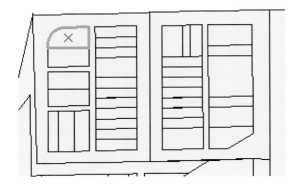

66. On the Editor toolbar, click the Attributes button. On the right-hand side of the Attributes dialog, scroll a short way down the list of attributes until you can see the four address fields, HOUSENRLO, DIR, STREET, and STTYPE. Using the reference

map as your source for the address attributes, add the values into the four fields of the selected parcel. (Use all capital letters, do not add periods at the end of the abbreviations, and truncate AVE to AV.)

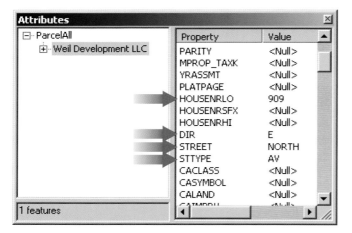

Adding the attributes to each parcel one-by-one is a tedious process. To speed the work up, you will add the street attributes to their associated parcels all at once.

You can add an attribute to several records at once by selecting a group of features, opening the Attributes dialog, clicking the layer name instead of the feature name, then typing in the attribute values. By selecting the layer name in the Attributes dialog, the attribute value you enter is applied to all the selected features instead of a single record.

Using this technique you will create attributes of the street names, street prefixes, and street types for the new parcels in the Weil addition.

67. Select all the parcels that will be addressed along N. Weil St. as shown in the graphic. (To select nonadjacent features with the Edit tool, hold down the Shift key while clicking the features to select.)

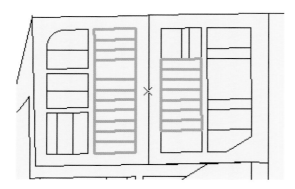

68. In the left-hand side of the Attributes dialog, click ParcelAll.

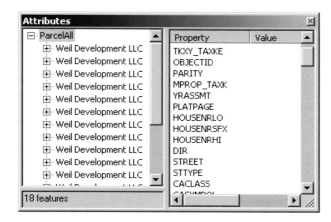

All of the field names in ParcelAll appear on the right-hand side of the dialog and the Value column is empty.

69. On the right-hand side of the dialog, scroll down until you see the DIR, STREET, and STTYPE fields.

70. Click in the Value column next to the DIR field. In the text box that appears, type **N,** then press the Enter key. (After you press Enter, the Value field will become blank again, but the value has been applied to the selected features.) Click in the Value column next to the STREET field, type **WEIL**, and press Enter. Click in the Value column next to the STTYPE field, type **ST**, and press Enter.

71. On the Tools toolbar, click the Identify tool, then click any of the selected parcels in the Map Display. In the Identify Results dialog, scroll through the list of fields and verify that the street attributes are present, then close the Identify Results dialog.

72. Select the parcels shown in the graphic below. Using the same technique you used in steps 68 through 70, attribute the DIR field with **E**, the STREET Field with **NORTH**, and the STTYPE field with **AV**. (Be sure to click the ParcelAll layer name in the left-hand side of the Attributes dialog before you add the attribute values.)

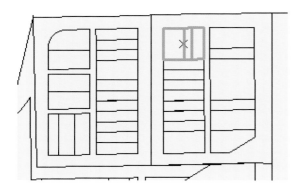

73. Select the parcels shown in the graphic below. Populate the DIR field with **N**, the STREET Field with **BREMEN**, and the STTYPE field with **ST**.

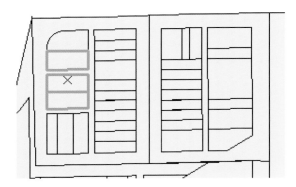

74. Select the parcels shown in the graphic below. Complete the DIR field with **E**, the STREET Field with **GARFIELD**, and the STTYPE field with **AV**.

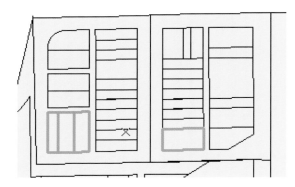

75. Select the parcels shown in the graphic below. Complete the DIR field with **N**, the STREET Field with **HUMBOLDT**, and the STTYPE field with **AV**.

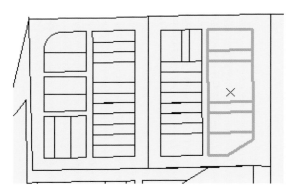

The parcel records now contain the street attributes, but you still must add the address numbers. This time there is no shortcut—you will have to add these attributes manually for each parcel.

76. Using the reference map, add the address numbers to the HOUSENRLO field for each parcel.

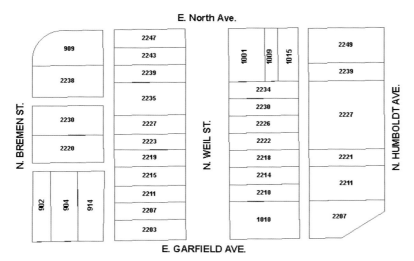

77. When you are finished adding the address numbers, from the Editor menu, choose Stop Editing. Click Yes to save your edits.

Check the new parcels for addressing errors

To make sure that you've entered the addresses correctly, you'll label the parcels with a concatenation of the four address fields.

78. Open the Properties of ParcelAll and click the Labels tab. In the Text String frame, click the Label Field drop-down arrow and choose HOUSENRLO, then click the Expression button.

79. In the Label Expression dialog, scroll across the Label Fields and locate the DIR field. Click the DIR field and click the Append button, click the STREET field, then click the Append button, click the STTYPE field, and click the Append button.

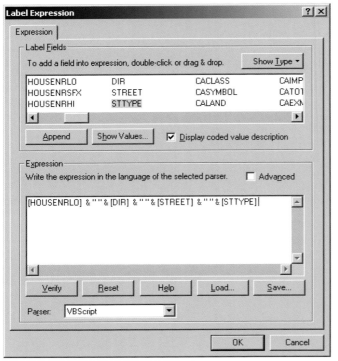

This label expression will concatenate the four fields into a single label string. This concatenation does not affect the underlying data and is only preserved with the map document.

80. Click OK in the Label Expression dialog, then click OK in the Layer Properties dialog.

81. In the table of contents, right-click ParcelAll and click Label Features.

At your current scale, the labels will overlap the parcel boundaries and in general look sloppy. However, if you zoom in to a few parcels at a time, the labels will fit within their respective parcels.

82. Zoom in to the northwest corner of the Weil addition and check the addresses against your index map.

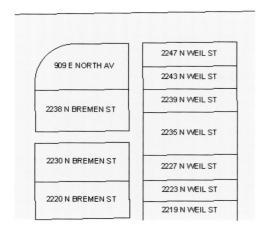

83. After you check the parcels in this area, use the Pan tool to bring more parcels into view and check their addresses. Mark any error you find on your index map. Once you have checked all the parcels, fix any errors you may have found.

84. When you have finished checking your work, turn off the labels and zoom to the full extent of ParcelAll.

Update the land-use statistics for District 1

With the addition of the Weil subdivision, the land use in District 1 has changed—there are now several new parcels with a vacant land use. Because of this, you should again summarize the land use in District 1.

The steps used to summarize the land use are the same as the steps you used in exercise 3a. If you need more information about how to perform a specific step, you should refer to that exercise.

85. Click the Add Data button, navigate to your **Arc City** geodatabase, and add the Ludesc table. (This table was created in exercise 3a.)

86. Join the Ludesc table to the Attributes of ParcelAll using LANDUSEGP as your key field.

87. Select all the parcels in District 1.

(The query expression should be [TKXY_TAXKE] <>"AND [DistrictID] = 1)

88. Open the Attributes of ParcelAll, then open the Summarize dialog from the Ludesc.LUDesc field. Within the Summarize dialog, do not choose to add any summary statistics. Save the output table to your Arc City geodatabase and name it **Dist1_LU**. (Click Yes if asked whether or not you want to overwrite the existing table.) Check the option to Summarize the selected records.

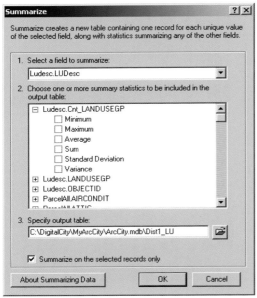

89. Click Yes and add the summary table to the map.

90. Close the Attributes of ParcelAll. Open the Attributes of Dist1_LU.

	Object ID*	LUDesc	Count_LUDesc
▶	1	Commercial	5
	2	Industrial	6
	3	Mixed Commercial and Residential	2
	4	Park	4
	5	Public	4
	6	Residential	103
	7	Vacant Land	38

You can now use this table to update the city's land-use report.
You should also determine how many parcels now exist within District 1.

91. In the Attributes of Dist1_LU, right-click the Count_LUDesc field and click Statistics.

Question: What is the total number of parcels in District 1?

92. Close the Statistics of Dist1_LU and the Attributes of Dist1_LU, then clear the selected features.

93. From the File menu, click Save As. Name the map **my_ex05b.mxd** and save it in your **C:\DigitalCity\MyArcCity** folder.

Print a new land-use map

Because the land use in Arc City has changed, you should also print an updated version of the city's land-use map.

You could create this map from scratch, but a quicker way is to open the land-use map document that you created at the end of exercise 3a. So instead of creating a new map, you can just rely on the one you created earlier and save some time.

94. From the File menu, click open. Navigate to your **C:\DigitalCity\MyArcCity** folder and open **my_ex03a.mxd**.

When you open this map, the original layout settings that you made earlier appear, and the map reflects the update to the ParcelAll feature class as well.

Feel free to make any adjustments to the map. Since this map will be recreated each time land use changes in Arc City, you should add a date element to the map.

95. Make any adjustments or additions to the map that you deem important.

96. Print the land-use map.

97. Close ArcMap. You do not need to save your changes to the map document.

Answers

☐ **Exercise 5b: Update the Arc City parcel data with new parcels in the Weil addition**

How many parcels are there now in Arc City?   **679 (To answer this question, you must run a query from the Attributes of ParcelAll that selects all the parcels and also excludes the right-of-way features from the results.)**

What is the total number of parcels in District 1?   **162**

Conclusion

You have now built a simple geographic information system database for local government from CAD drawings and data tables. You have also used the geodatabase in a few local government applications that are common within planning, building inspection, public works, police, health, and tax assessment departments.

Local governments that have already implemented a GIS have built upon these applications by adding more applications with the existing data and by adding more data to expand the number of applications. With this development, the GIS becomes an enterprise-wide resource, benefiting almost every function of the local government.

Expanded applications

Now that the basics are done, the parcel-level maps and attributes and the street center-lines and associated demographic data can be used in additional applications such as these three:

Economic development

The system you have created can be used to assist a developer who is looking for a vacant lot on which he plans to build a new commercial building. The lot must be zoned for an 80-foot tall building (ZONING ='IB85') and it must be at least 30,000 square feet in area (LOTAREA >= 30000). One lot is available, and its assessed value is $295,400. However, there are four smaller adjacent vacant lots whose combined area is 30,510 square feet and whose combined assessed value is only $152,600. You can help him find them by querying for all vacant lots (LANDUSEGP ='13'), then using the dissolve function to eliminate their common boundaries and create new parcels. When you query these features for LOTAREA >= 30000, the new bundle of lots is identified. Now that you have the skills, try it.

Vehicle dispatching

This task requires you to route the Arc City police chief from her current location at the restaurant located at 2176 N. Riverboat Rd. to a residence located at 1317 E. Hamilton where a call for service has just been made by the Locke family. As you can see from the street grid, there are many different routes the chief can take to get to the residence. Your task is to find the shortest route.

Public access to data

Moving the data and GIS capabilities out to the Internet is a good way to reduce the amount of time that local government staff spend on the telephone or in personal conversations with citizens seeking public information. It also promotes the local government because businesses, developers, real estate agents, and visitors can access information by themselves, wherever they are, about properties, streets, businesses, parks, public facilities, and more. Two good examples of Internet-based GIS capabilities for public access are the City of Milwaukee (*www.mapmilwaukee.com* for property data, and *www.milwaukee.gov/compass* for public safety, health, and other demographic data) and the City of Philadelphia

(citymaps.phila.gov for address-based maps, aerial photography, zoning and other land-use controls, service districts, and nearest facilities such as libraries, hospitals, etc.)

Expanded databases
As more applications are developed and implemented across additional departments and functional units, there will also be a desire to expand the database to include additional map and attribute data. This will create even more applications.

Digital orthophotos (DOPs)
Digital orthophotos are raster images of planimetric features such as curb lines, sidewalks, and building outlines. These aerial photos can be used in various applications from planning the location of a new park to identifying impermeable features for storm water management to tactical crime response. When they are georeferenced, they can be overlaid with cadastral maps to show the proximity of the planimetric features to parcel boundaries, rights-of-way, etc. In addition, DOPs can be used as a backdrop for digitizing additional features to expand the layers in the geodatabase. Further, draping DOPs over digital elevation models (DEMs) allows the image to be visualized in three dimensions.

Utilities

Public utility departments such as sewer, water, communications, and street lighting can benefit significantly from the use of GIS technology across the full range of public infrastructure services: planning, design, construction, maintenance, and usage. In addition to the obvious engineering design applications, local governments are using GIS technology to perform analyses that can identify sewer and water mains that are at high risk of collapse, identify the infiltration of storm water into sanitary sewers, plan efficient routes for maintenance crews, compute water consumption fees, and other innovative applications.

One jurisdiction used its GIS to identify properties that were illegally connected to public water mains, the owners of which were possibly stealing water from its water utility. Staff had determined that over 187 million gallons of water were lost in the previous year and wanted to know if they could recover some of the almost $500,000 cost by finding water thieves. The water billing database was joined with the water-main laterals layer and the parcel layer to identify parcels that did not have a water billing account, but did have a water lateral (the pipe that conveys the water from the main in the street to the property.) Eliminating vacant lots resulted in the identification of parcels having a building but not a water bill. A one square mile test area contained thirty-eight parcels that were using water but not being billed for it. In this one square mile alone, the potential annual recovery amount came to over $18,000!

Administrative, political, and other districts

As you learned, geocoding is a powerful function provided by geographic information systems technology. In chapter 3 you were easily able to append a district code to each of the parcel records in order to calculate land-use statistics by district in chapter 4. Local governments can have hundreds of such districts: aldermanic districts, voting districts, neighborhoods, school districts, zoning districts, watersheds, police beats and districts, fire and EMS districts, inspection districts, nursing districts, tree pruning districts, tax incremental financing (TIF) districts, and tax assessment districts. The many different offices of local government use these districts to manage their resources, report outcomes and changes over time, and analyze conditions. They even produce mailings to property owners, residents, and businesses in specific districts when new projects are planned. Adding layers in the geodatabase for these administrative, political, and management districts enhances the benefits that can be realized by GIS.

Current local government GIS applications

By now you are probably realizing that the list of applications of geographic information systems in local government is almost endless. In any particular agency, the number of applications grows as more government officials become aware of the potential of GIS and as more data is added to an agency's database. A survey of local governments completed in 2003 by Public Technology Incorporated, a Washington-based agency, provides a forum for raising the technology awareness levels of elected and appointed local government decision makers. They found the following applications most often in the 1,156 local governments responding:
- viewing aerial photography (77% of respondents)
- property records management and taxation (70% of respondents)

- public access to government data (57% of respondents)
- capital planning, design, and construction (41% of respondents)
- permitting services (38% of respondents)
- emergency preparedness and response (38% of respondents)
- computer-aided response (33% of respondents)
- crime tracking and investigation (28% of respondents)

The full list of applications reported as implemented in the PTI survey can be found at the PTI web site *www.pti.org*.

Another resource for learning about GIS applications in local government is *Beyond Maps*, which describes actual GIS applications implemented in specific governments (O'Looney 2000). These applications include:

Recycling	Water utilization equity analysis
Capital projects tracking	Attracting retail development
Watershed management	Economic development tax credit zone analysis
Capital planning	Property tax equity analysis
Garbage pickup	Storm water runoff fee determination
Crime pattern analysis	Siting youth and family services
Crime"hot spot"predictions	Planning for library expansion
Police resource allocation	Improving access to welfare services
Police dispatching using GPS	Applying for grants
Crime analysis studies	Redistricting
Travel demand forecasting	Siting unwanted facilities
Modeling transportation maintenance needs	Open space planning
Planning car pools	Airport noise analysis
Pavement management using video	Railroad noise analysis
Hurricane emergency response	Neighborhood planning
Park fire risk modeling	Historic preservation
Fire incident analysis	Brownfield redevelopment analysis
Fire station location analysis	Identifying health risks
Fire response analysis	Siting health facilities
Sewer inspection scheduling	Controlling mosquitoes
Time-of-use billing analysis	Housing program analysis
	Urban tree management

Towards an enterprise GIS

This book set out to give you the skills necessary to build and use a simple, parcel-based GIS and also, in chapter 3, show you how combining maps and data from different organizational functions in local government can enhance the use of that information. From the list of possible applications listed above, it should be clear that an enterprise-wide GIS implementation can provide benefits beyond those that could be realized if individual departments implemented their own systems.

When implementing a GIS in your local government, consider these words from the Enterprise GIS education and collaboration forum (*www.pti.org/gisforum.asp*) of Public Technology Incorporated:

The results of local governments that have implemented enterprise GIS are profound. Leading GIS government leaders will share their successes and lessons learned. Many local governments have saved millions of dollars by adopting an enterprise system. This cost saving, combined with the ability to provide faster, more accurate, and more efficient services to citizens, businesses, and other agencies is a compelling reason for all local governments to take the first steps toward an enterprise approach.

References

Huxhold, William E. 1991. *An introduction to urban geographic information systems.* New York: Oxford University Press.

Huxhold, William E., and Allan G. Levinsohn. 1995. *Managing geographic information systems projects.* New York: Oxford University Press.

Municipality of Burnaby. 1986. *Invitation to information* (brochure).

Nyerges, Timothy L., and Kenneth Dueker. 1988. *Geographic information systems in transportation.* Washington: U.S. Department of Transportation.

O'Looney, John. 2000. *Beyond maps: GIS and decision making in local government.* Redlands, Calif.: ESRI Press.

Ormsby, Tim, Eileen Napoleon, Robert Burke, Carolyn Groessl, Laura Feaster. 2001. *Getting to know ArcGIS.* Redlands, Calif: ESRI Press.

How to install data from the CD

ArcGIS and the Digital City includes one CD that contains the exercise data. The exercise data takes up about 20 megabytes of hard-disk space. The data installation process takes about five minutes.

⌐ Installing the data

Follow the steps below to install the exercise data. Do not copy the files directly from the CD to your hard drive.

1. Put the data CD in your computer's CD drive. In your file browser, click the icon for your CD drive to see the folders on the CD. Double-click the Setup.exe file to begin.

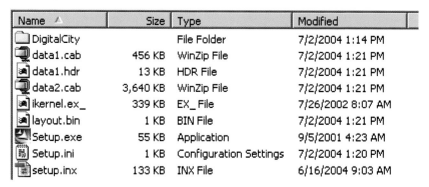

Name ⌐	Size	Type	Modified
DigitalCity		File Folder	7/2/2004 1:14 PM
data1.cab	456 KB	WinZip File	7/2/2004 1:21 PM
data1.hdr	13 KB	HDR File	7/2/2004 1:21 PM
data2.cab	3,640 KB	WinZip File	7/2/2004 1:21 PM
ikernel.ex_	339 KB	EX_ File	7/26/2002 8:07 AM
layout.bin	1 KB	BIN File	7/2/2004 1:21 PM
Setup.exe	55 KB	Application	9/5/2001 4:23 AM
Setup.ini	1 KB	Configuration Settings	7/2/2004 1:20 PM
setup.inx	133 KB	INX File	6/16/2004 9:03 AM

2. Read the Welcome.

InstallShield Wizard

Welcome to the InstallShield Wizard for ArcGIS and the Digital City exercise data

The InstallShield® Wizard will install ArcGIS and the Digital City exercise data on your computer. To continue, click Next.

< Back   Next >   Cancel

3. Click Next. Accept the default installation folder or navigate to the drive where you want to install the data.

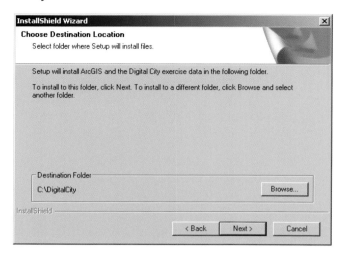

4. Click Next. The exercise data is installed on your computer in a folder called **DigitalCity**. When the installation is finished, you see the following message:

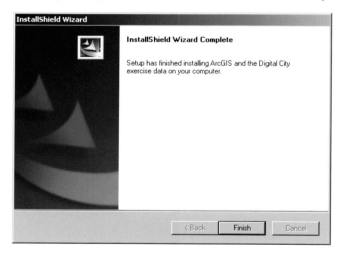

5. Click Finish.

If you have a licensed version of ArcInfo 9 software installed on your computer, you are ready to start the exercises.

⊐ Uninstalling the Data

To uninstall the exercise data from your computer, open your operating system's control panel and click the Add/Remove Programs icon. In the Add/Remove Programs Properties dialog, select the following entry and follow the prompts to remove it:

ArcGIS and the Digital City exercise data

ESRI Press publishes books about the science, application, and technology of GIS. Ask for these titles at your local bookstore or order by calling 1-800-447-9778. You can also read book descriptions, read reviews, and shop online at www.esri.com/esripress. Outside the United States, contact your local ESRI distributor. ESRI Press titles are distributed to the book trade by the Independent Publishers Group (800-888-4741 in the United States, 312-337-0747 outside the United States).

ESRI Press
380 New York Street, Redlands, California 92373-8100
www.esri.com/esripress

ArcGIS and the Digital City: A hands-on approach for local government
Cover design, book design, image editing, and production by Savitri Brant
Copyediting and proofreading by Tiffany Wilkerson
Printing coordination by Cliff Crabbe